AN AMERICAN JEWISH ODYSSEY

American Religious Freedom and

The Nathan Barnert Memorial Temple

For Kathy and Mike Gzzoro,
Phil was so fond of you, me too.
Happy New Year!
Cipora O. Schwartz   *7 December 2007*

Congregation B'nai Jeshurum
Paterson, New Jersey 1847–1987
Franklin Lakes, New Jersey 1987–2007

CIPORA O. SCHWARTZ

KTAV PUBLISHING HOUSE, INC.
JERSEY CITY, NJ 07306

An American Jewish Odyssey

The City of Paterson—Historic Preservation Commission and the Urban History Initiatives Making History Grant provided important support toward this publication. An Anonymous Foundation donated an exceptional grant. I would like to thank them both.

ACKNOWLEDGMENTS

Further acknowledgments appear on pages v–vi, which constitutes an extension of this copyright page.

KTAV Publishing House, Inc., 930 Newark Av., Jersey City, NJ 07306
201-963-9524 fax 201-963-0102
www.ktav.com   info@ktav.com

Copyright © 2007

Library of Congress Cataloging-in-Publication Data

Schwartz, Cipora O.

An American Jewish Odyssey : American religious freedoms and the Nathan Barnert Memorial Temple /
By Cipora O. Schwartz.   p. cm.

ISBN 0-88125-950-0

1. Nathan Barnert Memorial Temple (Franklin Lakes, N.J.) 2. Jews—New Jersey—History. 3. Reform Judaism—New Jersey—History. 4. Barnert, Nathan, 1838–1927. 5. Jewish businesspeople—New Jersey—Biography. 6. New Jersey—Ethnic relations. I. Title.

BM225.F732N387 2007   296.09749'21–dc22   2006038085

Printed in China

CONTENTS

Introduction v

CHAPTER 1   The Promised Land 1

CHAPTER 2   The City by the Falls 7

CHAPTER 3   The Early Years 21

CHAPTER 4   Nathan Barnert: B'nai Jeshurun's Benevolent Benefactor 27

CHAPTER 5   A New Home 39

CHAPTER 6   Rabbi Max Raisin: The Scholarly Theologian 47

CHAPTER 7   The Best of Times and the Worst of Times 59

CHAPTER 8   The Exodus from Paterson 73

CHAPTER 9   Rabbi Martin Freedman: The Renaissance Rabbi 97

CHAPTER 10   Moving On 125

Appendix 173

Rabbis 175

Temple Presidents 177

Oral Histories 179

Bibliography 181

Index 185

INTRODUCTION

America. God bless America! The history of Congregation B'nai Jeshurun, the Barnert Memorial Temple, is forever entwined with the history of our nation, the United States of America, our state, New Jersey, and our city, Paterson (1847–1987) and the borough of Franklin Lakes (1987–2007).

Our present congregation and the generations that preceded it are participants in a continuing American story. Jews have been a presence in the United States ever since the seventeenth century, and we have all participated in the growth of this great democracy of ours.

An ancient people in a new land, the Jews who settled in Paterson and started our congregation came to America seeking religious freedom and economic opportunity and dreaming of a better life. Generation after generation, our ancestors toiled so that their children could be educated and live in peace in a country in which religious freedom is constitutionally guaranteed.

The Barnert Memorial Temple spans three centuries as an American Jewish institution committed to service to our congregation and to the larger world as American Jews.

This history is for our children and our children's children. It is a chronicle of our ancestors' struggle and journey to reach a dream. These are our beginnings and their future.

This book is not intended, in any sense, to be a scholarly work. It is written mainly from secondary sources (see bibliography) and told primarily in the words of our congregants from oral histories obtained between 1978 and the present. We interviewed "elders," past presidents, individuals whose families had long ties with the congregation, and individuals who served the congregation in leadership roles.

It documents, through their words, a continuing American Jewish odyssey that I hope other writers will expand upon in the future, for much more can be written about the essence of Barnert Temple in Paterson and in Franklin Lakes.

In writing this book, I have been blessed with the generous support and encouragement of numerous esteemed friends, family and congregants. Their invaluable help can be acknowledged here only briefly with my deep, deep appreciation.

For their enthusiasm and commitment to the Oral History Project: Lenore Albert, Joel Bauer, Millie Cohen, Delight Dodyk, Ph.D., Janet Finke, Barry Freeman, Ph.D., Minna Greenberg, Susan Lane, Theodore Lobsenz, David Roth, M.D., Dorothy Starr, Jonah Zweig, and the late Ken Edelson. The oral histories quoted in this book have been edited; complete transcripts are available in the Barnert Temple archives. Barnert Temple bulletins, minutes, and other documents used as sources in this manuscript are also available in the Barnert Temple Archives.

For the loan of photographs, pamphlets, brochures, and other memorabilia: Joel Bauer, Morrill J. Cole, Judge Joseph Conn, Sarah Dunn, Janet Finke, Norma Hayman, Betsy Stott Kimmerlee, Alvin and Susan Sauer, Carole Ann Steiger, and the Barnert Temple archives. For contemporary photographs, my appreciation to Karen Galinko, Sherie Reiter, and James D. Schwartz.

For a brilliant high school term paper about our congregation, written in 1967, which became an important source, Rabbi Howard Allen Berman. The rabbi's insights and love for our congregation have been an inspiration for me. I am deeply indebted to him.

For her comments on an early draft of this history, my gratitude to Sally Yerkovich, Ph.D., executive director of the New Jersey Historical Society. For reviewing a partial manuscript and for her encouragement, Marlie Wasserman, director of the Rutgers University Press.

For her unstinting devotion to this project and to me, in helping with research at the Judaica Division of the New York Public Library, the research library of the New Jersey Historical Society, the library of the Passaic Historical Society at Lambert Castle, and the archives of the Barnert Memorial Temple, I am exceptionally indebted to my friend, Dorothy Starr. To Susan Adelman, Leonore Albert, Ellen Gutenstein, Susan Lane, and Sherie Reiter, who helped review the Barnert Archives material. For helping to organize research files, intern Andrea Brooks of Ramapo College. For Yiddish and Hebrew translations, Stuart Freedman. For valuable book design consultation, Evelyn Bauer. For their co-operation, administrator Alice Kintisch and the office staff of the Barnert Temple.

For copy editing the manuscript, Robert J. Milch. For digital photography Avics, Inc. For book design Susan Brorein. This manuscript has benefited greatly by their talent, expertise and professionalism. I am deeply appreciative for the contribution.

I wish to express my appreciation to Arnold Reiter, Esq., for attending to copyright and contractual matters, and to Charlotte Swift, Esq., for assistance with U.S. Supreme Court decisions research. To Stephen R. Schwartz for editorial and technical advice and for transferring the oral history transcripts onto computer disks as a gift to the Barnert Temple Archives. I am indebted to Rabbi Martin and Shirley Freedman for reading chapter 9 and correcting dates and spellings and ensuring factual accuracy. My profound thanks to the late Jay W. Levy, who during the early phase of my writing this book provided me with encouragement, and research, editorial and word processing assistance, which I found invaluable. For insightful comments, critical observations, and editorial notes, my abiding gratitude to manuscript readers Felicia E. Alpert B.A., Sherry Eldridge, Esq., Francis H. Schott, Ph.D., and Timothy O. Schwartz, M.B.A. To Elyssa Mosbacher, who sensitively edited my book, my deep gratitude. Though all these individuals have contributed to this book, I alone am responsible for its shortcomings.

For a generous grant in support of research expenses, to the City of Paterson–Historic Preservation Commission and the Urban History Initiatives Making History Grant. Their interest in the subject of American religious freedom as exemplified by the Barnert/Paterson story and the commission's patience during the research and writing period are greatly appreciated.

To a private family foundation, for their interest and exceptional financial support.

Any profits I receive from this book will be donated, equally, to the Barnert Temple Archives and the Paterson Main Public Library's Research and Archives Division.

Lastly, my deepest gratitude to the late Sam and Esther Schwartz, for their confidence in and love for me and their interest in the early history of Paterson and the Barnert Temple, and to my husband, Philip Schwartz, for his encouragement, moral support, and infinite patience.

Cipora O. Schwartz

DEDICATION

This book is dedicated to the memory of my beloved parents,
Margolis Musikant Fialkov Odentz and Zvi Odentz.

"And the glory of children are their parents."

Proverbs 17:6

CHAPTER ONE

The Promised Land

Lady Liberty welcoming Jewish Family to America.
1909 Postcard. Private collection.

Historians tell us that Joachim Gans was the first Jew to arrive in America. A native of Prague, and America's first metallurgical scientist, he reached the New World on June 26, 1585, some thirty-five years ahead of the Pilgrims, on one of Sir Walter Raleigh's ships under the command of Sir Richard Grenville, whose mission it was to survey North America.

In 1654, twenty-three Jewish emigrants, expelled from Brazil by the Portuguese because of the policies of the Inquisition, were saved at sea after their ship capsized in the Atlantic. They were brought to Nieuw Amsterdam, now New York, where they established Congregation Shearith Israel, the first Jewish congregation in America. (The 350th anniversary of this first permanent settlement was nationally celebrated in 2004.)

American Citizens Manual—the Constitution of the United States. Private collection.

Reuben Etting. Private collection.

They received a less than friendly reception from Governor Peter Stuyvesant, who opposed any religion other than the Dutch Reformed Church. Stuyvesant's intolerance was tempered somewhat by his employer, the Dutch West India Company in Holland. The company numbered many Jews among its investors, and its policy of "giving Jews and all other inhabitants of Nieuw Amsterdam the opportunity to live, work, travel and traffic" in the colonies it controlled prevailed. This action helped set a precedent for religious freedom as an idea that would expand and flourish in our nation's future.

By the time the Declaration of Independence was signed in 1776, there were approximately 2,000 Jews living in the thirteen colonies. By 1783, synagogues had been established in New York, Newport, Savannah, Charleston, and Philadelphia.

The ratification of the United States Constitution on September 17, 1787, guaranteed certain religious rights not only for Jews but for members of all religions. The two most significant parts of the Constitution in this respect were Article 6 and the First Amendment of the Bill of Rights.

Article 6 ensured that "no religious Test shall ever be required as a Qualification to any Office or public Trust." This legally ended the practice of prohibiting members of certain religious groups from holding governmental posts, although in reality religious discrimination of this kind did not end immediately. It would be many years and only after much struggle that Jews held public office in the colonies. One early officeholder was Reuben Etting, appointed by President Thomas Jefferson as a United States marshal in 1801. Etting, born in York, Pennsylvania, in 1762, served with distinction as first captain of the Baltimore Independent Blues, a militia regiment.

The First Amendment stated that "the Congress shall make no law respecting an establishment of religion, or prohibiting the free exercise thereof." But as important as the legal freedoms guaranteed by our Constitution was the early political, social, and cultural tone established, for example, by President George Washington and articulated in his famous letter to the Touro Synagogue in Newport, Rhode Island, in which religious freedom was laid down as a basic freedom of the new republic.

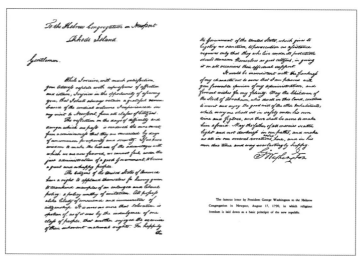

George Washington's famous letter to the Touro Synagogue.

The Citizens of the United States of America have a right to applaud themselves for having given to Mankind examples of an enlarged and liberal policy; a policy worthy of imitation.... For happily, the Government of the United States, which gives to bigotry no sanction, to persecution no assistance, requires only that they who live under its protection should demean themselves as good citizens, in giving it on all occasions their effectual support. May the children of the Stock of Abraham who dwell in this land continue to merit and enjoy the good will of the other inhabitants, while everyone shall sit in safety under his own vine and fig tree and there shall be none to make him afraid.

—George Washington
Letter to the Touro Synagogue
August 17, 1790

The colony of Rhode Island, founded by Roger Williams, was a hospitable environment for all religions, and the first Jews arrived in Newport in 1658. An active Jewish community developed there, and in the next century the well-known colonial architect Peter Harrison designed a synagogue for the Newport congregation. Now known as the Touro Synagogue in honor of its first rabbi, it was designated a National Historic Site in 1946. The Touro Synagogue was restored by a member of the Barnert Temple Congregation in 1958.

The Touro Synagogue

The tolerance expressed by Washington in his letter to the synagogue and his liberal policies as president set the tone for all Americans to accept the principle of religious freedom for all faiths. An early exponent of this principle was Dr. Ezra Stiles, a Congregational minister from Newport and later president of Yale University, who a few years before Washington's letter described the Touro Synagogue as "an edifice the most perfect of the Temple kind perhaps in America ... splendidly illuminated ... which could not but raise in the mind a faint idea of the majesty and grandeur of the ancient Jewish worship mentioned in the Scripture."

Despite the promising, if not total, freedom provided by the new Constitution, immigration of European Jews in the early 1800s, as in the preceding century, was slow. It picked up around 1830, but the first major wave of Jewish immigration began as a consequence of the failed Revolutions of 1848, and by 1869 some 144,000 German Jews had come to the United States.

Medal for the historical restoration of the Touro Synagogue awarded to a Barnert Temple congregant. Private collection.

Many immigrants became peddlers, and German-Jewish immigrants in particular made great progress toward financial independence, eventually building such retail empires as Macy's, Gimbels, and Altman's.

My father originally became a peddler and sold items to the farmers in the field out in the outskirts of the town.

I don't know how he sold a thing. He didn't know the language. I don't know how these guys took care of themselves.... They had the greatest courage imaginable. To get off a boat in a strange country, not knowing the language, not knowing the customs, not knowing the traditions, and making a living.

Then he met and married my mother. He managed to find some textile, some lace manufacturers who had extra merchandise ... and that he sold. My mother discovered that if you put a piece of lace on a common housedress you now have a party dress. Instead of selling the dress for a dollar and a half you could get two and a half dollars for it because, with the lace attached, it was a party dress. So my mother arranged to have a couple of ladies help her. She became the production staff in the apartment. She brought these ladies in and the three of them were sewing lace on these common housedresses, making party dresses, and my father went out and sold them. And they made a good living.

Medal commemorating 350 Years of Jewish Life in America, 2004. American Jewish History Society.

—Alvin Sauer
oral history

U.S. stamp dedicated to
Dr. Albert Sabin.

Judge Amy Herz Juviler, *on left,* as an intern
in Washington, D.C., office of New Jersey
Congressman Gordon Canfield, 1957.
Private collection.

Standing from left to right: Richard Neustadt,
Willard Wirtz, John Dunlap; *seated,* President
Harry Truman and David L. Cole.
Private collection.

Gains were also made in the areas of investment banking, meat-packing, and clothing manufacture. In the nineteenth century, Jews began to move westward to places like Chicago, where Sears and Roebuck developed the first national mail-order catalogue, and San Francisco, where Levi Strauss work clothing was born.

The next wave of mass Jewish immigration came from Poland and other parts of the Russian Empire in the late nineteenth century, when life there became especially difficult for Jews. Discrimination, famine, mass expulsions, and anti-Jewish pogroms were on the rise. Work was increasingly difficult to find. Two areas of Poland from which large numbers of Jewish immigrants arrived in America were the towns of Lodz and Bialystok. It is no coincidence that many of these immigrants settled in Paterson, New Jersey, which was already known for its textile manufacturing. Both of these towns had active textile industries.

> *My father came from an area close to Lodz. It was sometimes Polish; it was sometimes Russian. He was born in 1881. He came to this country in about 1896 or 1897. He was a weaver, and that's why he came to Paterson, because Paterson was the silk city of America, and if weaving was your trade this was certainly the place to come to.*
>
> —Samuel Schwartz,
> oral history

As early pioneers left Europe and stories of success began to make their way back home, the wave of immigration began to pick up steam. The new immigrants of the late 1800s would soon become not only the backbone of the textile industry of Paterson, but also an important part of its cultural heritage.

In the nineteenth and twentieth centuries, these mostly German, Polish, and Russian Jewish immigrants and their descendants made a great contribution to Paterson and to our country. Among them: Harry B. Haines, editor of the Paterson Evening News; his father, Edward B. Haines, who founded the Paterson Morning Call and the Evening News and served as a volunteer in the 19th Illinois Infantry Regiment during the Civil War; Hannah "Annie" Silverman, union leader and heroine of the 1913 Paterson silk strike; physician-scientist Dr. Albert Sabin, developer of the first live-virus oral polio vaccine; labor lawyer David L. Cole was appointed chairman of the United States Mediation and Conciliation Service by President Harry Truman and served as labor peace maker for every president from Franklin D. Roosevelt to John F. Kennedy; Burt Meyer, Paterson department store developer and philanthropist; poet Allen Ginsberg; Esther Schwartz, historian, and restorer of the Touro Synagogue; Dr. Irving Selikoff, chief investigator of the connection between asbestos and lung cancer; Judge Charles S. Joelson, four-term congressional representative from New Jersey and later judge of the New Jersey Superior Court; educator Joan Weiner Konner, dean of the Columbia Graduate School of Journalism; Amy Herz Juviler, criminal court judge and senior litigator for twenty years with the New York state attorney's office; and environmental activist Frank Lautenberg, president of ADP Systems and four-term U.S. senator. And, of course, philanthropist, real estate developer, and political activist Nathan Barnert, described as follows in the 1920 edition of Nelson and Shriner's *History of Paterson and Its Environs:* "He belongs not to Paterson, no business contains him, his Jewry cannot compass his spirit, for he is an American, a citizen of the world." The contributions of these American Jews were made possible by the religious freedom enjoyed by all Americans.

The Russian-Jewish migration to the United States was a very complex phenomenon. In 1880, about four million Jews, half of the world's Jewish population, lived in the Russian Empire, which included most of Poland, in addition to Ukraine, Belarus, and the Baltic states. Life was dismal for Russian Jewry because of pervasive anti-Semitism and an extraordinary series of restrictions that limited their economic and educational opportunities and confined their residency to a region known as the Pale of Settlement.

Dr. Morris Joelson's funeral, in August 1958 in 1894 Barnert Temple. Private collection.

> *My father, Morris Joelson, came from Russia when he was eleven in a pickle barrel, smuggled out, because they were conscripting twelve-year-olds. He and his younger brother, Harry ... became great Patersonians.*
>
> *His parents came with his sisters. He came at eleven in 1894, and in 1906 he graduated from Columbia Physicians and Surgeons. Came not speaking a word of English. I don't know how he did it. And he was one of the most beloved people in Paterson. He delivered 20,000 of its babies.*
>
> —Norma Joelson Hayman
> oral history

During the reign of Czar Alexander II (1855–1881), life for the Jews of Russia improved somewhat. New job opportunities opened up. Jews were now permitted to be merchants, bankers, and industrialists. Their contributions in these areas helped the stagnant Russian economy grow, and for this Alexander II rewarded them. Jews could now live in the formerly off-limits city of St. Petersburg. Universities were opened to Jewish students, giving them the opportunity to study medicine and law. Unfortunately, this period of relative tranquility was short-lived.

In 1881, Alexander II was assassinated, and his successor, Alexander III, began to reinstate the policies of the iron-fisted Nicholas I, especially in relation to Russia's Jews.

> *Alexander III's policy was to weed out all Jewish professionals by restricting the number of Jewish youths studying in the universities. Jews had to serve in the army and pay taxes, but were ignored and oppressed otherwise. They had no rights any of the officials would respect, and if life went on ... it was due primarily to the determination of the people to survive at all costs.*
>
> —Rabbi Max Raisin
> "My Fifty Years as a Rabbi,"

Under Alexander III, the Jews were blamed for all of Russia's problems, including the assassination of Alexander II. A wave of pogroms followed throughout the country, lasting until 1882. Most Jewish properties were confiscated or destroyed. Jewish women were raped, children were mutilated, and thousands of Jews were murdered. Twenty thousand Jews were left homeless, and a hundred thousand were economically destroyed. Anti-Semitism was rampant.

Russian Jews were left with little choice. Faced with such horrible acts of terrorism, one-third of Russia's Jewish population chose to emigrate, and a majority of them eventually came to America. Like those who had preceded them, they came to

America to work and to build a new life. Many chose New Jersey. In fact, New Jersey went from having the smallest number of Jews in the twenty-seven states in 1847, to a mass influx of Jews in the 1880s. Paterson's textile industry continued to be the major draw.

My dad's people came from Lithuania, which was then part of Russia. They had been wealthy people, but all of their earnings had been illegal. Jews were not permitted to own land in the czarist regime so that my grandfather acquired large tracts of land registered in the names of illiterate gentile retainers. Only he and the local czarist official, who apparently was bribed, knew of this situation. There was a huge home on this land. Jews were not permitted to be middlemen, but gentile farmers were often afraid to leave their homesteads to go to a port like Riga on the Baltic because if the weather turned bad the roads turned to quagmires and they couldn't get back and take care of the livestock on their farms. So they very often stopped overnight at my grandfather's home. More accurately, they sold to Jewish merchants who acted as the illegal middlemen as they would stop overnight at my grandfather's home on their way to the coastal cities. In addition, it was illegal to speculate. The main crop that was exported was flax for linen. My great-grandfather had a huge barn in which he bought and stored flax that he was buying for speculation. And he also had equipment upstairs in his barn for washing and drying the flax. Now, one of the major pieces of equipment was a huge drum that would spin around to dry out the flax by centrifugal force. When impressment gangs came down the road they would hide the children who might be considered eligible for military service into this huge drum.

—Joseph Shapiro, M.D.
oral history

CHAPTER TWO

The City by the Falls

The Great Falls of the Passaic River, 19th century image. Private collection.

The city that was to become Paterson, New Jersey, was founded in 1791 by Alexander Hamilton, along with an assortment of politicians, financiers, and adventurous merchants. The Great Falls of the Passaic River presented possibilities that appealed to their entrepreneurial spirit, and they envisioned the site as a manufacturing town.

Their instincts were right. The river and the area's other natural resources would lead to growth in lumbering, sawmills and grist mills, copper and iron mining, and eventually cotton and silk production. But it was the waves of immigrant labor that would prove to be the city's greatest natural resource.

As industry grew in the period before the American Revolution, labor was scarce. Workers were hard to find, since land was easy to obtain and most people were interested in farming. Slaves and redemptioners (indentured slaves who allowed the captain of the ship to sell their services for a designated number of years in exchange for passage to the colonies) were used to fill the gap.

By 1737, slaves made up nearly 10 percent of the population of New Jersey, with 90 percent born in the colonies. In 1804, the state passed a law requiring that the children of slaves be freed after reaching adulthood.

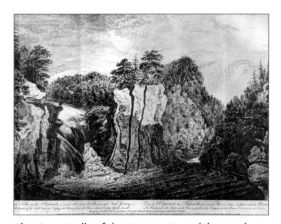

The Great Falls of the Passaic River, lithograph by Governor Pownal, London, ca. 1800. Private collection.

The Great Falls of the Passaic River, 19th century photograph. Private collection.

In the years before the Revolution, New Jersey became a prosperous colony. Passaic County, made up primarily of farmers, was not actively involved in the growing rebellion because the tariff laws that Parliament had imposed on the colonies did not affect farmers as much as merchants and traders.

But in 1765, Parliament passed an act requiring that troops be housed and fed in the province in which they were stationed. The impact this had on New Jersey, because of its strategic location as a route between the northern and southern colonies and as an entry to the western territories, inspired its farmers to join the rebel factions.

Winning the Revolution brought political independence, but economic autonomy had yet to be obtained. Economic independence from the British would only be won when America began to develop its own manufacturing capability.

In 1789, Alexander Hamilton was appointed secretary of the treasury by George Washington. One of his responsibilities was to develop the manufacturing capabilities necessary for the survival of the new country, for he understood that domestic manufacturing of essential products would be an essential underpinning of the new country's future.

Hamilton recognized that the major obstacle to industrial development in America was the lack of power to run its factories. He saw the waterpower potential of the Passaic River and its 75-foot falls as one answer to the nation's growing energy needs. Hamilton envisioned the area known as Ackquackanonk as a centralized manufacturing site, and convinced New Jersey legislators to grant a charter to create an industrial center.

On December 7, 1791, Hamilton, writing from Philadelphia, informed the Society for Establishing Useful Manufactures that he had made contracts on its behalf, subject to its revocation should the parties' performance not please it, with four gentlemen to oversee various facets of the industrial center's operation, thinking it "advisable to secure persons of whose usefulness there was occasion to entertain a favorable opinion, though on terms that may appear high, that the business might be early put in motion."

According to the society's minutes, on May 18, 1792, Ackquackanonk, an area near the Great Falls including the land within six miles of either sides of the Passaic River, was chosen because of "the natural lay of the land" which afforded hundreds of excellent sites for building mills.

Ackquackanonk had a number of advantages, first and foremost being the availability of waterpower to run the mills. In addition, both wood and iron ore could be found locally and sandstone could be quarried nearby for building. And the Passaic River provided easy transportation to New York City. The area was soon named Paterson after William Paterson, the governor of New Jersey, who was a stockholder in the Society for Establishing Useful Manufactures.

> *The advantages which Paterson possesses for a manufacturing town are obvious. An abundant and steady supply of water; a healthy, pleasant, and fruitful country, supplying its markets fully with excellent meats and vegetables; its proximity to New York, where it obtains the raw material, and sale for manufactured goods; and with which it is connected by the sloop navigation of the Passaic, by the Morris canal, by a turnpike-road, and by a rail-road—render it one of the most desirable sites in the Union.*
>
> —*Gazetteer of the State of New Jersey (1834)*

Paterson would soon become America's first industrial city and an active, thriving community. Plans for the construction of factories to accommodate cotton mills, buildings for spinning and weaving, and houses to accommodate workmen were approved at a meeting of the Society for Establishing Useful Manufactures held by General Philip Schuyler on May 29, 1792, at the house of Abraham Godwin, the Passaic Hotel.

Captain Abraham Godwin built and operated the Passaic Hotel in 1774, and his son, General Abraham Godwin, added a long room at the back of the hotel in 1820. Over the years, the hotel was to be the site of many important community functions. Earlier in 1792, the founders of the Society for Establishing Useful Manufactures had decided on the location of Paterson there. According to the *Trenton Federalist*, Governor DeWitt Clinton of New York was entertained there in 1823, and the Marquis de Lafayette, the French hero of the American Revolution, was feted there in July 1825.

Banner welcomes General Layfayette. The Passaic Hotel, Paterson, New Jersey, watercolor, 1825. Private collection.

At a meeting held on July 4, 1792, at the house of Abraham Godwin at Great Falls, the following report was presented: The committee appointed for the purpose of fixing upon a proper place the waters of the Passaick for the seat of the factory, for fixing the town Paterson and making the necessary purchases of land, Report: That on the 29th of May last, they went to the Great Falls of Passaick with General Schuyler and several other gentlemen well acquainted with the country and the nature of water works in general. The committee also reported having purchased and paid for the various tracts of lands constituting the township of Paterson. On July 5 the board resolved: That this Board do immediately cause the following works to be erected, namely, first, a building and machinery for carrying on the business of the cotton mill-second, the building and machinery for carrying on the printing business-thirdly, the building and machinery for carrying on the business of spinning, weft and weaving-fourthly, that a number of houses be erected for the accommodation of the workmen, to be employed by this Society.

—Nicholas Low
chairman of the Society for Establishing Useful Manufactures
July 4, 1792

The Great Falls of the Passaic River, Paterson, New Jersey. Postcard, 1905. Private collection.

The Gun Mill, 1835.

By the turn of the nineteenth century, Paterson's forges and furnaces were in full swing. Shoes, glassware, and cloth were being manufactured in small quantities. Fabric was in heavy demand after England cut off America's supply sources, and cloth began to be produced in the former colonies.

Because the society's charter made no legal provision for the city of Paterson, designating it as a corporation, the first industrial city of the world's greatest democracy had no local government for the first forty years of its existence.

It was not until 1831, after much agitation from the city's residents, that the New Jersey legislature finally granted Paterson a town charter. Paterson thus shares with Washington, D.C., the distinction of being one of the first two planned cities in the nation that began without their own municipal governments.

Hamilton's friend, Pierre L'Enfant, the engineer and architect of Washington, D.C., was initially retained to design Paterson. L'Enfant's proposals were too ambitious for the society, however, and his budget impractical. He was fired after two years and replaced with Peter Colt, the secretary of the treasury in Connecticut and an owner of some of the only cloth factories in New Jersey. He was one of the many Colts who would influence the development of Paterson, helping to lead the young city's industrial capabilities to maturity.

> *John Crawford, of Newark, came to Paterson in 1812 to complete the woodwork of the Peter Colt mansion (which was occupied from 1871–1896 as the city hall). He soon found some congenial associates whom he straightway organized into a branch "Garret" Society. Free, jovial and convivial, fond of company, and of discussion, he was nevertheless temperate himself. On one occasion he decreed that the " society" should meet on Wesel Mountain and salute the rising sun on the Fourth of July morning, with a salute from a four-pounder or six-pounder cannon. Crawford himself, a man six feet high, of powerful physique, tugged hard with the piece of ordnance up the mountain, and had the pleasure of touching it off in the early dawn, and of seeing the amazement and consternation with which the inhabitants of the little village at his feet rushed out of their houses to inquire the meaning of the explosion. When the story got abroad, the association of "The Garret" with the Mountain was inevitable, and the name, Garret Mountain, soon came into general use.*

> —Shriners
> *Chapters of Paterson History,* 1919

From another branch of the Colt family came Samuel, the inventor of the revolver, who built the Gun Mill in Paterson in 1835.

Peter Colt's son, John, developed a process for making cotton duck (a heavy canvas fabric) on a loom, thereby helping to extend the period that the cotton industry flourished in Paterson.

Christopher Colt was the first person to bring silk machinery to Paterson, beginning what was to become the city's major industry.

John Colt oversaw the building of the Bull Mill, the first mill in Paterson, which was completed in 1793. The mill's wheel was not turned initially by water, but by an ox on a treadmill—hence its name. The ox was replaced by waterpower a year later.

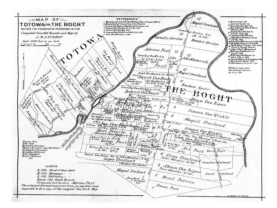

Partial map of Paterson, 1791.
Private collection.

In February, 1793, it was agreed to rent to John Campbell, of Philadelphia, sufficient space in the mill about to be erected for the introduction of the manufacture of stockings, and the superintendent was authorized to accommodate other intending manufacturers in a similar manner. Before cotton spinning was begun in the large mill, cotton was spun in a small temporary structure, the power being supplied by oxen, from which the building obtained its name as the "Bull Mill." In the meantime the building of the larger mill progressed; it was not occupied until the following year.

The mill stood on Mill Street—hence the name of the street north of Market, and was four stories high, with a high basement. A large bell in the cupola summoned the operatives to work. When in full operation there were four carders, four roving billies, four stubbing machines, twenty-five spinning jennies and sixty single looms. The bleaching and printing works stood on what is now Bridge Street, the bleach house being of frame, three stories high. Much of the machinery was imported, for there was hardly a machine shop in America. The workmen to set up the machinery, and the hands to operate it, were brought from Europe.

—Shriners
Paterson and It's Environs, 1920

Peter's sister, Sarah, began the first Sunday school in New Jersey in 1794, where she took it upon herself at the age of fifteen to teach the children of the mill workers to read and write in English.

Partial map of Paterson, 1882.
Private collection.

But of all the Colts, it was Roswell, another of Peter's sons, who would have the greatest impact on Paterson. "The greatest of all the Colts," for years Roswell L. Colt practically directed the future of Paterson. His name is attached to numerous deeds of real estate donated for churches, cemeteries, and educational purposes. Although his principles were thoroughly democratic, he ruled Paterson as an autocrat, and little was done without his consent and assistance, and frequently his initiative.

After several years of residence in Connecticut and in New York City, Roswell Colt decided to move to Paterson. With $150,000 borrowed from his father-in-law, he acquired large real estate holdings in the city and its vicinity. He now had ten children, and the question arose as to a proper home for his family.

He favored the small hill on Main Street, between Grand and Ward, the same spot that L'Enfant had looked upon as the proper central point for Paterson, from which streets and avenues were to radiate or circle. Mrs. Colt objected to this selection, expressing a decided preference for the top of Garret Mountain, from which a magnificent view could be had of all the surrounding country. Their differences were irreconcilable and resulted in a separation.

Grand Street Mill

Dexter Mill

Barbour Flax Mill

Colt carried out his original plan for a residence. For many months numerous laborers were employed carting soil to the small sand hill that formed the nucleus of what was later known as "Colt's Hill." Trees and shrubbery were removed from the mountain, and exotic plants of all kinds were crowded into the spacious hothouses. On the plateau on the top, a large mansion was erected in the Colonial style, and for years the mansion rivaled in social affairs the best-known homes in New York, the large stocks of foreign wines in the cellar doing their part to promote sociability.

Nearly all the prominent men of the day at some time or other were the guests of Roswell L. Colt. Among the more frequent visitors was Daniel Webster, who, in one of his letters speaks in enthusiastic terms of the present of a fine bull he had received from Mr. Colt. There is an interesting story connected with what followed one of Webster's visits.

Webster had tarried longer than had been expected in the genial companionship of Roswell L. Colt, and it was late when he arrived in New York, where he had promised to escort Mrs. Webster to Castle Garden to attend a concert in which Jenny Lind was the bright particular star. When Miss Lind sang "The Star Spangled Banner," Webster's enthusiastic patriotism asserted itself. He arose in his seat and joined in the chorus. Remonstrances on the part of Mrs. Webster were not heeded. Webster urged the audience to join him, which they did, all rising in their seats.

It is a fond belief, deeply rooted in the hearts of many people of Paterson and elsewhere, that it was this occasion that established the custom of audiences rising and singing at the rendition of the national hymn.

—Nelson and Shriner
History of Paterson, vol. 1

When the War of 1812 cut off the flow of manufactured goods from Europe, it helped Paterson's economy by creating a need for cloth to make soldiers' uniforms. Peter Colt encouraged the establishment of cotton mills, as the city of Paterson already had its factories built in the time of Alexander Hamilton, more than fifty years earlier.

The cotton industry was boosted by John Colt in 1832 when he made the first cotton duck that did not require special dressing to protect it against mildew. This fabric was especially suited for sails because it stood up well against moisture. The demand was so great that Colt developed a process for manufacturing it on a power loom. By the 1830s all the sails used by the United States Navy were being made in Paterson. In 1851, the yacht America won a victory under Colt sails that became the first in a series of international competitions known ever afterwards as the America's Cup race.

By 1881, raw cotton production in Paterson had increased to 3,850,000 pounds a year and employed nearly 1,000 workers. Bleaching and dyeing had become a significant part of Paterson's cotton industry, which remained active well into the twentieth century.

Despite the gradual eclipse of cotton as Paterson's dominant product, R.H. Addams and Company would go on to produce cotton for years. In 1872, S. Hold and Sons developed Turkish towels, also known as terry cloth. And George and Alexander McLean were producing mosquito netting and buckram, a material used for the backing of rugs and the making of sacks.

As for the silk industry, England's King James I had encouraged its production in Virginia as early as 1608. Silk had been tried unsuccessfully in England, and he looked to the colonies for a more suitable environment for raising silkworms and producing raw silk.

Later, the American government attempted to promote raw silk production by encouraging the growth of mulberry trees, but the cultivation of mulberry trees would prove unsuccessful, and a large number of investors who had hoped to make their fortunes producing raw silk lost money.

John Ryle

Manufacturers of silk goods turned to importing raw materials from the Orient and the Mediterranean. Silk industry professionals were brought over as well, and there was a renewed interest in manufacturing.

The skills and equipment utilized for cotton production were easily transferable to the silk industry. Christopher Colt is credited with bringing the first silk-making machinery to Paterson in 1838. He established his business in a section of the Gun Mill. He would later sell the business and the facilities to George Murray, whose own silk business had recently been destroyed by a fire.

Murray hired a young man named John Ryle to run the business. By 1843, Murray and Ryle were partners and built two more structures near the original Gun Mill, where the first Colt revolver was made, and soon employed over 500 workers.

John Ryle was a leader in Paterson's burgeoning silk industry and its growing fame as "The Silk City." He was the first person in the United States to put silk on a spool and was also the maker of the first silk American flag, which would fly over the Crystal Palace at the 1853 World's Fair in New York. Ryle also built the Murray Mill and, despite another devastating fire in 1869, and other financial setbacks, went on to establish John Ryle and Sons, which later merged with the Pioneer Silk Company.

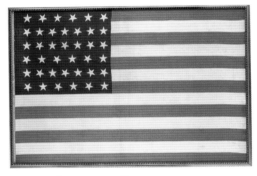

39-star silk American flag.
Private collection.

Ryle became the silk industry's most powerful proponent and lobbied for the repeal of a tariff on imported raw materials. In 1864, he went to Washington, where he was successful in having the tariff removed, putting Paterson manufacturers into competition with foreign firms.

Betsy Ross making the first United States Flag, woven silk,
Anderson Brothers, Paterson. Private collection.

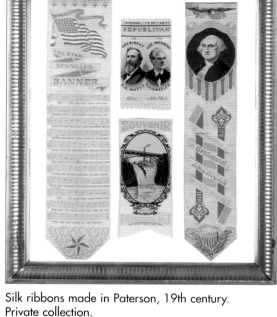

Silk ribbons made in Paterson, 19th century.
Private collection.

Silk Mill of the Paterson Ribbon Co.
Private collection.

Jacob Wiedman Mill.
Private collection.

Private collection.

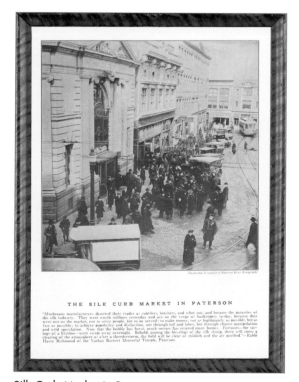

Silk Curb Market in Paterson.
Barnert Temple Archives.

In the 1850s, Ryle bought the romantic valley and heights surrounding the Passaic Falls, spent considerable money enhancing their already magnificent beauty, and opened it to the people of Paterson, who until then had had no public park.

Paterson continued to attract ambitious and talented entrepreneurs, who employed large numbers of men and women and became wealthy industrialists. In 1876, Catholina Lambert, a clerk and eventual partner at a Boston firm that made silk products for military uniforms, convinced his employers to move to Paterson. By 1882, Dexter, Lambert, and Company had facilities in both Paterson and Pennsylvania, where they did more than $1 million worth of business annually and employed more than a thousand workers.

Photograph of Belle Vista as it was in 1896 by Paterson photographer John Reid. Passaic County Historical Society.

Catholina Lambert would become one of Paterson's best-known "silk barons." He constructed Belle Vista Castle, which still stands today on Garrett Mountain and is known as Lambert's Castle. It was sold to the city of Paterson when Lambert died in 1923 and later was acquired by the Passaic County Park Commission. The Passaic County Historical Society now has its headquarters in the Castle, which is being restored to its original condition.

Among the main features of Lambert Castle were its colonnade and the galleries devoted to the display of Lambert's extensive collection of art. Lambert engaged for many years in collecting works of the old masters and many specimens of the work of modern schools, and once the large halls in his residence were filled he had an art gallery among the finest in the country. His art collection, which included works by Rembrandt, Botticelli, Velasquez, Rubens, Constable, Monet, Pissarro, and Renoir, was sold by the American Art Galleries at the Plaza Hotel in New York City in February 1916.

Mr. Lambert's home is one of the landmarks of the city, a magnificent residence erected thirty-five years ago and constructed along the lines of an English castle. Its grounds comprise 125 acres, beautifully and artistically planted with trees and shrubbery, and the building is of stone from his own quarries. The interior decorations and furnishings of the castle are all that discriminating taste and unlimited means can provide, among its art objects a collection of paintings of great value. Mr. Lambert is an art connoisseur and critic of no small knowledge and ability, and in the course of a score of trips abroad has acquired many canvases, precious artistically and from a financial standpoint. Period furniture and statuary of excellent choice contribute their share to the attractiveness of the Lambert mansion, and the acquisition of these art treasures has been one of his most enjoyable pleasures.

—*Nelson and Shriner*
History of Paterson, vol. 2

ON FREE PUBLIC VIEW
AT THE
AMERICAN ART GALLERIES
MADISON SQUARE SOUTH, NEW YORK
BEGINNING SATURDAY, FEBRUARY 12th, 1916
(LINCOLN'S BIRTHDAY)
AND CONTINUING UNTIL THE MORNING OF
THE DATE OF SALE, INCLUSIVE

THE FAMOUS
CATHOLINA LAMBERT
COLLECTION

TO BE SOLD AT UNRESTRICTED PUBLIC SALE
IN THE GRAND BALLROOM OF
THE PLAZA HOTEL
FIFTH AVENUE, 58th TO 59th STREET, NEW YORK
ON MONDAY, TUESDAY, WEDNESDAY AND THURSDAY EVENINGS
FEBRUARY 21st, 22nd (Washington's Birthday), 23rd AND 24th
BEGINNING PROMPTLY AT 8 O'CLOCK

Catalog, Catholina Lambert Collection Auction, 1916. Private collection.

Model of the Paterson train station, ca. 1910.
Private collection.

Cadillac Textiles Inc. medal, 1946.
Private collection.

Cadillac Textiles Inc. medal, 1971.
Descendants honor a textile founder born
in 1881. Private collection.

While England's silk industry suffered a severe decline in the nineteenth century, Paterson's continued to grow. Between 1872 and 1881, the annual output of silk products grew from $9.5 million to almost $16.5 million. By 1881, there were 121 firms in Paterson involved in silk manufacturing, silk dyeing, and the manufacture of supplies and equipment for silk production. According to *The Silk Industry of America*, a history prepared by Dr. L. P. Brockett for the 1876 Philadelphia Centennial Exposition, Paterson's silk firms employed nearly 8,000 "operatives" in 1875. Two-thirds of them were female and one-fourth were under sixteen years of age. All told, they earned just over $2.5 million (an average of $312 per worker per year). Nearly $6 million was invested in the mills, machinery, and manufacturing.

In fact, until the turn of the twentieth century, Paterson was the fastest-growing city on the East Coast, its population increasing dramatically every decade. And while the silk industry was rising, other areas of manufacturing were beginning to prosper in Paterson as well, including machine tools, locomotives, submarines, paper, soap, candles, and chemicals.

The Machine Works, built by Joseph C. Todd, who started in 1836 in a small machine shop in Paterson (Godwin, Clark & Co.), manufactured the first successful hemp-spinning machine. Boat engines, steam engines, and machinery for flax, hemp, jute, rope, and silk made there were sold all over the world.

Paterson even had a major brewery. The Katz Brewery began operations in July 1877, on the corner of Godwin and Bridge streets, with capacity of twenty-five barrels a day. It soon could not keep up with demand, and bought the Burton Brewery on Straight and Governor streets, which it also soon outgrew. The firm opened stores in New York and other cities, expanding to 130,000 barrels a year. In the 1890s an English syndicate offered $1 million for the business.

Once again, it was people that were Paterson's greatest asset. What all of the immigrants brought with them to Paterson was a strong work ethic and the willingness to make sacrifices for their children's education and futures. Great appreciation for the opportunities available to them in their new land, and for the religious and civil freedoms of America, made these new Americans committed and connected to their new country. In the following centuries many of these Paterson descendants honored their ancestors for the opportunities they received as American Jews.

> *My grandfather came to Paterson sometime in the early 1900s. He was working in a foundry making parts for coal stoves, and he had an opportunity to come to Paterson, New Jersey, and to go into business for himself to sell the parts that they made in the foundry. That's how our business started. I remember my father working six days a week and never on Sunday. Hated to even think about working on Sunday.*
>
> —Alan Kessler
> oral history

Machine Works of J. C. Todd

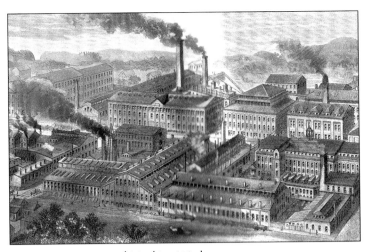

Rogers Locomotive and Machine Works

Exhibit of the Phoenix Silk Manufacturing Co. at the Paris Exhibition of 1878

Edison Electric Illuminating Co.

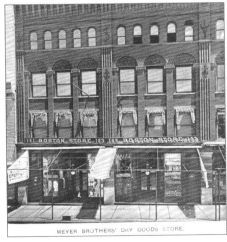

The first Meyer Brothers' department store, 181–187 Main Street.

Katz Brothers Brewery, later the Consolidated Brewing Co.

Residence of Rev. G. W. I. Landau

Broadway and Graham Streets

Residence of Hon. Garret A. Hobart

When the family came to America, my great-grandfather didn't come, because he was getting a pension from the German government and he didn't want to give it up. But my mother came because she had older sisters and all of a sudden there was a decree passed that the Jewish children couldn't go to the school where they lived. So her mother—my grandmother—got upset and said to her father, "We'll go to America."

My mother came over in 1886 when she was two. They lived on River Street, although I don't think it was called River Street to begin with. They had money, and they bought a barrel of kerosene. And then they got a barrel of herring and that's how they had the first Jewish-owned grocery store in Paterson. And my grandmother used to bake bread herself and sell it. But then around the corner, a group of Jews started The Cooperative Bakery. That cooperative was really wonderful. Such bread you never had!

—Esther Schwartz
oral history

In turn, Paterson's affluence was reflected in its large, handsome homes on wide, tree-lined, landscaped avenues, attesting to the success of its industrial and professional families. Its new public buildings—the City Hall, a remarkable example of Beaux Arts architecture; St. John the Baptist Cathedral; the Danforth Library; its schools; Eastside and Westside Parks; and, in 1894, the Nathan Barnert Memorial Temple—were all examples of the success of this great industrial city.

My mother bought a house on 34th Street in Paterson. When we moved in, it was very nice. As a matter of fact, the street, while in those days it wasn't even paved, was lined with trees, so it was a very nice neighborhood. Paterson at that time was a real royal city.

I remember we would go to the empty lots and you could pick buttercups and daisies right in the street practically. I used to go to the library on Broadway almost every day. I remember the books I used to pick out. I started with the A's and the B's and I got to D and I got to Dickens and I thought he was wonderful. I was just a youngster and it was a big walk from our house to the library. There were no radios. There was no television.

—Esther Schwartz
oral history

Paterson City Hall

First National Bank

Court House

Paterson Free Public Library

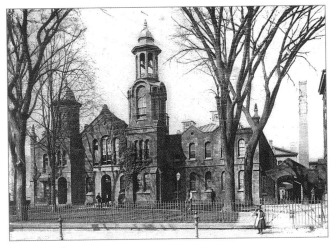

County Jail

Public School No. 2

Masonic Hall

Interior of St. John's Cathedral

Interior of Temple B'nai Jeshurun—The Nathan Barnert Memorial Temple

CHAPTER THREE

The Early Years

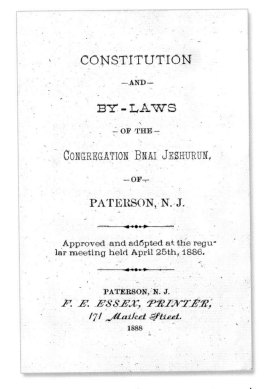

Congregation B'nai Jeshurun Constitution and
By-Laws, April 25, 1886. Barnert Temple Archives.

P rior to 1847, the Jews of Paterson met their religious needs privately, with Sabbath and festival worship taking place in individual homes. Some Paterson Jews would journey into New York City on the High Holidays to attend services in one of the synagogues there—no easy task then, as transportation was by horse and carriage or by boat.

The Jewish population in Paterson was still rather small—a religious census compiled in 1827 by the Rev. Samuel Fisher, pastor of the First Presbyterian Church, did not even have a category for "Hebrews" and listed one Joseph Shannon in the catch-all category "Infidels." But the early Paterson Jews nonetheless felt the moral and traditional responsibility to establish their own synagogue.

Congregation B'nai Jeshurun deeds and
mortgages,1889, 1891, and 1892.
Barnert Temple Archives.

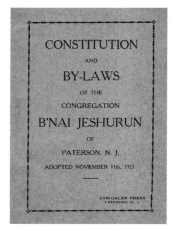

Congregation B'nai Jeshurun constitution
and by-laws,1925. Barnert Temple Archives.

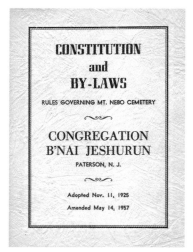

Congregation B'nai Jeshurun constitution
and by-laws,1957. Barnert Temple Archives.

Our nation was not yet seventy-two years old, and the president of our young, twenty-nine-state republic was James Polk, when, on November 26, 1847, five leading "Hebrew" citizens were elected as trustees of Congregation B'nai Jeshurun: Edward Harris, Sigmund Blunauer, Barnhard Raskam, Abraham Steiber, and Jacob Rheim. Eight days later, the trustees drew up the certificate of incorporation, which was delivered to the town clerk, Absolom B. Woodruff, and submitted to the New Jersey State Legislature on December 3, 1847.

It certified that the signators "have taken upon themselves and hereby assume the name of 'The Trustees of the Congregation B'nai Jeshurun of the Town of Paterson,' and by that name desire to become incorporated under and by virtue of the act of the legislature of the State of New Jersey, in such case made and provided."

The petition for incorporation was approved on December 22, 1847, and thus B'nai Jeshurun was legally established.

When I was president of the temple, there was a great debate whether our temple or the one in Newark was the oldest congregation in New Jersey. So I wrote to the secretary of state and got copies of the two certificates of incorporation, and, by George, we were three months older than the one in Newark. The interesting part, however, is that of the people required to sign the certificate in 1847, three of them could write, two of them made their X on the certificate.

—Daniel Lieblich
oral history

Hyman Grinstein reports in The Rise of the Jewish Community of New York, 1654–1860, that according to the official minutes of the New York City Jewish Council, in 1849 a request was granted for the loan of a Torah scroll to "the Synagogue in the town of Paterson, New Jersey."

The first official action taken by B'nai Jeshurun was the acquisition of land for a cemetery. Clifton, New Jersey, records show that on December 23, 1847, a plot of land 50 x 110 feet in Acquackanock Township (now Clifton) was purchased by the congregation from Dr. Joseph W. Ashman for $50. The Clifton city file is marked "Hebrew Cemetery."

One of the earliest headstones reads: "Post–Wife of Mac Rosenstien. Died March 19, 1876. Aged 42 years." Another: "In Memory of Rosa Goldstein, who died September, 1873. Aged 68 years."

The plot in Acquackanock, overlooking the New York City skyline, is still maintained by the congregation, although fragments of some headstones have been relocated to Mount Nebo Cemetery, a 22-acre tract of land purchased in 1867.

From 1847, services were held in private homes. Then, in 1853, ten citizens of Paterson gathered over a shoe store on Main Street, near Bank Street, and held services conforming to the Jewish religion. Services were held here for several years until 1858, when a room in a building on West Street was obtained.

In the early years of the congregation there was no rabbi, and members officiated at services. In 1860, they bought a private residence on the east side of Mulberry Street, adjoining the Dagger Bobbin Mills, and fitted it up as a synagogue, where they held readings and prayers for seventeen years.

Building at 9 Mulberry Street, used as B'nai Jeshurun Synagogue, 1860–1877. Photograph by Albert H. Heuser, 1925. Private collection.

> *"Yesterday afternoon the very unusual spectacle of a wedding "according to the laws of Moses and of Israel" was witnessed in the Jewish Synagogue on Mulberry Street, in this city. The event, unusual as it was, with such a complete observance of minute detail, was still further remarkable on account of the great brilliance and even splendor of all the accompaniments.*
>
> *The synagogue is in the upper chamber of a plain two-story building in Mulberry Street, near River. The room is furnished with plain benches with high backs. At the eastern end of the chamber is a raised platform, enclosed by a railing. On this platform is a reading desk, and back of the desk hangs a heavy, white, silk damask curtain—supposed to guard the ark of the Covenant from profane gaze; this being somewhat modeled after the original Temple at Jerusalem. On this curtain is embroidered a golden crown—emblem of the Crown of the Law, or the Covenant. Above the curtain is a double Table of the Decalogue, on red stained glass, and as this is in front of a window, the effect of the light shining through is very pretty.*
>
> —*Paterson Daily News*
> *January 11, 1872*

Works of John R. Daggers. Barnert Temple Archives.

The new temple on Mulberry Street did not at first enjoy the support of the wealthier Hebrews, who preferred to retain their connections with New York synagogues. Therefore the attendance was not large, and there was often no rabbi, with services conducted by lay members of the congregation. Among the early rabbis were Herman Blichrode, Jacob S. Jacobson, Solomon Bergman, and A. Brasch, all of whom are listed in various editions of Boyd's Paterson Directory, 1870 through 1877, albeit as "Pastors," a designation not corrected until the 1878 edition, when Rev. Max Molle was listed as "Rabbi."

In another section of Boyd's Directory, 1875–1876, Nathan Barnert, who was to become the temple's most famous benefactor, is listed with three of his relatives, Boas, Morris, and Meyer, all of whom were employed as clerks at his clothing store on Main Street.

Evidence shows that the congregation was still small in the year 1860. Nathan Barnert recalled in his personal memoirs that "there were often times that men from the congregation had to travel into Passaic on Sabbath mornings, which was no easy journey in those days, to gather sufficient fellow Jews for a minyan," the quorum required for public prayer.

1847 Mount Nebo Cemetery.
Author photo, 2005. Private collection.

1867 Mount Nebo Cemetery.
Author photo. Barnert Temple Archives.

1867 Mount Nebo Cemetery.
Author photo. Private collection.

With the great influx of German Jews into Paterson in the early 1860s, the congregation entered into its first real stage of growth. In 1867, a new plot of land was purchased for cemetery purposes from the Bensen Farm for $8,000.

The 22-acre tract of land was incorporated as Mount Nebo Cemetery, named after the site of Moses' death in the Bible. By June 15, 1919, there had already been 238 interments in Mount Nebo, which remains the congregational burial ground today.

The congregation worshipped on Mulberry Street until 1878, when it acquired its first permanent building, a one-story frame structure at 124 Van Houten Street, between Bridge and Washington streets. The building had previously housed the Society of Independents (a political organization), a church, and a private school for girls.

While some of the early rabbis of the congregation were ordained clergymen from Europe, most were devout, educated laymen, elected by the congregation to conduct worship, preach sermons, and give religious instruction to the children.

In 1881, Rev. Moses Cohen was elected to serve as rabbi, as noted in the 1882 edition of Turnbill's History of Industrial Paterson. He was followed in 1884 by the Rev. B. Newmark, who served the congregation until 1887. In 1883, the first official Hebrew school in the history of Paterson was established at the Van Houten Street synagogue. Myer S. Hood of Newark was engaged to teach the children Hebrew, German, and Bible. In 1887, Hood accepted the additional duties of rabbi and served in this capacity until 1892.

But Congregation B'nai Jeshurun would soon undergo a fundamental change in its religious orientation—a change that has lasted to the present day.

When founded in 1847, the congregation was organized as an Orthodox synagogue, following the Ashkenazic ritual of the German Jewish community. Reform Judaism was, at the time, in its infancy.

By 1880, however, Reform Judaism, a response to the strict doctrines of Orthodoxy that allowed for the accommodation of new scientific ideas and social practices, revision of the liturgy to allow prayers and sermons in the local vernacular (in this case English), and a ritual more in tune with life in America, was already established as a force on the American religious scene.

The Reform philosophy also reflected the openness and progressive aspects of American society. Jews, like other immigrant groups, remembered bitterly their second-class citizenship in Europe and embraced their American freedoms, which transformed and reformed all religions. They became American Jews.

The Orthodox Jews of Paterson were beginning to feel the impact of this new movement, and Congregation B'nai Jeshurun would soon make the transition. In fact, B'nai Jeshurun was a very Americanized role model for Reform. The people actively involved in the temple tended to be laymen rather than religious, and English began to be used more in the services. After 1877, while the congregation was still housed in the Van Houten Street synagogue, the change toward Reform began.

I don't know how early my people started with the Barnert Temple, but because my mother came from a town where her family was the only Jewish family and she didn't know Hebrew, didn't know Yiddish, and had very little if any religious training, my dad, who came from an Orthodox Jewish background, took her to a [Reform] congregation where most of the services were in English and she would be comfortable. They had been members for some time before I was ready to go to Sunday school there. I went to Sunday school and I had my bar mitzvah at the Barnert Temple.

—Joseph Shapiro, M.D.
oral history

Some of the restrictions in Jewish law were relaxed, such as the dietary laws, which proved impractical in an evolving setting. Two innovations were the use of family pews in the synagogue (previously the worshipers, in Orthodox tradition, had been separated by sex) and the inclusion of women in the choir.

A small gallery at the west end—originally intended for the exclusive occupancy of the ladies, who were according to the ancient law, kept apart from the men in the Synagogue. This distinction is now generally ignored, we believe.

—Paterson Daily News
January 11, 1872

The role of the religious leader, the rabbi, changed as well. Traditionally, in Europe, the local rabbi was primarily a decisor on questions of Jewish law and the judge in disputes between members of the community. In the United States, the traditional power of this authority figure diminished greatly because fewer people felt bound by Jewish law except perhaps in strictly religious matters. On all other matters Jews were regarded as individual citizens rather than members of an autonomous community and therefore were subject to the same civil and criminal law as everyone else.

Thus rabbis in the United States were "protestantized." They relinquished many of their customary legal functions and, like Christian pastors, now concentrated on conducting religious services, teaching, and officiating at the life-cycle events of their congregants, such as marriages and funerals. Involvement in the larger community, social action, and interfaith cooperation now became standard commitments of rabbis in Paterson and elsewhere.

...the Reform movement in Judaism, which began at the end of the eighteenth and beginning of the nineteenth centuries, was primarily a movement of the laity. The rabbis, erudite scholars, were immersed in the vast maze of Hebrew learning and devoted their self-sacrificing energies to the maintenance of Jewish traditions against all the forces of a changing and unpredictable age. But Jewish laymen, being men of affairs, were not confined to the enchanted garden of Talmudic lore but were in constant contact with the new age. They realized more than the rabbis could possibly realize the vast gulf between Jewish tradition and the actualities of life in the changing era. To the extent that the rabbis appreciated the contradiction between the environment and tradition, they would naturally insist that the life of the Jew in the modern world must be made

Mrs. J. Lieblich, 1912. Barnert Temple Archives.

Left to right: Max Rosen and Jacob Rosen, 1910.
Barnert Temple Archives.

to fit the requirements of tradition. The laymen naturally concluded that the Jewish tradition must be modified to fit into a changing world. Thus it came about that the laymen were the pioneers of the Reform Movement....

The strength of Reform is precisely in the fact that it is not one set of changes determined upon and ordained, but the spirit of living growth. Therefore it must not be referred to as "Reformed" Judaism, but as "Reform" Judaism.

—Rabbi Solomon B. Freehof
"What Is Reform Judaism?"

Congregation became synonymous with community. The synagogue offered a historic look at the past in this vast new land so distant from the members' ancestral surroundings. First-generation American Jews recollected painfully their humiliating and dangerous experiences in Europe and relished the many precious religious and civil freedoms of their newfound country. The Old World, with its quaint and often restrictive ways, was their past. As American Jews they were avidly energized by the freedom of American society and firmly committed to their future as American Jews.

Though no records of a formal adoption of Reform Judaism by the Paterson community are available, the change had apparently taken place by 1890. The most significant evidence in support of this assumption is the fact that in 1886 a second, more Orthodox, synagogue was organized in Paterson.

My mother's entire family, the Aronsohns, was in the textile business. Her father [Israel Aronsohn] was the president of the Orthodox shul, the big shul on Fair Street. I can remember when people used to get very dressed up for the holidays. Everybody had new clothes.... I mean dressed up—hats, gloves.

—Norma Joelson Hayman
oral history

The Orthodox shul, Congregation B'nai Israel, was organized in 1886, at the home of Moshe Kassel on River Street, by Russian and Polish Jews who did not wish to affiliate with B'nai Jeshurun because of its increasing trend toward Reform.

Along with the change in orientation, the existing quarters of B'nai Jeshurun would soon prove to be too small. The cramped facilities did nothing to attract the wealthier Paterson Jews, who could have contributed much-needed financial assistance but were instead worshiping in the more established synagogues in New York City. But the congregation's physical situation was about to change, thanks to a forward-thinking member and benefactor—Nathan Barnert.

CHAPTER FOUR

Nathan Barnert
B'nai Jeshurun's Benevolent Benefactor

Oil portrait of Nathan Barnert. Barnert Temple collection.

Nathan Barnert, the most influential and generous member in the congregation's history, was an illustrious figure. He was born in Posen, Germany (now Poznan, Poland), on September 20, 1838—Yom Kippur, the Day of Atonement, and the most sacred day in the Jewish calendar. Barnert, always a devout Jew, took great pride in this fact.

Ida Barnert. Barnert Temple Archives.

Meyer Barnert. Barnert Temple Archives.

Barnert came to the United States with his parents, Ida and Meyer Barnert, in 1849, when he was eleven years old. He was schooled at home in New York City, studied Torah on Henry Street, and worked in his father's tailoring shop on Forsythe Street, near Grand. Nathan was ambitious, resourceful, energetic, and focused.

As a young man he set out for California and the Hawaiian Islands via Nicaragua in search of gold and his vocation in life. He made his way to Nicaragua by steamer, working as a coal passer on the ship to earn meal money. When he got to California he was too young to stake a claim, so his first job was in a general store, sweeping the floor.

Almost immediately he decided that gold mining was a risky venture at which few men were likely to succeed, so he became a peddler. He went out to the miners with a pack on his back, carrying small items like needles, soap, candles, and thread.

Within a very short time, he had a horse and wagon and could take out heavier things like spades, lanterns, and kerosene. By the end of this period he was much wealthier than most of the miners.

However, neither the Hawaiian Islands nor the gold rush made Barnert the truly wealthy man he aspired to be, so he returned to New York in 1856 and entered the clothing business.

In 1858, when he was twenty, he moved to Paterson, the great industrial city, and in several years he had built a successful tailoring business on Main Street. Barnert's business interests were diverse. He invested in real estate and textile mills for rental spaces and founded the Annondale Screen Plate Co., which furnished supplies for paper mills. He was greatly admired, both for his business success and for his assistance in helping the community to solve some of its employment problems.

In 1860, "King Cotton," which until then had reigned in Paterson, was about to be dethroned as the city's leading industry in favor of "the arm of iron"—locomotives. The "sleeve of silk," what would eventually become Paterson's highly successful silk industry, was still in its infancy. Then came the attack on Fort Sumter in April of 1861, and the Civil War.

With the outbreak of war came hard times for Paterson. Business was stagnant, and unemployment was high. Nathan Barnert worked hard to aid the many men and their families in need of assistance. The opportunity came when he succeeded in securing large contracts to clothe the Union forces, thus giving employment to hundreds of poor people on the verge of starvation and re-energizing Paterson's cotton industry.

Barnert Silk Mill. Barnert Temple Archives.

When he got to Paterson he got there with money, but there was a period of economic disorientation. It seemed like a good time to buy mill space. So he bought mill space, and when things got straightened out and it was a period of prosperity a few years later, he owned a very good proportion of the mills, and after renting out mill space all over the place he had a substantial income and had made a similar fortune making uniforms during the Civil War.

—Joseph Shapiro, M.D.
oral history

Barnert continued in mercantile life until 1878, when he retired to devote his entire attention to his extensive real estate interests, from which he would build his fortune, purchasing textile mills and other properties which he rented to commercial interests.

I remember that I could have bought all of Main Street on one side of the street, from Market Street down to Ellison Street, forty-seven years ago for $100 a foot front. I bought the property where the five-and-ten-cent store is now located for $50,000 and people thought I was crazy, that something was wrong in my head.

—Nathan Barnert,
from Baum, Paterson's Most Useful Citizen

Medal of Treasurer, Silk Workers' Benevolent Association. Private collection.

Nathan Barnert married Miriam Phillips, the daughter of a wealthy English family, on September 2, 1863. One of her brothers was twice Lord Mayor of London, and another was a London alderman for several terms. But for most of her life Miriam lived in America, most of it in Paterson. Her father, Henry L. Phillips, was a furrier on Grand Street in New York City and a property owner in Paterson.

The 1914 edition of Michael Baum's biography of Nathan Barnert described Miriam Barnert as "a domestic woman who believed in a home; a patriotic woman who believed in the American flag and a social woman who believed in human relations—the relation of humanity to humanity. She went through the world doing good, leaving behind her a path of light. It was not her wealth or position that counted for her; it was her use of both for doing good."

Nathan Barnert was a civic-minded American Jew who felt compelled to concentrate his energy, insights, and funds on helping his community. Miriam Barnert was Nathan's partner in life and actively participated in their common goals of improving the welfare of Paterson's citizens.

Paterson in the 1870s was a Republican city. Notwithstanding, Barnert, a sturdy Democrat, was appointed by the board of aldermen to make a special investigation of the city's finances and tax accounts. It was a common suspicion at the time that city government was being conducted for the financial benefit of the politicians and their friends.

Barnert's investigations confirmed these suspicions; in fact, so thorough was his work that the city prosecuted a number of officials, who, as a result, landed in New Jersey State Prison. Gradually, Barnert increased his sphere of activity and influence in the city, and in 1876 he was elected alderman of the Sixth Ward, serving two terms. He was so successful in bringing about sorely needed reforms that he was nominated for the office of mayor and was overwhelmingly elected on April 9, 1883—the first Jewish mayor of Paterson.

My political aspirations are overestimated. Public office has no charm for me. To be serviceable to the people who have put their trust in me as executive is my aim. It is my only object to accomplish a more careful, honest, systematic method of business.

—Nathan Barnert
on his election as mayor

On April 16, 1883, one week after his election, Barnert used his first message to the board of aldermen to present one of his first recommendations, that the city construct a commodious park where "the working men of the city, together with their wives and children, may resort to for comfort and refreshment after their labors are over." Eastside Park, as it was to be named, would also provide a place where sick and convalescent children might be taken to enjoy fresh air and pure water.

On one occasion, Barnert refused to sign bonds for the Eastside sewer, contending that it should be constructed of brick and not of cement. The matter was taken to court, and the mayor eventually won. It was estimated that he saved the city over $100,000 in this matter alone.

As mayor of a then-corrupt city government, Barnert worked tirelessly to institute political reforms and efficiency procedures. He was defeated in 1885 by a highly regarded Republican who ran a dynamic campaign, but Barnert was again drafted to run for mayor in April 1887. Running on an unpopular platform of "municipal reform," he was nonetheless re-elected by a narrow margin. During both terms, he labored to develop Paterson's cultural and social services, donating his salary each month to local charities, hospitals, libraries and orphanages, an example of political liberality rarely known at that time.

Eastside Park, postcard. Private collection.

The citizens of Paterson are to be congratulated upon Nathan Barnert's reelection to the mayoralty. He was elected because a majority of the people remembered his former administration of the office, and wished it repeated. They believed that he would be watchful of their interests and earnestly strive to promote the progress of the city. Mr. Barnert holds that the taxpayers should get a dollar's worth for every dollar entrusted to their official representatives, but he also believes that money judiciously spent for public improvements is wisely spent.

It is the first time in the history of the Republican Party in this city that they were ever frightened out of buying the purchasable vote. There was a large corruption fund raised, but they were afraid to use it. Mr. Barnert spent no money except to pay for his printing.

—Paterson Daily Guardian
April 9–10, 1889

Westside Park, postcard. Private collection.

The acrostic reproduced in part below, composed by one A. Blyerelland in 1890 after reading of Mayor Barnert's visit to the almshouse, shows the esteem in which he was held by his fellow citizens.

> **N**–oblest and gentlest of thy noble race,
> **A**–t the head of the 'Aldermanic Board,
> **T**–hou shalt endure when others in disgrace
> **H**–ave left the riches they unjustly hoard,
> **A**–nd long in homes and hearts of men,
> **N**–athan, thy name and deeds shall live.

Miriam Barnert.
Barnert Temple Archives.

Memorial window, from Barnert Temple
in Paterson. Now hangs in
the Barnert Temple in Franklin Lakes.
Photo by Karen Galinko.

Sanctuary of Barnert Memorial Temple,
Broadway at Straight Streets.
Barnert Temple Archives.

The similarly flattering acrostic below was composed by congregation member Jane Jacobson nearly twenty-five years later, on the occasion of Nathan Barnert's seventy-sixth birthday. As in the years to follow, the celebration of his birthday was a communal event, "a source of much rejoicing to Jew and Gentile alike."

B–oaz — A descendant of Judah, a man of the highest character and integrity, who married Ruth, the Moabite, from whence came the Royal House of David.

A–braham — Who by his obedience to God's will, through him the seed of all Israel was blessed.

R–euben — Jacob's eldest son.

N–ehemiah — A distinquished Jew born in captivity, becoming cup bearer to King Artaxerxes, by his wondrous influence with the King, he was commissioned to visit Jerusalem and repair its ruins. He was made Governor forthwith.

E–zra — A priest and scribe who with Nehemiah was instrumental in restoring once again the worship of Israel, and the Sacred Books were compiled and collected under their direction.

R–iches — And honors are with me; yea durable riches and righteousness. Proverbs, Chap. 8 v. 18.

T–he — Tishbite Elijah, favored by God with miraculous power, transported to heaven in the presence of Elisha and fifty other persons.

Nathan and Miriam Barnert were known throughout Paterson for their kindness and devotion to Judaism and the community at large, as evidenced, for example, by their building of the Barnert Memorial Temple (completed in 1894) for the congregation where they had been active members for decades.

In the deed transferring the land for the new building to the congregation, Nathan Barnert made several stipulations about the ritual observances that were to take place in the new temple. He also included a provision that when he and Miriam were deceased, the memorial prayer, Kaddish, was to be recited in the synagogue on each and every anniversary of their deaths.

It was a provision fulfilled all too soon. On March 31, 1901, after a lengthy illness, Miriam Barnert passed away. Miriam Barnert was known throughout the city of Paterson for her saintly and pious ways, and her death was a blow to thousands of people who knew and loved her. She had long served the charitable institutions of Paterson, and had devoted much of her time to personal acts of righteousness.

It had been her practice every Friday afternoon to invite the poorer Jews of the city to her doorstep, where she would dispense money for the Sabbath meal. She also made it her custom to pay the dowries of young Jewish girls in the city. On April 1, 1901, for the first time in its history, a funeral for a woman took place in the sanctuary proper of Barnert Temple. Thousands, rich and poor, members of all religions, came to pay homage to their friend and benefactor. The funeral, in keeping with her lovable character, was unostentatious.

She was a cheerful light in the world and did not confine herself to her own blood and race, but was just as kindly and generously disposed towards all sects and races, and she never tired in doing good.

—Orrin Vanderhoven,
Paterson Evening News,
September 26, 1892

On April 20, 1902, a beautiful memorial window in honor of Miriam Barnert was placed in the side wall of the Barnert Memorial Temple, a gift of the temple trustees. At the top of the stained glass were Moorish ornamentations, and directly beneath were two simple scrolls bearing the inscription "In Memory of Miriam Barnert." After his wife's death, Nathan Barnert undertook many more charitable projects, among the most important of which were the establishment of the Miriam Barnert Memorial Hebrew Free School and the Miriam Barnert Dispensary Association, which later became Barnert Memorial Hospital.

The Miriam Barnert Memorial Hebrew Free School was dedicated on September 27, 1904. The school offered instruction in biblical and post-biblical history, reading and translation of Hebrew, and a comprehensive study of Jewish ritual and ceremonies.

The first requirement was that applicants must be attending a public school. The Barnert school quickly attained a national reputation for the scope of its answer to the challenge of religious instruction. At its inception, an average of 500 students, ranging in age from six to fourteen, attended the school. All expenses and salaries were defrayed by voluntary contributions, many from gentiles.

On October 19, 1914, the cornerstone was laid for the $250,000 Nathan and Miriam Barnert Hospital, a magnificent facility that serves as a monument to Barnert and his wife, to whom it is dedicated.

It has been my ambition since the death of my wife to erect a hospital where the sufferings of all, regardless of sect or religion, race or color, could receive proper care and medical attention. I pray almighty God that I may live to see this hospital fulfilling the purpose for which it is erected.

—Nathan Barnert,
dedication of Miriam Barnert Memorial Hospital

Miriam Barnert Memorial Hebrew Free School.
Barnert Temple Archives.

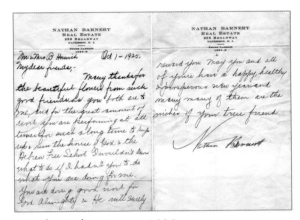

Letter by Nathan Barnert, 1925.
Private collection.

Daughters of Miriam.
Barnert Temple Archives.

Original Barnert Dispensary, 1908.
Barnert Temple Archives.

Community response to this great gift, which would benefit all Paterson citizens, was immediate and overwhelming.

You and your deceased wife have been models of benefactors of the poor. The hospital will be a crowning act of your generosity.

—Rev. W. McNulty
St. Johns Rectory
October 17, 1914

A significant circumstance in the history of the city will occur today in the breaking of ground for the new Barnert Memorial Hospital on upper Broadway. The munificence of Nathan Barnert to supply the ground and money for this handsome and attractive institution is only another evidence of the good in this distinguished citizen.

—Paterson Morning Call
July 20, 1914

Barnert Memorial Hospital. Barnert Temple Archives.

Paterson is indeed fortunate in having among its citizens a philanthropist of the quality of Nathan Barnert. The impressive ceremonies attending the laying of the cornerstone yesterday afternoon of the magnificent hospital to be erected for the use of our city without respect of creed, class or color, signaled the beginning—or rather the development into its full flower—of a beneficent work which will, through all the coming years, stand as a monument to Mr. Barnert and the great-hearted wife to whose fragrant memory this hospital was yesterday dedicated.

—Paterson Press
October 20, 1914

Board of Directors, Nathan and Miriam Barnert Memorial Hospital. *Top row: left to right:* Jacob Rosensweig, John Charney, David Yedwab, Henry Marelli, John Kaufman, Herman Heinrichs, David Atkind, Sigmund M. Cohan, Morris Scher, Abram I. Bluestein, Gustav D. Mikola, Herman Haimowicz. *Center row:* Samuel Neinken, Joseph T. Lieblich, Albert H. Slater, Hon. Abram Klenert, Hon. Nathan Barnert, Boas Barnert, Rabbi Israel Rosenberg, Jacob Fabian, Arnold Levy. *Bottom row:* Phillip Dimond, Sender Federbush, Isadore Horowitz, Louis Spitz, Max Rosen, David Agins, Joseph Kassel, Max Menein, Samuel Friedlander. Barnert Temple Archives.

In 1908, when the original Barnert dispensary was planned, it was decided that English, German, French, Jewish, Italian, Hungarian, and other foreign languages should be spoken so that the patients, often handicapped in making themselves understood by physicians with whom they were unable to converse in their mother tongue, could be given proper treatment.

The Barnert Memorial Hospital was an imposing structure, occupying one entire block, also contributed by Barnert, on Broadway between 30th and 31st streets and Thirteenth Avenue. Standing on a plot of land allowing for ample air and light, it had an initial capacity of seventy-five patients, a figure that has grown to several hundred today. But perhaps its most striking feature was that its entire cost was borne by one man—not a single dollar was asked or desired of the public. For the rest of his life, Nathan Barnert continued his public endeavors to benefit all Paterson's citizens.

On November 6, 1925, Friday night services included a "Nathan Barnert Gratitude Service," at which he was the recipient of special honors tendered by the Jewish people of Paterson. The eighty-seven-year-old Barnert received an ovation when he rose to speak, evidence of the affection held for the "Grand Old Man."

In October of 1926 a statue of Nathan Barnert was unveiled in front of the Paterson City Hall. The bronze monument was placed in the company of similar tributes to Andrew F. McBride, M.D., twice mayor of Paterson (1908–1914) and Garret A. Hobart, a Patersonian who served as vice president during the administration of William McKinley. Paid for by contributions from all sectors of the populace, the statue was unique in that it was erected while its honoree was still alive.

Nathan Barnert was to outlive his beloved Miriam by nearly twenty-seven years, passing away on Friday morning, December 23, 1927, at the age of eighty-nine. Those twenty-seven years Nathan Barnert devoted to the public good.

As news of his death spread throughout Paterson, the entire city went into deep mourning for its former mayor and devoted friend.

Nathan Barnert's funeral was held on a Sunday afternoon. All the flags in the city were at half-mast, and the temple was draped in black. Three separate services were conducted: a private family ceremony at the Barnert home, a public funeral at the temple, and Masonic rites at the cemetery. Barnert had been an active Mason for many decades. He also held memberships in Jephta Lodge No. 143, Independent Order of B'nai B'rith, organized in Paterson on May 15, 1870; the Paterson Orange Lodge of Masons; the Independent Order of the Odd Fellows; and the Knights of Pythias.

The police and fire department's guard of honor, the hundreds of gentiles who crowded the temple on the day of his burial, the half-masted flag at the City Hall and on other public buildings of Paterson—all bore eloquent testimony to the city's profound sorrow at the passing of this great and highly regarded American Jew.

Not since Vice President Garret A. Hobart was laid to rest had Paterson seen a funeral so large or one where the entire community was so deeply and completely affected.

Nathan Barnert reading a speech of appreciation at the 1925 unveiling of his statue in front of Paterson City Hall. Barnert Temple Archives.

Statue of Nathan Barnert in front of Paterson City Hall. Photo by James D. Schwartz, 2005.

Paterson City Hall. Photo by James D. Schwartz, 2005.

Maquette for the Nathan Barnert statue in front of Paterson City Hall, by sculptor Gaetano Federici. Photo by James D. Schwartz, 2005. Barnert Temple collection.

His pallbearers included the mayor of Paterson and the most eminent judges, merchants, lawyers, and physicians of the city.

Among them was also Gaetano Federici, the sculptor who fashioned and executed the statute of Nathan Barnert which now stands at the City Hall.

Nurses from the hospital he built, children of the school he erected, members of the temple which bears his name, residents of the orphanage and old people's home which he brought about—all were there to do honor to the man who for three generations symbolized what is best and noblest in American Jewish life and achievement.

> It is appropriate that the very first words in memory of Nathan Barnert be said from this pulpit. For Nathan Barnert was, for a longer time than even the oldest among us remember, indissolubly bound up with the life of B'nai Jeshurun. He was our patron saint, the life-long and devoted friend of B'nai Jeshurun, a pillar of strength in our midst even as he was throughout our city and our State.
>
> With my mental eye I can see Nathan Barnert time and again discoursing from this pulpit. I can picture his ministering to this congregation at the time the corner of this edifice was laid and again at the time of its consecration, and I can see his face abeam whenever anything unusual took place here.
>
> He blessed our boys and girls when they went through the sacred rite of Confirmation, he mingled with our men and women in times of joy and he joined our people in times of great sorrow.
>
> And I see before me a picture of that Friday evening some twenty-eight years ago when this prince of wondrous deeds walked down the aisle with a President of the United States, William McKinley, and I see before me now the tablet which marks the spot where he sat....
>
> Much will be said in days to come about Nathan Barnert's life and deeds. Let us pause tonight and reflect on what he has meant to us as a congregation. In a large sense Nathan Barnert was the founder, the formulator and fashioner of B'nai Jeshurun.
>
> Seventy years ago, this congregation already existed, but it was a frail structure and needed building up from the very foundation. This Nathan Barnert did. Like Moses he fused our people together with the might of his own spirit. Nathan Barnert occupied himself greatly with the construction of buildings, but he succeeded even more as a builder of souls.
>
> He built well. It has been said of him that he was orthodox in Jewish sympathies. I would rather say that he was extremely Jewish. He loved ceremony, rite and custom. But he was also progressive and adaptive. It was he who was instrumental in introducing a mixed choir, the use of a pipe organ, and family pews. It was he who sought to harmonize Jewish custom with the American spirit.
>
> —Rabbi Dr. Max Raisin,
> Sabbath sermon after the death of Nathan Barnert

Nathan Barnert was buried not showily but solemnly and impressively. The customary Jewish rites were carried out at the end in the temple, and the Masonic fraternity reverently played its part at the cemetery.

According to his wishes, Nathan Barnert was buried in a plain cedar coffin, which he had purchased almost twenty-seven years before, when his wife died. The coffin was draped with an American flag and the blue-and-white banner of Zion. In the fulfillment of Barnert's wish, Rabbi Max Raisin spoke no sermon, but read selections from the Book of Psalms. Thousands of mourners then joined the rabbi in the *Kaddish* prayer.

Tomb of Miriam and Nathan Barnert.
Barnert Temple Archives.

At the age of eighty-nine, Nathan Barnert passed on to the Great Beyond. Born on Yom Kippur, 5599 (1838), he yielded his great spirit on the early morning of Rosh Hodesh Kislev 5688, Friday, December 23, 1927. He died as he lived, amidst plain and humble surroundings. He cared not for the glitter of earthly things during his days of health and strength, and his deathbed scene mirrored this attitude towards life and the things that go to make life worthwhile.

The man who used his money to make others happy was very parsimonious where his own comfort was concerned. He spent a million on others; he hesitated to spend a dollar on himself.

And he died like he lived—also from the Jewish point of view. Always the staunch, loyal and proud Jew, he ordered in his last will that his funeral rites be conducted as simply and inexpensively as possible. No eulogy to be delivered and only selections from the Book of Psalms should be read.

—Michael T. Baum
"Paterson's Most Useful Citizen", 1914

גתן ברנרט
נולד ביום הכפורים תקצ"ט
נפטר בשיבה גדולה ובשם טוב בכ"ט כסלו תרפ"ח
נתן לאבי ונים. צדקתו עומדת לעד. קרנו תרום בכבוד
תהלים קי"ב

NATHAN BARNERT
PHILANTHROPIST, TWICE MAYOR OF PATERSON
1838 ——— 1927
SANTO MICHEL   PATERSON
תנצבה

Nathan Barnert Memorial Plaque. Author photo, 2003.
Barnert Temple collection.

Not a flower was anywhere in evidence. Instead two large flags, the star-spangled banner of his beloved America and the white-blue banner of Zion, with its lone star, covered his casket.

And thus slept the sleep eternal the man who gave Paterson and the entire country the finest example of American and Jewish manhood: an American who twice stood at the head of the city he helped to make great and prosperous; and with it all a Jew—every inch of him a staunch, devoted, unflinching son of the people of Israel....

The thousands of men, women, children who passed round his bier, lingering to look at the earthly features of Paterson's great Ex-Mayor, saw in him that which he truly was: "A Prince and a Great Man in Israel."

B'nai Jeshurun Weekly Bulletin
January 1928

Home of Miriam and Nathan Barnert on Broadway.
Barnert Temple Archives.

My parents, Albert and Anna Del Guidice, were neighbors of Nathan Barnert. They lived in an old Victorian house at 266 Broadway that had been converted to apartments. My father's barber shop was on the ground floor. Mr. Barnert's house was at 270 Broadway.

I was born in 1921, and to commemorate the occasion, Mr. Barnert gave my mother a $5 gold coin. I remember Mr. Barnert's house well, it had two iron hitching posts where people tied their horses when they came to visit. I often saw Mr. Barnert on the porch of his house. He was a kindly, well dressed gentleman.

—Vincent Del Guidice, M.D.
Author Interview January 27, 2000

There is the extraordinary example given to us a century ago by Nathan Barnert and his wife, Miriam. It was their vision, their wisdom and their generosity which became the bedrock upon which the institution we know as the Barnert Temple was created. They were an outstanding couple for their time and all time.

—Susan Low Sauer
Barnert Temple bulletin
May 2002

Dedication of portrait of Nathan Barnert at sisterhood meeting, 1953. Rabbi Granison;
Mrs. Jacob Politinsky, corresponding secretary; Judge Filbert L. Rosenstein, counsel to Mr. Barnert during his lifetime; Mr. Haines, Dr. Alan Barnert, Mrs. Philip Miller, president; Mrs. Sigmond Schwartz, vice-president; Mrs. Harold Einhorn, treasurer, and Mrs. Max Baker, recording secretary. Photo courtesy of *Paterson Evening News*. Barnert Temple Archives.

CHAPTER FIVE

A New Home

Sanctuary of Barnert Memorial Temple, Broadway at Straight Street, 1894.
Barnert Temple Archives.

In 1889, Nathan Barnert (then mayor of Paterson) announced that he and his wife, Miriam, were going to build a new temple for the congregation. Its completion would not only provide the congregation with desperately needed extra space, but it would secure the congregation's place at the center of Paterson Jewish life.

Throughout his many years in Paterson, Nathan Barnert was a leading member of Congregation B'nai Jeshurun. The Barnerts' devotion to their faith and to their Jewish community was reaffirmed on May 16, 1889, when they deeded a plot of land at the southeast corner of Broadway and Straight Street for the erection of a synagogue to be designated as "The Nathan Barnert Memorial Congregation B'nai Jeshurun."

The deed of transfer stipulated that regular services, chiefly in the Hebrew language, were to be held every Friday evening and Saturday morning and that all men in attendance were to keep their heads covered. Three years later, on October 24, 1892, the deed was amended so that the service could be read in English as well as Hebrew and men in attendance were not required to cover their heads.

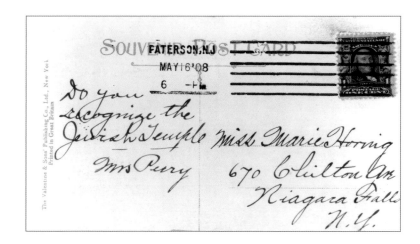

Front and back of postcard showing Barnert Temple, Broadway, dated May 16, 1908. Private collection.

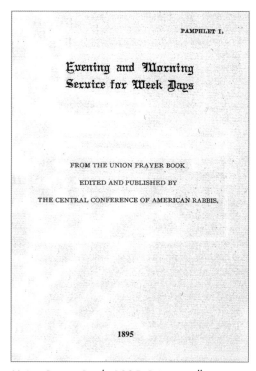

PAMPHLET I.

Evening and Morning Service for Week Days

FROM THE UNION PRAYER BOOK

EDITED AND PUBLISHED BY

THE CENTRAL CONFERENCE OF AMERICAN RABBIS.

1895

Union Prayer Book, 1895. Private collection.

These amendments signaled the congregation's shift to Reform Judaism, a move confirmed in 1920 with its adoption of the *Union Prayer Book.* (In fact, *Evening and Morning Services for Weekdays*, a reprint from the *Union Prayer Book*, had been used by the congregation as early as 1910.) While the change surely did not please Barnert, an Orthodox Jew, he nonetheless accepted it. Nathan Barnert was always a progressive, forward-looking man, and the common good always superseded his personal needs.

The groundbreaking ceremony, held at 7:30 a.m. on October 18, 1892, was attended by prominent Christians and Jews. It is reported that Rabbi Eisenberg delivered "a brief but appropriate address, and offered a simple prayer" at the groundbreaking.

> *Ground was broken this morning for the erection of a new Hebrew Temple on the corner of Broadway and Straight Street. The building has already been fully described in these columns. The contract for the mason work has been awarded to Jas. S. Van Ness for $13,176.00, and the carpenter work to J.M. Rogers for $12,541.00.*
>
> *—Paterson Evening News*
> *October 18, 1892*

> *The first ceremonious laying of the corner stone of a Jewish house of worship that has ever taken place in Paterson occurred this forenoon, when the corner stone of the new synagogue of the Congregation B'nai Jeshurun, on the corner of Broadway and Straight street, was placed in position by ex-Mayor Nathan Barnert in the presence of about 500 persons. Every Hebrew of prominence in this city participated in the ceremony, which was interesting and impressive. There were a considerable number of Christians present, and Rev. Harvey Wood, pastor of the Park Avenue Baptist Church, took an active part in the ceremonies. This is perhaps the first time in this State or in this country that a Baptist minister has participated in the laying of the corner stone of a synagogue.*

Rev. Dr. Abram S. Isaacs
Barnert Temple Archives

Rev. Dr. Ely Mayer
Barnert Temple Archives

Dedication tablet, 1894, Barnert Temple,
Paterson. Photo by James D. Schwartz, 2005.
Barnert Temple collection.

When the exercises began, shortly after ten o'clock, the platform was crowded, among those in the gathering being Mayor Braun, ex-Mayor Barnert, Rev. Dr. F. de Sola Mendes of New York, Rev. Hervey Wood, Rev. M. Hood of Newark, formerly of this city, and Rev. S. Eisenberg, rabbi of the Congregation B'nai Jeshurun....

The articles placed in the corner stone were issues of all the local papers, a copy of the Hebrew Standard, list of the city officials, membership list and constitution and by-laws of the congregation, coins of the present date and membership lists of all Jewish organizations in this city.

—Paterson Daily Guardian
July 12, 1893

The actual construction of the building took about two years, and was completed early in the summer of 1894. The architect was a Patersonian, John H. Post, who also supervised the construction on the site. Before the completion of the building, Nathan Barnert purchased the lots surrounding it, and presented them to the congregation for future expansion. He also paid off the first debt on the furnishings of the temple.

The Barnert Memorial Temple of Congregation B'nai Jeshurun was dedicated on September 17, 1894, just in time for the High Holidays. It was hailed all over the state, and even in many parts of the country, as one of the finest Jewish sanctuaries in the United States. Hundreds of Paterson citizens came to see the building and attended the joyous ceremonies. Its magnificent interior, fine stained glass, and pipe organ captured the attention of the town and soon the synagogue became a city showplace, featured in magazines, newspapers, and Paterson postcards.

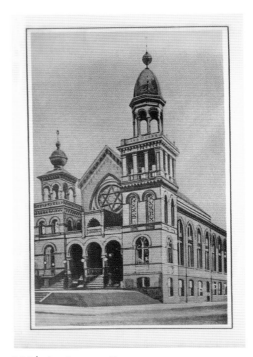

135th Anniversary Program cover,
Barnert Temple, Broadway.
Private collection.

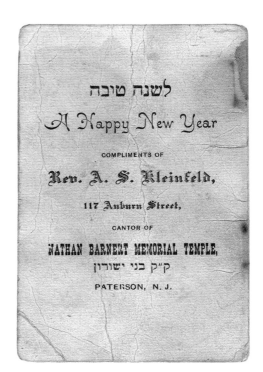

Early Barnert Temple New Year card (*front*).
Private collection.

Early Barnert Temple New Year card (*inside*).
Private collection.

We have completed the glorious work of building the House of the Lord. Our task is so far done, and we have met today to celebrate the event by public manifestations of rejoicings. You who have so earnestly labored to help achieve this long deferred end are worthy of unstinted praise.

The need for a new Temple has long been felt, and now that it is at our disposal, let us resolve to inaugurate a new era by our unfeigned piety; by a strict adherence to the principles of Judaism; by paying proper homage to the God of Israel in the House of Worship.

—Nathan Barnert
dedication of Barnert Memorial Temple
September 17, 1894

That temple was so beautiful. And you know the lights were not electrified, some of them, because when they had some holidays ... they lit the candles in the temple.

—Dorothy Doblin
oral history

With the dedication of the new temple, which had a seating capacity of 1,000, Congregation B'nai Jeshurun took its place as a major force in the religious, cultural, and social life of Paterson. Known as "The Mayor's Congregation," B'nai Jeshurun was the outstanding symbol of the Jewish community, and it quickly became the center of Paterson's Jewish activities.

In 1899, Congregation B'nai Jeshurun elected Abram S. Isaacs to its pulpit, following the resignation of Rabbi William Muetter, who had preached since 1896. Rabbi Isaacs was a distinguished scholar and author from New York, and one of the first truly Reform-oriented rabbis of the congregation. He introduced the use of the Siddur Avodath Israel to the temple early in his tenure.

This was one of the more popular liberal prayer books of the time, arranged by Marcus Jastrow of Philadelphia, an early Reform leader, and published in 1870. The "Jastrow prayer book" was quickly accepted by the members of B'nai Jeshurun, who welcomed the shortened services, hymnal supplement, and beautiful English translations.

One of the most important events in the history of the congregation occurred on April 20, 1900, when the president of the United States, William McKinley, paid a visit to the temple. Nathan Barnert had written to the White House inviting President McKinley, who was to be in New York and New Jersey on official business, to be his guest at a Sabbath dinner that Friday evening and to accompany the Barnert family to the Sabbath evening service at the temple that night.

The president's visit was supposed to have been kept secret, to avoid the crowds that would inevitably assemble and disturb the worship. However, word of the president's plans did leak out, and a crowd began assembling around the temple late that afternoon. By 7:30 p.m., over a thousand people had gathered in front of the temple on Broadway to catch a glimpse of the nation's twenty-fourth president.

The entire police force was on hand to maintain order, and the president obliged the crowd by pausing on the top step of the temple and waving to them.

According to *The Call* newspaper on April 21, 1900, "Temple officers, who had called for the President at the Caroll Hall Hotel, all dressed in formal attire, entered the sanctuary, and Mr. Barnert, arm in arm with the President, escorted him to the Barnert family pew, as the entire Congregation rose in the President's honor." Others in attendance included Governor Foster M. Voorhees, Mayor John V. Hinchcliffe of Paterson, and congregational trustees Nathan Fleisher, Leopold Maeyer, Colonel William Barbour, and General Joseph Congdon. Rabbi Dr. Isaacs's sermon was devoted to "Springtime."

The Passover Sabbath of President McKinley's visit has remained a memorable date in the history of Paterson and Congregation B'nai Jeshurun. In the Barnert Temple sanctuary, a plaque commemorating the historic event was affixed to the pew occupied by the president. The plaque has held a prominent place amongst the memorial and honorary plaques displayed in every Barnert Memorial Temple building since then.

The congregation was growing steadily in the early years of the new century. The beautiful building, Reform services, and the prestige of the presidential visit attracted many of the Jewish families who were moving into Paterson in the midst of the great Eastern European immigration of the early 1900s. The ethnic make-up of the congregation began to change during this period, as Russian and Polish Jewish names were placed on the membership rolls alongside the mostly German Jews.

In the winter of 1902, Paterson experienced the worst catastrophe in its history—the great fire. Soon after midnight on February 9, an overheated stove in a trolley shed caught fire. Fanned by 60-mile-an-hour winds, the blaze consumed most of downtown Paterson—almost all of the city's commercial district—and spread into the Sandy Hill residential area.

Though there were only two deaths ascribed to the fire, the toll in property was significant: twenty-six city blocks and 459 buildings—more than a quarter of Paterson's structures were destroyed.

Stores, churches, banks, and homes were burned to the ground. The City Hall, the old Paterson News building, the Hamilton Club, and the Danforth Library—the first public library in New Jersey—and its 37,000 volumes were lost. Saint Joseph's Catholic Church and the Second Presbyterian Church were among the houses of worship consumed before the blaze burned itself out. It was, at that time, the worst fire in New Jersey's history. Yet, remarkably, the Barnert Memorial Temple was not damaged at all.

After the fire, the city of Paterson was forced to rebuild. Individual members of Congregation B'nai Jeshurun contributed to the effort with money for relief programs to aid the injured and the homeless. And in a spontaneous and caring outreach act, the congregation performed a great act of community service by providing for three years a temporary home for the Second Presbyterian Church.

B'nai Jeshurun offered the church the use of its building for worship services and Sunday school until a new church could be built. During the three years that the congregation of the Second Presbyterian Church used the Barnert Temple, they were offered complete access to the sanctuary and the schoolrooms. The B'nai Jeshurun Sunday school changed to a split session so that the Christian

Plaque commemorating President McKinley's visit. April 20, 1900. Photo by James D. Schwartz, 2005.

Ex-Mayor Nathan Barnert
Barnert Temple Archives

Illuminated letter of thanks from the Second Presbyterian Church, March 12, 1905. Barnert Temple collection. Photo by James D. Schwartz, 2005.

Illuminated letter of thanks from the Second Presbyterian Church in original frame. Barnert Temple brass Hanukkah menorah with American Eagle over Star of David, March 8, 1908. Barnert Temple collection. Photo by author, 2003.

Sunday school could be accommodated in half of the temple's classrooms. All offers from the church to pay rent or share gas and maintenance expenses were declined.

From one standpoint, one of the most overdue meetings the civilized world has ever seen was held last week as the Second Presbyterian Church held services on the first floor of the Barnert Memorial Temple at the corner of Broadway and Straight Street. So far as it is able to ascertain, it was the first time a Protestant congregation had ever worshipped in a building devoted to the exercises of the Hebrew faith.

—*Paterson Evening News*
February 13, 1902

After the church was rebuilt, the minister, Rev. Charles D. Shaw, sent a letter to Nathan Barnert to be read to the congregation. It said in part, "Our great Father Abraham could not have been more courteous, more kind, or more helpful to the passing stranger, whom he invited to his tent, washed his feet, and gave him to eat, than you have been to us. You are a Prince in Israel and a leader in any company of men."

A magnificent, illuminated letter of thanks, signed by the president of the church, Joseph Wadsworth, the church's officers and trustees, and Rev. Charles D. Shaw, and with a background design including Hebrew lettering and symbols, was also given to the temple. It is a precious part of the Barnert Temple heritage and hangs proudly in its present building.

...Dear friends, your God is our God. The great men of your race are examples to us of faith, patience and fidelity. We recognize the glory of your past history, and we and you look forward to a greater glory yet to be.

For your unparalleled kindness to us we thank you and we bless you in the name of the Lord God of Israel. May He return into your bosoms the kindness you have manifested to us and show His mercy to you as you showed it unto us when we were stricken, afflicted and desolate.

—*From letter of thanks of*
Second Presbyterian Church
March 12, 1905

In 1904, the congregation engaged its first organist, George Benz. He was loved and respected by the members of the temple and served until well into the 1940s. Beyond doubt one of the most popular figures in the musical life of Paterson and vicinity, the ecumenical Benz, who was a silk weaver before he turned to music, also served as organist and choirmaster of St. Mary's Episcopal Church in Haledon, the Second Reformed Church in Paterson, Christ Church in Ridgewood, and the First Presbyterian Church in Paterson.

In early November of 1929, George Benz was honored with a reception commemorating his twenty-five years of service to the temple. A beautiful silver flower dish and two magnificent silver candlesticks were presented to him and Mrs. Benz. To the great delight of the audience, Mrs. Benz joined temple president Jacob Rosen in singing a beautiful duet dedicated to the organist/choirmaster.

In 1906, Rabbi Ely Mayer of Philadelphia succeeded Rabbi Isaacs. Rabbi Mayer occupied the pulpit for three years until 1909, when he was succeeded by Rabbi Leo Mannheimer of Chicago. Subsequent spiritual leaders of B'nai Jeshurun in the early 1900s included Rabbi Marius Ranson in 1915 and Rabbi Harry R. Richmond in 1919.

Two laymen who contributed significantly to the culture and benefit of the Paterson community were Harry Haines and Jacob Fabian.

Haines, who was president of the Barnert Temple Men's Club and very active in temple affairs, possessed considerable literary ability which he inherited from his father, who was the founder of the Paterson Morning Call and the Evening News, both popular and enterprising newspapers.

Among his peers, as Nelson and Shriner observe in their history of Paterson, he was regarded as "a good fellow … a congenial friend, bright of intellect, quick to see the funny side of every circumstance, and cheerful and loyal to every trust."

Fabian operated Paterson's first movie theater and ultimately built a national cinema chain. He was prominent in philanthropic work, both in the Jewish community and in Paterson in general. He was very successful in organizing substantial charities, giving his personal services to the projects, and contributing liberally from his material wealth. Along with Max Rosen, Jacob Fabian was one of the prime movers in the building of Barnert Memorial Hospital, where he was appointed permanent officer of the hospital. He also served on the board of St. Joseph's Hospital.

A number of important temple organizations began functioning between 1900 and 1920. The choir of B'nai Jeshurun had, for the most part, been a paid professional quartet since 1895, usually made up of both Christians and Jews. However, as Reform Judaism grew and its musical liturgy developed, the increased use of traditional Hebrew modes and responses made it desirable to organize a choir of temple members. A volunteer choir was attempted in 1904, but it remained a small, inactive group until 1907. In that year, Jacob Rosen, a temple member, took charge of the volunteer choir. Rosen, who would later become president of the congregation, had an extensive musical background, and often acted as cantor at services.

George Benz

Jacob Rosen,
President of B'nai Jeshurun
Barnert Temple Archives

BOARD OF EDUCATION—1913

Names	Addresses	Term Expires
FREDERICK AIMONE..	37 Vine Street......	Feb. 1, 1915
WILLIAM J. ANDERSON	67 Jasper Street......	Feb. 1, 1914
ROBERT BARBOUR......	44 Prince Street......	Feb. 1, 1914
LOUIS F. BRAUN......	354 Darcon Avenue...	Feb. 1, 1914
WILLIAM J. BRIDGES..	1242 Madison Avenue	Feb. 1, 1916
WILLIAM HAND.......	225 Broadway........	Feb. 1, 1914
RABBI L. MANNHEIMER	446 East 29th Street..	Feb. 1, 1915
JOHN M. NOLAN......	359 East 23rd Street..	Feb. 1, 1916
LEONARD STOLK......	249 North 4th Street..	Feb. 1, 1915

OFFICERS

WILLIAM J. ANDERSON....	President
WILLIAM HAND..........	Vice-President
JOHN R. WILSON........	Superintendent of Schools
HENRY RIDGWAY........	Secretary
JAMES P. DUMPHEY......	Assistant Secretary
THOMAS F. KELLEY......	Office Assistant
MISS MARY McBRIDE.....	Stenographer
MISS ELLA NIXON.......	Stenographer
CHARLES KEATING.......	Truant Officer
PATRICK J. CLUNE.......	Truant Officer

Office of the Board.......Room No. 22, City Hall
Office of the Superintendent..Room No. 22, City Hall
The regular meetings of the Board are held on the last Monday of each month at eight o'clock P. M.
3

Rabbi Mannheimer was active in educational and philanthropic affairs in the city and state. Private collection.

Heike Oppen, World War I orphan. Barnert Temple Archives.

"My grandfather, Jacob Rosen, had a wonderful singing voice, so I think he started the choir and later became president for fifteen years. And I guess he used to pitch in if the rabbi or cantor weren't there."

—Daniel Lieblich
oral history

The Banner, a monthly publication "devoted to the interests of the Jewish community of Paterson," mainly represented by the B'nai Jeshurun population, made its debut in 1913, with Rabbi Mannheimer, a capable and devoted minister and a man of wide civic interests, as its inspiration and first editor.

It reported Rabbi Mannheimer's active role in the educational and philanthropic affairs of the city and state. In January of 1913 he was appointed to the Commission on Education by Mayor Andrew McBride. (Nearly seventy years later, history would repeat itself when Rabbi Martin Freedman was appointed a trustee of the State Board of Higher Education by Governor Richard Hughes.) In February of 1913, Rabbi Mannheimer lunched with President-elect Woodrow Wilson.

The Barnert Temple was an important civic center for Jewish citizens during this period. Among the organizations meeting in the temple were the Hebrew Ladies' Benevolent Society (founded in 1883 with seventeen inaugural members and Miriam Barnert as president to help the needy of Paterson; it had more than 200 members by 1914), the Barnert Hospital Ladies' Auxiliary, the Junior Temple, the Alumnal Club, the Council of Jewish Women, the Helping Hand Society, the Zionist District of Paterson, Miss Fannie Barnert's Girl Scout Troop 7, and, of course the Barnert Temple Sisterhood, which, as is the case in so many American congregations, has always been one of the most active organizations in B'nai Jeshurun.

The Sisterhood was founded on November 9, 1915, under the guidance of Rabbi Ranson. The first officers were Mrs. William Jacobus, Mrs. I. Jacobs, Mrs. Lewis Levy, and Mrs. J. L. Stern. By 1920, the Sisterhood had over a hundred active members. Its activities ranged from directing Sunday school programs to sponsoring community cultural events. The Sisterhood was especially active during World War I, contributing to many relief causes and adopting an orphan, Heike Oppen, after the war.

In 1920, Rabbi Richmond resigned from his post to teach. The temple was in need of fresh, new leadership, and in May of 1921, Rabbi Max Raisin, a noted speaker, scholar, and Hebraist, was called from a temple in Brooklyn to take charge of the congregation.

Rabbi Raisin, who was to serve for more than twenty-five years, would bring about a new era at B'nai Jeshurun.

CHAPTER SIX

Rabbi Max Raisin
The Scholarly Theologian

Rabbi Max Raisin
Barnert Temple Archives

Rabbi Mordecai (Max) Ze'ev Raisin was born in Nesvizh, Russian Poland (now Niasvizh, Belarus), on July 15, 1881. Even during his early childhood in the "old country" his parents began to lay the foundation for his life in America as a Reform rabbi.

Max's father, Aaron Solomon Raisin, was a Hebrew teacher and tutor. A secular man who believed in disseminating knowledge through Hebrew language and literature, he spoke several languages and was interested in secular and world issues and liberal causes. Max's mother, Tova Slotsky Raisin, a devoted practicing Jew, was a homemaker and ran a small grocery store to augment the family's income.

Both of his parents were proud of their long and distinguished ancestry of rabbis and communal leaders. Tova Raisin was the granddaughter of Reb Zalmonke, a noted sage and saintly man, and Aaron Raisin could trace his lineage back to the Vilna Gaon, the outstanding intellectual figure of East European Jewry in the eighteenth century.

In his memoirs, Rabbi Max Raisin recalled that Nesvizh "was a biblical city, full of synagogues, *midrashim and yeshivot*." He remembered fondly the joyous holiday festivals and weddings. "The synagogue was not only a house of worship, a school and a place where law was dispensed to the congregants, but also a community center and a hostelry, where a poor stranger could spend the night on a bench and be served a meal by the women of the congregation the next morning."

To supplement his Hebrew studies, Max was sent to a Russian school for Jewish children, where he learned Russian and studied a variety of secular subjects, including arithmetic, geography, and Russian history.

As the oppression of the Jews in Russia increased, with the expulsion of Jews from Moscow mandated in 1891, Max's father, in anticipation of worsening conditions, went to America in 1889 to escape the lack of work, serfdom, and Russian barbarism that afflicted the Jewish people.

Working and saving his earnings, Aaron brought the family to America piecemeal, as his funds permitted, starting with Max's older brother Jack (Jacob) and sister Rose in 1890, and his sister Annie the next year. Finally, in 1893, four years after he had arrived in America, the rest of the family—Tova, Max, and the youngest daughter, Sadie—joined Aaron, settling on New York City's Lower East Side.

In later years, Rabbi Max Raisin was to say that the greatest influence in his life was his father, whose love of Judaism, general knowledge, literature, and the Hebrew language had a huge impact on his career and life; but most of all he thanked his father for bringing the family to the "blessed shores" of the United States.

When my father came to America as an impecunious immigrant, he went to an evening school and sat among youngsters to acquire a knowledge of English and of the history of the United States of which he was such a great admirer.

It was his emigration to the United States, in 1889, which constitutes our greatest measure of gratitude to him. For, as he repeatedly told us, he did it solely to save his family from Russian barbarism and especially his boys from serving in the Czar's army.

For years he had hoarded his meager savings to enable him to make the trip. To emigrate across the ocean some 65 or 70 years ago was a truly heroic feat of courage. It meant a two to three weeks' voyage in the steerage conditions of those days, where as an observant Jew he could only subsist on dry bread and tea. But he was impelled by the desire to be a free man and to free his children from the disgrace of Russian serfdom.

—Rabbi Max Raisin
"My Fifty Years as a Rabbi"
Hebrew Union College Archives, Cincinnati, Ohio

There were five Raisin children to protect and raise as American Jews in New York. Everyone in the family worked. At age twelve, Max attended New York City public schools and the Machzike Talmud Torah in the afternoon. After high school, to earn money, he worked for Western Union for a year, delivering telegrams throughout the city.

It was at this time that he came in contact with the Hebrew Alliance, where the classes aroused his interest in Hebrew literature. He was soon writing articles and essays for Hebrew journals and periodicals in American and Europe. He also expanded his knowledge of Hebrew and of religious and secular subjects with independent studies prior to enrolling as a second-year student at the Hebrew Union College (HUC) rabbinic seminary in Cincinnati in 1898.

Many wealthy American Jews of German ancestry were concerned with keeping Judaism alive in America. To this end they supported and built beautiful synagogues, hospitals, homes for the aged, and schools, including HUC, where a scholarship fund established by Temple Emanu-El in New York City helped finance Max's studies. Max and his brother, Jacob, who was also to become a rabbi, divided their studies between HUC and the University of Cincinnati. Max's rabbinic dissertation, "A History of the Jews in America," was the first submitted in Hebrew at HUC. He was ordained in 1903. Max had chosen HUC because he felt that he would become "Americanized" more rapidly in Cincinnati. Max's brother, Rabbi Jacob Raisin, was the rabbi of the first Reform Congregation in America, Congregation Beth Elohim, Charleston, South Carolina from 1919 to 1944.

First Reformed Congregation in the United States, Charleston, South Carolina Synagogue, 1795, lithograph. Private collection.

Max's years at the seminary were happy ones, and he revered its founder and president, Dr. Isaac M. Wise, for his openness, his love for his students, and his progressive and encouraging attitude toward general knowledge and other faiths and peoples.

In remembering Dr. Wise, Rabbi Raisin observed of his fellow students at the seminary that "American students did not have the background of the alien-born students as 'learned Jews,' but had many priceless human qualities, an interest in the situation of others and a participation in their sorrows."

This "characteristic aspect of their spirit," he believed, was the force that moved them to become Reform rabbis—"pastors who would serve their generation and their faith, wishing with all of their heart to be a moral help to their congregants."

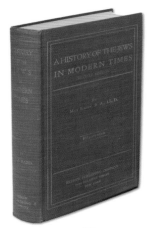

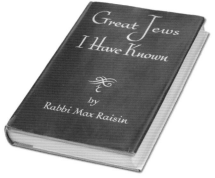

Books by Rabbi Max Raisin.
Private collection.

Upon graduation and ordination in 1903, Rabbi Raisin assumed the pulpit of his first congregation in Stockton, California. Long afterward, in "My Fifty Years as a Rabbi," he observed that while Hebrew Union College had trained him to be a religious leader, able to deliver sermons, minister at life-cycle events, and organize study groups on Jewish history and the Bible, it had not prepared him for the practical aspects of rabbinic service—the congregational politics, the social expectations, and the one-year contract without benefits that were the standard in those years.

Further, he was disturbed by the attitude of his Stockton congregants toward their spiritual leader and their lack of attendance at weekly services. Thus, he was not surprised when, after he took a post-graduate course at the University of California at Berkeley under the noted Bible scholar Max L. Margolis, that instead of commending him for his effort, the congregation, which had not interviewed the twenty-two-year-old before hiring him, let him go without even discussing the issue with him.

Rabbi Raisin was pleased to return to the East Coast, where he served a congregation in Philadelphia for a year before becoming the rabbi of a congregation in Meridian, Mississippi, in 1905, a position he would hold for eight years. He had already married Florence Steinhardt of New York, and they had three daughters, Beatrice, Maxine, and Louise, who were born in New York City, Meridian, and Brooklyn, respectively.

In Meridian, he found second- and third-generation Jews who appreciated an intellectual rabbi who also related to the general community. There, in addition to tending to his rabbinic responsibilities, he completed a book in Hebrew on the English poet John Milton and was involved in many ecumenical endeavors, including the cause of black Americans, working for changes in the labor laws affecting black children, and encouraging fellow members of the clergy and state officials to end the economic persecution of their black brothers, an activism for which he was both praised and criticized by members of his congregation.

He had some success when his efforts contributed to the passage of a law limiting the number of hours a week black women and their children were permitted to work.

In 1912, Rabbi Raisin actively supported B'nai B'rith's petition to cancel the United States trade agreement with Russia because it would not honor the passports of American Jews, a far less controversial action for which he was awarded an honorary law degree at the University of Mississippi at the direction of the state's governor.

Rabbi Raisin's daughter Louise Grabow recalls that when he left Meridian in 1913 to return to New York to serve a congregation in Brooklyn, the Meridian congregation held "a lovely function and gave the family a beautiful sterling silver tea set as a going-away gift."

He served New York congregations for eight years, until in 1921 he received a call from an "old and settled Reform congregation," B'nai Jeshurun, whose Barnert Memorial Temple was located in Paterson, New Jersey.

He was to serve the Paterson congregation for twenty-five years as rabbi and seven years as rabbi emeritus. "My stay in Paterson was the most fruitful of my entire ministry," wrote Rabbi Raisin. "While there, I wrote most of my books and did most of my global travel. I sought to make of my temple a truly Jewish house of worship, which, while Reform in every way as regards ritual and the accepted standard of the American temple, was none too radical."

"We used the Union Prayer Book and observed only one day of Rosh Hashanah. I preached the sermon on the second day at the Orthodox services at the Hebrew Free School, without in the least compromising my Reform convictions. We did not make an issue of the wearing of the hat, so that the parents and grandparents of the members could come to services and feel they were in a synagogue. My pulpit was a sounding board for the questions of the day. I mingled with Jews who were not members of the congregation and made them feel that I was one of them during my entire length of my Paterson rabbinate."

Initially, Raisin was an oddity in the Reform movement in America. His involvement with Zionism and the modern Hebrew language was a rarity in the Reform rabbinate. By the end of his career, however, the interests of many, if not most, American Reform Jews were beginning to coincide with his.

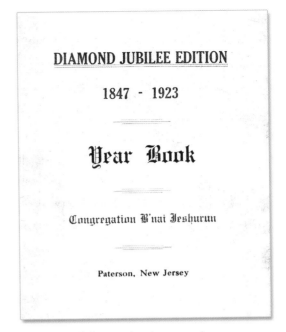

DIAMOND JUBILEE EDITION

1847 - 1923

Year Book

Congregation B'nai Jeshurun

Paterson, New Jersey

Diamond Jubilee Yearbook, written by Rabbi Dr. Max Raisin, 1923. Barnert Temple Archives.

> *If I was [known as] the Hebraist Rabbi, I was always the American Rabbi, face to face with the problems of Jewish life. I wanted America, as the one last refuge of democracy, to rise above the cannibalism which anti-Semitism foreshadowed and often led to.*
>
> *—Rabbi Max Raisin*
> *"My 50 Years as a Rabbi"*
> *Hebrew Union College Archives, Cincinnati, Ohio*

Raisin's love of Hebrew and its literature and his involvement in the field of Jewish scholarship were fulfilled by his hundreds of contributions to periodicals in Europe and America and his association with many of the most important Hebrew writers of his day.

> *My Uncle Max [great-uncle] was very much a scholar. He did a lot of his writing in Hebrew, in the same way that Galileo wrote backwards.*
>
> *It was rough for rabbis in those days. They were given one-year contracts. Never knew from year to year whether they would be reappointed. The rabbi's wife, the rebbetzin, was supposed to be an auxiliary, come along as a freebee, a twofer kind of thing; hire me, you get my wife, too. Things have changed very dramatically.*
>
> *—Ted Lobsenz*
> *oral history*

In addition to leading his congregation, he continued to serve the Zionist cause, organizing a branch of the American Jewish Congress and serving as its representative in Geneva in 1936.

In his autobiography, Rabbi Raisin was to later write:

> As an American Jew, I am very proud of the rebirth of the State of Israel—my five visits to Eretz Israel were the most beautiful days of my life. Indeed, this is the most wonderful event in the history of nations—that an ancient people like Israel, spread throughout the ends of the earth, harassed daily, could raise up on its two feet once again and establish its fallen sovereignty.
>
> I am overflowing with gratitude because of the role my American brothers played in this magnificent accomplishment. And furthermore, I thank God for enabling more than five million Jews to be gathered in America, to find here refuge and accommodation, and to dedicate themselves to the foundation of the Jewish state. I believe this to be an act of Providence. Finally, Bless the State of Israel, in which lies our future as a people and as a religious community. And Bless America, for all that She has done for us.

At a time when there was little discussion on the subject of intermarriage, Max Raisin read a paper stating his views on the matter before the Association of Reform Rabbis of New York and Vicinity, sometime during his tenure in Paterson. He said, in part:

> I do agree that intermarriage should be tolerated so long as the parties to the marriage agree to raise their children in the Jewish faith.
>
> By tolerating intermarriage I mean that rabbis should even officiate at mixed marriages without insisting that the non-Jewish party first go through a formal conversion to Judaism, provided the promise is first obtained about the religious up-bringing of the offspring. To insist on such a pre-nuptial conversion would indeed be to follow good Bible and Talmudic doctrine, but it would be questionable ethics.… Conversion should always be a matter of conviction and not of coercion.

Rabbi Raisin also found time for literary work in English, Hebrew, and Yiddish, and served as co-editor with S. Melamed of the American Jewish Chronicle. He traveled to Europe and Israel several times, where his meetings with Hebrew literary figures became fodder for his own later writings.

And he remained politically outspoken in defense of causes and freedoms that he deeply believed in. In 1922, at a service of the Baptist church on Washington Street in Paterson, Rabbi Raisin spoke out against the Ku Klux Klan, warning that it stood for race hatred against Jews, Catholics, and blacks, and urging the state of New Jersey to be very diligent. And in 1924, the Barnert Temple's Alumnal Club, started by Rabbi Raisin, resolved after debate "that segregation in the Paterson High School should be abolished."

When the Nazi Party began holding meetings and rallies in Passaic and Bergen counties, the Jewish War Veterans led a number of Jewish groups in demanding that such meetings be outlawed. However, Rabbi Raisin, speaking before the Barnert Hospital Association, denounced the idea of banning the Nazi gatherings.

Barnert Temple's 87th anniversary dinner, February 12, 1935. *Left to right:* Jacob Rosen, Rabbi Max Raisin, Mrs. Florence Raisin, Rev. Dr. Steven S. Wise, Joseph T. Lieblich, Mrs. Stephen Wise, Mrs. Moe I. Fuld, Mr. Moe I. Fuld. Barnert Temple Archives.

The rabbi asserted that the freedom of speech was "too precious to jeopardize." He said, too, that as an American and a Jew, he loathed the Nazis and everything they stood for, but that he "was not afraid of them."

> *There speaks a true American. If only outstanding radio and press people would see the light as this God-fearing Rabbi, the "ism" bubble would soon burst of its own accord. Would to the Almighty that there were more of Dr. Raisin's stamp. Gentlemen, scholars and teachers of his kind would soon dissipate the specter that is shaking our country to its foundations. May his utterances show the way to others, for by his very words he has proven his Americanism is the only "ism" we have room for.*
>
> *—North Jersey Times*
> *March 2, 1939*

Long before the onset of Word War II, Rabbi Raisin was keenly aware of the impending disaster European Jews and all humankind faced. He articulated his concerns to his congregation and all Patersonians through his sermons, speeches, and writings.

> *"War is in the air," says Dr. Raisin on returning home from Europe. The atmosphere is tense and the nervousness which has taken hold of the European frequently takes the form of panic.*
>
> *—Paterson News*
> *September 2, 1936*

Rabbi Max Raisin receives an honorary doctorate of divinity, Hebrew Union College, Cincinnati, December 8, 1945. Barnert Temple Archives.

Rabbi Raisin (*right*), served as guest chaplain and gave the invocation in the United States House of Representatives, January 30, 1947. Barnert Temple Archives.

The time has come for the liberty loving nations to make common cause in behalf of their liberties. We are perhaps nearer disaster than any of us realize.

—Rabbi Max Raisin
Yom Kippur sermon, 1936

I believe that Lincoln, were he alive today, would have spoken in no uncertain language, of what he thinks of the Fascist and Nazi regimes, as well as the Communist reign of slavery.

—Rabbi Max Raisin
sermon, February 12, 1937

Communism and Fascism are twin brothers who were conceived in sin and born in inequity. Whatever difference they may have in ideology, they are identical in their methods of enslaving and oppressing, of humiliating and degrading the people they rule.

—Rabbi Max Raisin
sermon, April 16, 1937

Hitler is the greatest menace to general civilization that has risen up in many centuries.

—Rabbi Max Raisin
address to Non-Sectarian Anti-Nazi League
June 28, 1937

World democracy could have frustrated Hitler's plans had it acted 10 years ago. Let no one say that we did not know what Nazism meant or what its designs were. Hitler clearly stated it in his book.

—Rabbi Max Raisin
sermon, February 7, 1943

In his memoirs, Raisin cites two dates as outstanding in his life. The first was December 8, 1945, when the man who had once been an impoverished immigrant student on scholarship received an honorary doctorate of divinity from Hebrew Union College. His fellow honorees on this unforgettable day were Henry Morgenthau Jr., secretary of the treasury in Franklin Roosevelt's administration, and Rabbi Stephen S. Wise, a great liberal and Reform Jew who had founded the Hebrew Free Synagogue in New York and was admired by both Jews and Christians. The degree was presented on the occasion of the College's seventieth anniversary by its president, Dr. Julian Morgenstern.

The second was January 30, 1947, when, at the invitation of New Jersey Congressman Gordon Canfield, he served as guest chaplain and gave the invocation in the United States House of Representatives. In his memoirs, Rabbi Raisin wrote, "I believe that nothing so reveals the greatness and the true spirit of

America as the sight of a one-time immigrant boy from far-away Poland uttering words of prayer before the men and women who legislate for the noblest and mightiest country in the world."

But despite these honors, he was to say, "My greatest satisfaction is in the family I have raised, the children and grandchildren we have given to America, who have added such joy to myself and my dear wife."

An American rabbi, a modest man, with a life-long commitment to the betterment of humankind, Raisin established his integrity and progressive outlook, actively promoting ecumenical harmony in Paterson and throughout the country.

Diamond Jubilee of Girl Scout Troop, 1923.
Barnert Temple Archives.

Rabbi Raisin urges support of The Salvation Army, which "is doing noble work among people who are often overlooked or cannot be reached by other agencies."

—B'nai Jeshurun bulletin
May 1924

Rabbi Raisin appeals to Temple members to buy and use as many Christmas Seals, the proceeds of which were used to prevent the spread of tuberculosis, as possible.

— B'nai Jeshurun bulletin
December 1925

Jewish Girl Scout Troop at Barnert Temple, 1925, organized by Florence Raisin. Photograph of Miriam Barnert on wall left of American flag.
Barnert Temple Archives.

Rabbi Raisin preached last Sunday in the pulpit of the Calvary Baptist Church on East 18th Street, the guest of the Rev. A. A. Watts.... This Sunday evening at eight, Rabbi Raisin will occupy the pulpit of the Trinity Methodist Church, of which the Rev. F. S. Garris is the pastor.... An invitation has been received by Rabbi Raisin to attend the exercises at the laying of the cornerstone of the new Saint Athanasios Greek Orthodox Church, at 20–24 Southard Street.... Rabbi Raisin has been invited to attend the installation of the Right Reverend Thomas Joseph Walsh, D.D., the new Bishop of Newark, at the New Cathedral of Newark, on Tuesday, May 1.... Rabbi Raisin has been elected a member of the Paterson Rotary Club, the third clergyman to be so honored, the other two representing the Protestant and Catholic faiths, respectively.

—B'nai Jeshurun bulletins
1928–1930

Christian Clergy Joins Rabbis in Honoring Rabbi Max Raisin on 15th Anniversary as Spiritual Head of Barnert Temple

"My ministry has given me great satisfaction, because it has enabled me to do things both as a Jew and as an American."

—Paterson News
May 23, 1936

Rabbi Max Raisin Memorial Plaque.
Barnert Temple collection.

The Community Chest is above all a unifying force in our communal life. It helps us to bridge over the parochial gaps that tend to divide us.

—Rabbi Max Raisin
sermon, October 9, 1942

We have a lovely relationship with the non-Jews of this city, for we all realize we are all headed for the same goal. This is why this occurrence is such an unusual one, and of great moment to the city of Paterson.

—Rabbi Max Raisin
on temple's ninety-fifth anniversary
December 12, 1942

The sidebar of the temple's weekly bulletin, which Rabbi Raisin expanded, wrote, and served as editor, underlines his reaching out to all people: "To one and all who would worship with us, whether members seat-holders or strangers, the Rabbi and officers of Temple B'nai Jeshurun extend a most cordial welcome."

It has been my privilege to come in personal touch with Mr. [William Howard] Taft and to get to know him well. My first meeting with him was some twenty-one years ago, shortly after his election to the Presidency. I have a vivid recollection of that episode in my life. Mr. Taft was essentially a true friend who never forgot anyone with whom he was in any way associated.

—Rabbi Max Raisin
B'nai Jeshurun bulletin
March 14, 1930

I do remember Rabbi Raisin very, very well. I remember going to his home with one or two of my friends to prepare for the bar mitzvah. Rabbi Raisin was a very serious man. I understand he was a Hebrew scholar, and I remember him telling us how impressed he was when he walked down the aisle with Mrs. Eleanor Roosevelt (who received an honorary law degree from Columbia University on the same day in the late 1930s as he), and how impressed he was with her, as many of us were. That was Rabbi Raisin.

—Alan Kessler
oral history

In 1946, as he approached his sixty-fifth birthday, Rabbi Raisin informed the congregation that he wished to retire, and he was appointed rabbi emeritus for life. During his retirement, he published three additional books, adding to a collection of books and articles on the Jewish people in modern times and the Reform movement that fills one and a half shelves in the Library of Congress in Washington, D.C. A partial list of his books includes *A History of the Jews in Modern Times, The Jew and His Place in the World, John Milton, Israel in America,*

Light from the Diaspora, *Great Jews I Have Known*, and *Out of the Book of My Life*. His paper "The Reform Movement as Reflected in Neo-Hebraic Literature," written in 1905, is still significant and meaningful today. All of Rabbi Raisin's books are enduring works of scholarship and history.

Both the *Morning Call* and the *Evening News*, Paterson's two leading newspapers, bemoaned Rabbi Raisin's retirement. The Call's editorial read in part, "Thousands of Paterson's citizens as well as members of the Barnert Memorial Temple Congregation regretfully heard of the decision of Dr. Raisin to retire. This is due to the fact that in addition to his service to the people of his congregation, Rabbi Raisin devoted much of his time to the study of community needs and was a leader in many of the improvements that have been brought about in our city."

And in the *Evening News*, "It is a matter of great community regret that Rabbi Raisin finds it desirable to seek retirement, because he has been one of our most fervent leaders, liberal in thought, energetic in action and generally helpful in everything worthwhile."

In his farewell address in the Temple Bulletin in June 1946, Rabbi Raisin wrote that he was retiring with the deepest goodwill and sincerest good wishes toward the congregation he had led for a quarter of a century. "To the new Rabbi I extend my fraternal greetings and best wishes for the greatest measure of success. Under his guidance may the Barnert Memorial Temple go from strength to strength and continue as a precious milestone on the road to noble living."

After his retirement, when called on by the Placement Committee of the Hebrew Union College, he agreed to serve as an interim rabbi to relieve rabbis during their sabbaticals. He served in Oshkosh, Wisconsin; Curaçao, Dutch West Indies; Tarrytown, New York; and Florence, Alabama, where he died in 1957 at the age of seventy-five.

It was during Max Raisin's lifetime that the full effect of the emigration of Eastern European Jews to America was felt, as they made their mark not just on the established German-Jewish population but also on Americans of all religions. His social activism prepared the way for similarly inclined rabbis who followed him, notably Rabbi Martin Freedman, by accustoming the congregation to rabbis who spoke and got involved in activities outside the temple walls.

He used the Barnert pulpit to instruct and enlighten generations of students and congregants on social and racial issues. An inspiration and mentor to them all, his true legacy was in opening their eyes to the larger world around them.

Rabbi Raisin, the scholar, was intimately acquainted with the texts and meaning of our American Constitution and our guaranteed religious and civil freedoms. He understood that each moment in the life of a democracy is an opportunity to serve others. Remembering his family's immigration to the "blessed shores of the United States," his philosophy and commitment of service to his fellow human beings was a fulfillment of his love for our country and its freedoms.

CHAPTER SEVEN

The Best of Times
and the Worst of Times

Rabbi Dr. Max Raisin and Barnert Temple School, 1925.
Barnert Temple Archives.

As Rabbi Raisin began his tenure in Paterson, the decade of the 1920s would prove to be one of continual growth and community service for B'nai Jeshurun. With a waiting list to join the temple, a shortage of pews for purchase, and children being turned away from the religious school, the congregational leadership turned its attention to enlarging the temple. "The present expansion is makeshift, soon present dimensions of building will prove inadequate and the only remedy will be a new Temple in that part of the city where majority of our people have taken up their homes," predicted Rabbi Raisin. It was a prophecy that was to come true, and a course of action that would be followed at least twice more in the congregation's life.

In December 1921, Rabbi Raisin was authorized to communicate with an architect regarding the imperative need to enlarge the temple. In March of the next year, architect Crosby appeared before the board with plans and sketches.

In 1922, a major renovation of the sanctuary began. Additional pews were added because the membership was now 120 families. A photograph of the Sunday school, taken in 1925, shows more than 100 smiling children assembled on the front steps of the temple.

In the teens and twenties, concurrent with the growth of the congregation, the weekly Temple Bulletin, edited and mostly written initially by Rabbi Harry R. Richmond and later by Rabbi Max Raisin, recorded the diverse interests and contemporary themes that had already become part of the culture of this historic American Jewish congregation. Among them:

- ecumenical outreach
- integration of Jews in community life
- support of Jewish statehood in Palestine
- conversion to Judaism
- aid to immigrant mothers and children

The Barnert Temple Bulletins recorded in great detail the varied and complex issues of the decade and the congregation's responses, and reported on visiting speakers. Among them were Dr. Walter Laidlaw, registrar of the New York Clergy Club, on "The Message of Micah for Today"; Dr. Julian Morgenstern, president of the Reform seminary in Cincinnati, on "The Hebrew Union College"; and Rabbi Julius Silberfeld of Newark, on "The Four Pillars of Liberty."

Also heard at the synagogue was Colonel John Henry Patterson, a gentile officer in the British army who had commanded a unit of Jewish volunteers, the 38th Battalion, Royal Fusiliers, later known as the 1st Judean Regiment, in the successful campaign to liberate Palestine from Turkish domination. A supporter of Jewish statehood and a delegate of the Zionist movement in the United States, he wrote a book praising the idealism and valor of his Jewish soldiers.

Princess Catharine Radziwill, a descendant of the once powerful and politically progressive Polish family and herself a political activist, on whose parents' estate in the town of Nesvizh Rabbi Max Raisin had played as a child, also addressed the congregation.

B'nai Jeshurun's involvement in community affairs outside the temple was, in the 1920s just as today, an important part of its agenda. Rabbi Raisin's activities "supplementary to his pulpit and congregational work" fill three pages in the congregation's Diamond Jubilee Yearbook of 1922–1923. The range of Rabbi Raisin's activities that year included meeting with Mayor Frank J. Van Noort of Paterson and appearing before the New Jersey State Legislature in an effort to get the state to take over the Paterson Normal School, later to become William Paterson University; taking part in a reception in New York honoring the Zionist leader Dr. Chaim Weizmann; and addressing the congregation at the A.M.E. Zion Church in Paterson on the subject of "The Religion of Love Versus the Religion of Hate."

In April 1921, temple membership dues were raised 50 percent, in part to pay for the expenses of some of its "extracurricular affairs":

> In 1920, the children's group put on a Chanukah program at the Paterson Lyceum theater to rave reviews. "Their excellent work elicited unbound admiration and thunderous applause every minute they were behind the footlights," reports the Temple Bulletin. "Thanks also to the admirable corps of teachers, who worked with superhuman zeal and energy for the good of the entertainment. All of the proceeds from the show were earmarked for community charities."

> *Will you please express to the children of the religious school of B'nai Jeshurun, Barnert Memorial Temple of Paterson, our sincere appreciation of their thought of the sick people at this hospital.... To think early of the needs of the less fortunate, [the children] will grow into very fine men and women.*
>
> *—S. Pinsko*
> *Secretary, National Jewish Hospital of Denver*
> *May 11, 1928*

In a further effort to enrich its religious musical program, the congregation decided to engage a cantor, Joseph Koppell. Cantor Koppell was elected in 1922 and served with distinction until 1939.

> *Before Joe Posner came, there was a cantor named Koppell. When he stood before the ark with Rabbi Raisin, and chanted the "Eitz Chayim," I used to get goose bumps. It was all so beautiful.*
>
> *Leonore Albert*
> *oral history*

- The congregation's support of the quest for a Jewish state in Palestine was unflagging. On September 29, 1922, a parade was held in Paterson in celebration of the Palestine Mandate and the possible establishment of a Jewish homeland. The congregation was represented by Nathan Barnert, Rabbi Raisin, and the religious school principal, Raleigh Weintraub. And that same year, the temple welcomed Nahum Sokolow, the Zionist leader and probably the most distinguished Jewish diplomat of the day, and his assistant, Dr. Alexander Goldstein. In Paterson, $15,000 was collected for the Jews of Palestine.

- Care for the well-being of Paterson's mothers in need and their children was always high on the congregation's agenda. Barnert Temple's Helping Hand Sewing Society regularly distributed underwear, stockings, dresses, and petticoats to poor children and their mothers. The Hebrew Ladies Benevolent Society asked its members to contribute 10 cents on each rainy day to be used to provide milk for ill-nourished mothers and babies.

- The temple's first family Passover seder, organized and run by the Sisterhood, was held on April 1, 1923, with 125 congregants and their families and friends in attendance. Tickets were $2.00 for adults and 50 cents for children. It was a rousing success.

- The Paterson Council of Jewish Women, which held its first meeting on September 27, 1923, listed Americanization and aid to immigrant mothers as its two top priorities. And in July 1921, the children of the religious school adopted a second war orphan with $100 collected in nickels and dimes.

- A "flying squad" of 100 prominent Jews to visit 200 cities across the country in order to evaluate the state of Judaism in America and generate publicity on its behalf was established and Paterson was one of the 200 cities selected, and Judge Abram Kleinert represented B'nai Jeshurun as one of the "Committee of One Hundred."

- "News of the Local Jewish Circle," a special weekly feature, was established in the Paterson Sunday Chronicle in 1925, and radio broadcasts of the temple's services were a thorough success. Thousands listened, and countless encouraging messages from the press and public were received. "Never did the voices of Rabbi Raisin, Cantor Rothman and the choir sound better," said one listener.

- In 1924, Max Liffsitz was named commissioner of city planning by Mayor Colin McLean. Mayor McLean was welcomed by more than 500 temple members when he attended services and worshiped with the B'nai Jeshurun congregation that same year. In 1913, Governor Woodrow Wilson named Barnert Temple member Abram Kleinert a judge of the Court of Common Pleas.

The congregation had undergone a steady evolution in its orientation, from Orthodox to Conservative-progressive to Reform. It was the only congregation in Passaic County to employ a mixed choir and to use the Union Prayer Book, adopted in April 1920. The change was inevitable in a congregation situated in the midst of a strictly American environment. Its leaders appreciated the needs of the American-born generation of Jews.

The congregation's commitment to the Union of American Hebrew Congregations (now the Union for Reform Judaism), which it had joined in 1913, was strong. A promoter of religious schools and preserver of the Jewish spirit in the busy life of America, the UAHC/URJ was (and still is) a powerful force for the conservation of American Judaism.

But the commitment at times needed reinforcement, as in May of 1921, when Rabbi Richmond had to remind the congregation that while it was one of richest in America, it was among the least bountiful in giving generously to support and preserve Judaism.

"Our UAHC quota is $1395. We didn't even collect a third of it last year," Richmond chastised. "Let us raise that and more to wipe out that stain on our record. In responding to their appeal for financial support, you carry forward the banner of liberal Judaism in America, first unfurled by UAHC founder Rabbi Isaac M. Wise."

B'nai Jeshurun's delegates to the UAHC convention included Jacob Rosen and Joseph T. Lieblich. Descendants of both men are still members of the congregation.

"The growth and prosperity of B'nai Jeshurun is not just due to growth of the Jewish population in Paterson but also the labors and sacrifices of Nathan Barnert and others like him," said Rabbi Raisin on the celebration of the seventy-fifth anniversary of the congregation in the 1922–1923 journal. "We have grown old but remained young and helped make Paterson the great and thriving community it is today."

Two years after Nathan Barnert's death in 1927 came the crash of the stock market, which had a grave impact on the congregation, as well as our nation and the world. On October 24, 1929, the unstable prosperity that had dominated American life in the 1920s began to disintegrate rapidly. The fall of 1929 was a devastating one for the entire nation as the United States entered into the worst depression in its history. The 1930s saw hard times for all Americans, and the city of Paterson was no exception.

An indication that fiscal instability was already present was an appeal to members in February of 1926, in which the temple reported a $4,250 deficit accumulated over the past four years due to insufficient revenues.

When I grew up in my college years the economy was very bad. But I had a father who was a doctor. He was needed. And although the stories are that he was handing out more money to his patients than they were handing to him, still he was busy and he was working and he was making a living. And things were very bad. That was in the '30s.

—Norma Joelson Hayman
oral history

I guess when the crash hit in 1929 I was about eleven or twelve years old. And gradually all the things that I had taken as my due were being slowly but surely eroded. The expensive summer camp became the Girl Scout camp, which was fine. I loved it just as much. But the live-in help was gone. The summer vacations at the seashore, gone. My mother's jewelry, gone. The house we lived in, ultimately, gone. My father's business, gone.

But it's a funny thing, despite that fact that everything went, we managed. We moved to a much more humble abode. My father went to work for someone else, and my mother, give her due, studied like mad and passed her RN, which she had never done when she graduated from the Beth Israel. She was going to get married. She didn't need her RN. But this time she studied, she passed. And then my mother went back to work, and we all went to work. I went to a teachers' college instead of going to an expensive college, and somehow you manage.

On Saturdays I used to work downtown in Paterson in Behrman's or Stenchever's selling. It was a long, long day. It was a twelve-hour day, nine to nine. Summers I worked on the playgrounds in Paterson, and later on I was a camp counselor at [Camp] NAH-JEE-WAH, which is a New Jersey Y camp. Somehow you manage to survive. Your standard of living might be somewhat strained, but you survive.

—Leonore Albert
oral history

I was born in 1917, so I was twelve years old when the Depression hit. I do remember very well people selling apples. It got so bad that I think for a period my uncle (Jacob Rosen) paid the rabbi's salary out of his own pocket. I'll never forget that. And it's interesting that my sister and I still turn off lights when we leave a room; we make our calls after five o'clock—it's so ingrained in us from those Depression years.

—Daniel Lieblich
oral history

Mrs. Stearns asked for volunteers to help distribute clothes for the unemployed at School #1, the week of Feb. 22nd, beginning Feb. 20th, as the 22nd is a holiday. The following ladies volunteered: Fuld, Greenberg and Raisin.

—Minutes of Barnert Temple Sisterhood
February 1, 1932

In an effort to help meet congregational expenses, primarily Rabbi Raisin's salary, the Sisterhood, organized in 1914 and now boasting a membership of 107, inaugurated the Barnert Temple Thrift Shop, which sold good used clothing and inexpensive household items.

The Sisterhood also provided topical programs at its meetings, featuring lecturers of prominence or persons of great musical ability. And its annual musical follies served as fundraisers and bonded temple members in fun and camaraderie. In 1921, the Sisterhood had committed to finance all of the expenses involved in administration of the temple's religious school.

In 1939, the congregation engaged a new cantor, Joseph Posner. Cantor Posner's musical background was evident in his ability to produce beautiful musical programs at the temple, and he also became the director of the choirs.

On February 24, 1945, Cantor Posner presented a musical recital in New York City's Town Hall, attended by many members of the temple and the musical world. "This is the first time in the history of our congregation that we have had a cantor with the artistic ability of this caliber," said the congregation's president, Frank Stave.

Joe Posner taught me Hebrew. He was my Hebrew teacher back when. And he was a very relaxed, laid-back individual and he did not get angry at some of the obstreperousness of the boys in the class. Rather calm.... He had a beautiful voice, magnificent voice. I have a recording of two of his [Kol Nidre] services ... which I took with a tape recorder sitting in the front row on the floor, and I had a clicker in my hand. I'd turn it on and off so that just the music would come through. It's a terrible recording but you hear Joe Posner.

—Ted Lobsenz
oral history

Evelyn, my older daughter, was one of the last pupils Joe Posner prepared for bat mitzvah. And they set up a little rapport. He was somewhat intimidating to some of his students, but Evelyn liked him and got along very well with him. She told me that after they finished her lessons, they would sit down to play a game of chess for a while. So she got to know him quite well.

—Dorothy Starr
oral history

Cantor Joseph Posner and Youth Choir, Barnert Temple, Broadway, 1958. Barnert Temple Archives.

Cantor Posner would continue to guide generations of students through their preparation for bar/bat mitzvah at the Barnert Temple, eventually retiring in 1979, after more than forty years leading services with his glorious voice. He died on September 9, 1982.

Meanwhile, Americans were increasingly concerned by the disturbing news of Hitler's persecution of Germany's Jews. The wave of hatred that emanated from Nazi Germany caused many European Jews to flee to America in the period between 1935 and 1939. At the same time, northern New Jersey was the scene of many of the American Nazi Bund operations that were becoming popular among hate-mongers all over the country. Jews, other concerned Americans, and anti-Nazis in other countries sought ways to help rescue Jews and anti-Nazis from Europe. Their concern would prove to be prophetic.

My father, Louis G. Shapiro, M.D., had principles, and one of them was that he wouldn't send American dollars in as "schmeergelt" [bribery money] to the Nazis. Now at that time they hadn't yet decided to exterminate the Jews. If you just get rid of them it was fine, and if you take them that was fine. There was a little money available to be paid.

Unfortunately, the Depression wasn't completely over and America didn't want too many Jews; England didn't want too many, France didn't want too many. But my dad extorted money from well-to-do Jews and he was sponsoring German Jews. He seemed to know just what everybody's background had been. He had the papers sponsoring this man. If anybody came along who needed passage, he'd pay the passage. If they needed clothing, he'd buy it for them.

—Joseph Shapiro, M.D.
oral history

"On Sunday, June 26 [2005], the Village of Ridgewood will name a street after Varian Fry, the only American named as "Righteous Among the Nations" by Yad Vashem (Holocaust Memorial Center)....

Varian Fry went to Marseille in 1940 as the representative of a private American relief committee, with $3,000 in his pocket and a list of refugees in France who were in great danger from the advancing Nazis....

In Marseille he met thousands of refugees needing help to evade the Gestapo ... he extended his stay to 13 months, using every means he could find—from forgery to black marketeering to creating secret escape routes—to help 2,000 people leave France.

Among them were notable European intellectuals, writers, artists, scientists, philosophers, and musicians, including Marc Chagall, Max Ernst, Hannah Arendt, Franz Werfel, Marcel Duchamp, Jacques Lipschitz, and André Breton.

—Jewish Standard
June 24, 2005

The Best of Times and the Worst of Times   **65**

The threat of war became a reality to America on December 7, 1941, when the Japanese bombed Pearl Harbor. As Barnert Temple members had served during World War I, and other wars since the Civil War, by 1943, sixty-one members of B'nai Jeshurun were serving in our country's armed forces. The temple bulletins of 1944 through 1946—publication had been suspended during the early war years—recorded the congregation's involvement in the war: the tragedies, the commendations, the valor and travail.

Congregants learned that Private Herman Spitz was wounded on the German front ... that Lieutenant Sam Phillips, grandson of Mr. and Mrs. Sam Aronsohn, died in an airplane accident ... that Second Lieutenant Robert H. Joelson had graduated as a pilot of a B-24 Liberator bomber and would do combat duty with the Army Air Force ... that Private First Class Alvin Cohen was home on furlough ... that Sergeant Robert Haines Levine had been assigned as a special agent in the U.S. Counter Intelligence Corps in the European theater ... that Major Daniel Lieblich, who would retire as an Air Force colonel, had been promoted to a squadron executive officer with the overseas forces ... that David Roth, M.D. was serving with the Army in Guam ... and that Joseph Shapiro, M.D. attended the wounded of the Battle of the Bulge and later served as a consultant to the U.S. Medical Service at Los Alamos.

I was an eighteen year old sergeant in the Third Army in Europe during World War II. Two of my most interesting duties were guarding prisoners going to the Nurenburg Trials and setting up temporary facilities for individuals who survived the concentration camps. I met many courageous children and adults who endured the horrors of the camps and were appreciative of any kindness we were able to provide. We went into the army as kids and returned considerable more mature. I was awarded the Distinguished Service Medal from the State of New Jersey for serving in Europe.

Kenneth Herman, Ph. D.
letter to author

The bulletin also reported on the ongoing religious and life-cycle events of the congregation and the community at large during the war.

- In October of 1944, it reported that plans were underway for a "Fifty Years at Barnert Temple" celebration (the temple at Straight Street and Broadway had been dedicated in 1894). The celebration called for alterations and renovations to the interior of the building, and the Sisterhood had already begun work on beautifying the altar with new covers, designed and embroidered by Sisterhood members. Moe Fuld and Max Bodner were appointed co-chairmen of the project.

- A program and reception were held at the Paterson YMHA in observance of Jewish Book Month and honoring Paterson authors Rabbi Max Raisin, Louis Ginsberg, and P. Goodman, with Dr. Joshua Block, head of the Judaic division of the New York Public Library, the evening's speaker.

Promotion of Morris M. Cohn to corporal, June 16, 1918,
Camp de Meucon, France. Private collection.

World War I *Victory* lithograph.
Private collection.

M. Metz Cohn, World War I, American
Expeditionary Force 1917, France.
Private collection.

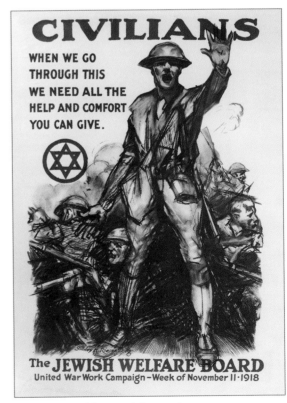

Civilians, World War I lithograph,
November 11, 1918. Private collection.

Rabbi Martin Freedman, World War II.
Private collection.

Barnert Hospital and Barnert Temple, World War II Red Cross Gray Ladies, 1942. Many of the nurses
were members of Barnert Temple. Some identified here are: Anne Brawer, Esther Bluestein, Lilian
Thieberg, Rose Pink, Jane Roth, Dorothy Doblin, Isabelle Gruber, Esther Schwartz, Claire Konner,
Annette Katz, Louis Roth, Dora Cohen, Abram I. Bluestein. Private collection.

Kenneth Herman, World War II, Germany, 1945.
Private collection.

Judge Joseph Conn, World War II, Guam, 1946.
Private collection.

Robert Gutenstein, Korean War, 1956.
Private collection.

- On December 11, 1944, an "Institute on Judaism" was held at the temple and was a huge success, as the fundamentals of Judaism, its symbols and ceremonial objects were explained and discussed before more than 120 Christian ministers and civic and cultural lay leaders of the community. Speakers included Rabbi M. J. Bloom of Newburgh, New York, Rabbi Bernard Heller of New York City, Rabbi Reuben Kaufman of Paterson, Rabbis Julius Silberfeld and David H. Wise of Newark, and Rabbi Irving Siman of Hackensack.

- Also heard from were Rev. W. L. Griffin, rector of St. Paul's Church of Paterson; Rev. Ernest A. Elwell, rector of the Broadway Baptist Church of Paterson; Rev. Charles J. Child; Rev. James C. Taylor, pastor of the A.M.E. Zion Church of Paterson; Robert Williams, publisher of the Paterson Morning Call; Harry B. Haines, publisher of the Paterson Evening News; former Paterson mayor Dr. Andrew F. McBride; Barnert Temple president Frank Stave; and Sisterhood president Florence Fuld.

- Other events reported by the bulletin during the war years included the appointment in 1946 by Mayor William P. Furrey of Charles Goodman to a three-year term on the board of adjustment, the retirement that same year of Fire and Police Commissioner Jack Stern after many years of service to the Paterson community, and temple president Max Rosen's observation, during the 1946 Kol Nidre service, that "Judaism is synonymous with democracy. The practice of democracy begins in the house of God."

While America was undergoing a massive struggle for the preservation of democracy in the world, the Jewish people was experiencing an even more profound struggle for its very survival. On May 12, 1943, a city-wide "Solemn Assembly of Mourning and Intercession" on behalf of the Jews suffering at the hands of the Nazis in Europe was held at Eastside High School in Paterson.

Brotherhood and youth activities were suspended during the war, but the Sisterhood carried on, sponsoring a Dutch supper to provide cheer kits for military personnel and constant support for the work of the Red Cross. Two VE-Day services, a congregational public seder, and a joint Thanksgiving service with Temple Emanuel, now known as Temple Emanuel of North Jersey, were held in 1945. All were well attended.

And on November 8, 1946, an Armistice Sabbath Service conducted by congregational war veterans was held. The topic of the sermon was "What I Learned from the War," and participants included Stuart Alexander, M.D., Alvin Cohen, Louis Guttens, Daniel Lieblich, Jack Stern, and Harry Zax.

In March of 1946, the UJA started a campaign for the rehabilitation of the surviving Jews in Europe, with $100 million its goal nationwide. Paterson Jews were asked to raise the huge sum of $650,000, and active participation by Barnert Temple members was expected. Barnert Temple's Sam Schwartz was chairman of the Paterson drive. Paterson's Jewish Community and the Barnert Temple Congregation led this effort for many decades.

United Jewish Appeal of Paterson, 1945. *Standing, left to right:* Benjamin Stave, Dr. Alan Yaeger, Lawrence Dimond, Dr. Sandor Levensohn, Rabbi Max Raisin, Louis Schotz, Jack Gruber, Rabbi Reuben Kaufman, Bibby Blank, George Abrash, David Bograd, Joseph Schulman, Frank Stave, Charles Bromberg, Jack Stern. *Seated, left to right:* Archie Marcus, Mary Goodman, Anna Maskowitz, Irving Brawer, Guest speaker Congressman Gordon Canfield, Samuel Schwartz, and Philip Dimond. Private collection.

Backbone of Israel's Economic Dinner, ca. 1958, Community and Barnert Temple members. *Standing, left to right:* Irving Brower, unidentified, unidentified, unidentified, Anthony Grossi, unidentified, Herman Yucht, Rabbi David Panitz, Rabbi Martin Freedman, Mayor Frank Graves. *Seated, left to right:* Jack Stern, Doris Stern, unidentified, Judge Mendon Morrill, Ray Joelson, Congressman Charles Joelson, Abe Green. Barnert Temple Archives.

UJA function, in support of new State of Israel, October 15, 1963. *Left to right:* Herman Yucht, Saul Rosen, Samuel Schwartz, Philip Dimond, Paul Segal. Private collection.

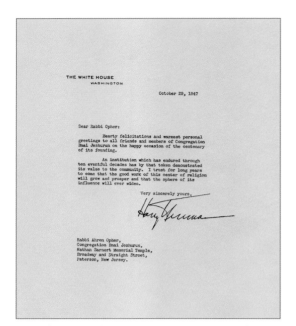

Letter from President Truman on Barnert Temple's
100th anniversary.
Barnert Temple Archives.

Barnert Temple 100th Anniversary, 1947.
Illuminated sign on temple building.
Barnert Temple Archives.

In 1945, Rabbi Raisin had informed the congregation of his intention to retire on July 1, 1946, saying that after twenty-five years of service, he wanted to take things easier on reaching the age of sixty-five. He promised, however, to remain active in temple affairs, and to continue to write, lecture, and support the many causes that held his interest. At its annual meeting on November 25, 1945, the temple board unanimously elected him rabbi emeritus for life.

In June of 1946, Rabbi Aaron Opher was appointed to succeed Rabbi Raisin. The new rabbi assumed his duties in September. In his message to the congregation at his installation on October 18, which was attended by Dr. Stephen Wise, president of the Jewish Institute of Religion, Rabbi Reuben Kaufman of Temple Emanuel, Rev. William L. Griffin Jr. of St. Paul's Church, and Mayor William P. Furrey, Rabbi Opher affirmed "the great tradition of this congregation, and the great humility with which he was stepping into the post held for a quarter of a century by one of the greatest scholars in the American rabbinate."

As America and its allies succeeded in their heroic effort to liberate the world from Nazism and fascism, and World War II finally ended, the Jews of America were overcome with a sense of joy and relief, but also an overpowering sense of grief and loss. They set about in a determined effort to commit themselves to Judaism, for the United States was now the world center of Jewish religion and culture. It was in this spirit that Congregation B'nai Jeshurun prepared for the centennial anniversary of its temple in this great nation of religious freedom.

The board of trustees held a general meeting of the congregation on March 6, 1947, to consider plans for expansion of the temple as part of the centennial festivities. George Schottland was appointed general chairman of the Centennial Committee, with Moe Fuld and Frank Stave as co-chairmen.

The first official event of the centennial celebration was a concert of liturgical music presented at Friday evening services on March 7, 1947. The printed program for the evening included greetings from President Harry S. Truman, and New Jersey Governor Alfred E. Driscoll delivered the keynote speech at the service.

The press gave the centennial events extensive coverage throughout the next year. On March 10, 1947, Men's Club president William Levine, a long-time member of B'nai Jeshurun, presented the congregation with an electrically illuminated "100" sign, which was placed above the portals in front of the temple. The sign remained illuminated throughout the year 1947, proclaiming to all the people of Paterson the congregation's one-hundredth anniversary.

In January 1947, the centennial year of the congregation was marked with many celebratory events and plans for construction of Fellerman Hall, which would house a social hall and Sunday school addition to the temple. It would be the first major addition to the temple since 1894.

Fellerman Hall, housing a social hall and auditorium, was completed in 1948, made possible by an initial donation to the building fund by Isidore and Blanche Fellerman, and a fundraising effort by the congregation. A second phase of the centennial building program provided for a minor renovation and remodeling of the sanctuary.

Fellerman Hall was an addition to the Barnert Temple on Straight Street. Fellerman Hall was built somewhere in the 1940s as a social hall because there was really no place for social gatherings in the Barnert Temple as I remember.

Today, of course, the Barnert Temple on Straight Street has been long forgotten.... There's a White Castle on the corner that was recently built about a year ago, but Fellerman Hall still exists—it's no longer Fellerman Hall, it's a tobacco warehouse.

How well I remember the sermons of Rabbis Raisin, Opher, and Granison on the High Holidays, when the trains from the Erie Railroad shook the leaded glass panes of the temple.

—Alan Kessler
oral history

Barnert Temple 100th anniversary bulletin,
September 26, 1947.
Barnert Temple Archives.

My sister was the first bride married in Fellerman Hall [in June 1948]. This is when I met Lena Struth, who was a delightful woman. I used to help her when we catered large things. I remember the trays and trays of chicken that she used to make.... I was confirmed in 1934, and I remember my mother's insistence that we do not carry peonies, that we carry calla lilies, and we did.

—Leonore Albert
oral history

The Barnert Temple had a theater group. They had it at night. Anita Cantor and Fritzy, my late wife, were two of the girls who were taught to dance in a line-up, like the Rockettes, and all that sort of stuff. And we had a lot of fun as kids in Fellerman Hall.

—George Sauer
oral history

In 1946, a membership campaign was inaugurated by chairman Raymond Kramer. More than sixty new families joined Barnert Temple between October 1946 and January 1947, and the total membership stood at more than 250 families.

As the congregation entered the second half of the twentieth century, its members recognized that they had inherited from their ancestors a tradition of liberal Reform Judaism, a sense of philanthropic obligation to the congregation and the community at large, and a responsibility to uphold the tradition of service to the temple established over generations. This was typified by the Rosen family, who, with their descendants, the Lieblichs, Bauers, and Kramers, have served as presidents of the congregation and its Sisterhood for more than fifty years.

My sister Selma has a grandson, Jason Kramer, who just started Sunday school, and he is the sixth generation at the temple—my grandparents, my parents, my sister, her son—six generations.

—Daniel Lieblich
oral history

Barnert Temple 100th anniversary plaque.
Barnert Temple collection.

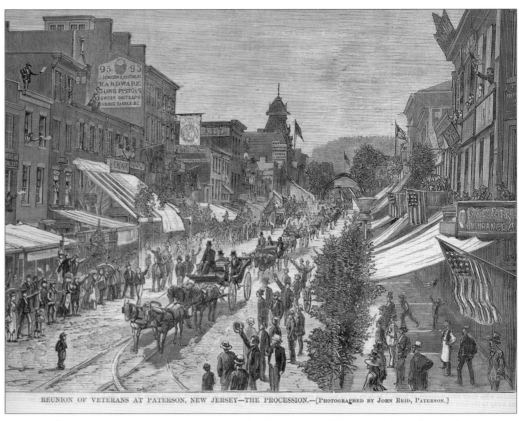

REUNION OF VETERANS AT PATERSON, NEW JERSEY—THE PROCESSION.—[Photographed by John Reid, Paterson.]

Reunion of veterans in Paterson, New Jersey—*The Procession*—[Photograph by John Reid, Paterson]
Lithograph 19th century. Private collection.

In one century, a profound change had taken place among the nineteenth-century Paterson Jews. They had succeeded, as had other immigrant groups, in educating their children and establishing themselves in professional, commercial, and academic fields, always driven by their work ethic and the opportunity for self and family improvement. The religious and civil freedom lacking in their homelands, they found in this great land of America.

They were partners with other American immigrants in protecting the American dream of religious and personal freedom. These Paterson Jews and their descendants had already defended their nation through service in the Civil War, the Spanish-American War, World War I, and World War II, the war that nearly annihilated the world's Jews.

America's religious and personal freedoms made possible the development of these Paterson Jews, and unified and changed them from their original, homogeneous community into a composite American model. In those 100 years, they became *American* Jews.

The Exodus from Paterson

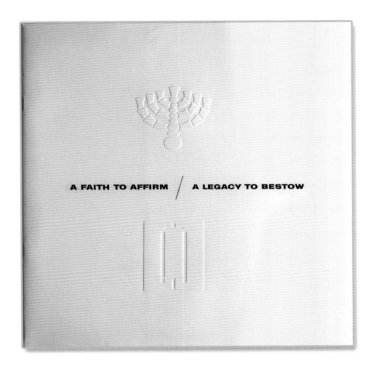

Cover of campaign pamphlet to move Barnert Temple, 1964.
Barnert Temple Archives.

In 1940, Paterson had the largest Jewish population in the city's history, numbering 25,000. But after World War II, just as many of our nation's larger, older population patterns changed from largely city dwellers to suburban residents, the northern New Jersey suburbs began a rapid process of growth and development. The towns of Fair Lawn, East Paterson, Paramus, Wayne, Ridgewood, and Glen Rock all experienced population booms in the years after 1945.

Most of the new residents in these suburban communities were young families from New York and surrounding metropolitan cities, including Paterson. The Jewish population in these suburban towns also grew steadily, and by 1955, at least one synagogue had been built in each of the boroughs surrounding Paterson.

The natural result was a shift in the number of Jews who stayed in Paterson, and by 1958, the Jewish residents of Paterson numbered only 11,350. The decline in the mid-1950s was becoming increasingly serious. By 1955 the membership of the Barnert Temple had decreased dramatically to 140 families.

To me, the most significant change in the past fifty years has been the demise of Paterson and how it has changed from what it was when I grew up. Then it was 20,000 Jews, and everybody knew everybody—it was a real community. It's gone down to practically zero, they've all moved to the suburbs and the temple has moved to Franklin Lakes. We've all spread out all over the place, and become more accepted, more affluent. That's the change.

—Harold Polton
oral history

In addition, much of the industry that congregation members owned or were dependent upon for their livelihoods was leaving Paterson.

We owned a dye plant from about 1948 to 1960, and because of union rules a dyer would only handle twelve feet of box. In New England they were running twenty-four and thirty feet of the same materials—they were getting twice as much productivity. So there was no point in making improvements in Paterson. There was nothing to do but move into the areas where workers would take the load they could handle. And this is what made Paterson a ghost of its former self

—Samuel Schwartz
oral history

Another pressing concern was the location of the temple. When it was erected in the 1890s, the location on Broadway and Straight Streets was in the center of a middle- and upper-class residential section of the city. However, after World War I and during the following decades, the downtown business district had expanded to the point where it almost surrounded the temple area.

Friday evening service attendance dropped markedly, since parking space was on the street and at a premium, and few members would walk through the area after dark.

The neighborhood comes back to me very vividly. Parking became so difficult. We had to walk for blocks and actually after dark it wasn't too safe, and that's why we moved.

—Warren Bauer
oral history

With the deterioration of the neighborhood, the building itself began to deteriorate. Maintenance costs were high because of the difficulty of caring for the ornamentation both inside and outside the building. It was evident by 1955 that the congregation would have to cope with this new reality.

During this period, there were several changes in the leadership at Barnert Temple. Rabbi Raisin had retired and resigned from his post in 1946 after twenty-five years of exemplary service to the temple and was elected rabbi emeritus for life.

Rabbi Aaron Opher, who served the Barnert congregation from 1946 to 1953, left to lead a larger congregation. Rabbis Abram Granison and Murray Blackman each served the congregation on an interim basis between 1954 and 1956. During the five-month period while the trustees searched for a new spiritual leader, Rabbis Albert Baum, Samuel Cook, and Eugene Lipman occupied the pulpit and conducted services.

Late in 1956, the congregation engaged Rabbi Martin Freedman of Temple Beth El in Elizabeth, New Jersey. (For full discussion of Rabbi Freedman's legacy, see chapter 9.)

American-born and descended from a long line of rabbis, Rabbi Freedman's devotion to B'nai Jeshurun was evident early in his ministry as he set about leading the congregation into serious consideration of its problems and options.

One problem the congregation faced was that while there was a sharply declining membership and attendance (as the communities surrounding Paterson experienced a dramatic expansion and shift in population), Paterson's Eastside section, surrounding Eastside Park, remained populated by a majority of Barnert Temple's congregants, dictating that any move considered should be within the Eastside area.

I don't think the congregation would have survived if it had moved Straight Street right to Franklin Lakes. Never in a million years. They needed to have that move in between, because it kept people from Paterson there. And it was a home for Reform Jews in other communities to come to. If you're a Reform Jew, you're a Reform Jew.

—Susan Sauer
oral history

And so, early in 1959, under Rabbi Freedman's leadership, a building fund campaign called "A Faith to Affirm—A Legacy to Bestow," chaired by Samuel Schwartz, was undertaken to make a move possible. The campaign's leadership included Miss Terese Bauer, Warren G. Bauer, Morrill Cole, Arnold Doblin, Rabbi Martin Freedman, Mrs. Carl Joseph, Nathan Kluger, Raymond Kramer, Norman Lappin, Daniel Parke Lieblich, Milton Makowsky, Frank Stave, Jack Stern, and Samuel Wolff.

The spirit of the campaign was articulated by Rabbi Freedman, who said, "A temple is a monument to the heritage of history, an endowment for generations to come and the testimony of a congregation's indomitable faith. The existing Nathan Barnert Memorial Temple has served as our house of worship for seven epochal decades. It will endure—in reality or in memory—as a symbol of our steadfastness in the past. But the advancement of our congregation and the dignity of our modern faith demand that we build anew."

Carroll Estate Passes to Barnert Temple

STEPHEN W. CARROLL signs the closing papers officially transferring the property of the $125,-000 Carroll estate to Barnert Memorial Temple. The Temple will relocate at the new site, the block encompassing Broadway, Derrom, Wall and 13th Aves. Left to right at the closing, seated are: Barnet Zalon, president, Barnert Temple; Carroll and Herman Singer, attorneys for the Carroll estate. Standing are Daniel P. Lieblich, attorney for the Temple; George Rosenthal, treasurer; Frank Stave, past president and Rabbi Martin Freedman, spiritual leader of the Temple.

Paterson news photo of transfer of Carroll estates, 1959. Barnert Temple Archives.

Carroll estate house—Barnert Temple school annex, 1959. Barnert Temple Archives.

Contract signing with Visbeen Contracting Co. for building of Barnert Temple Derrom Avenue, November 1962. *Seated, left to right:* George Rosenthal, Adrian M. Visbeen Sr., Norman Lappin, Samuel Wolff. *Standing, left to right:* Adrian M. Visbeen Jr., Theodore Ruser, Murray Glasgall, Rabbi Martin Freedman, Ellis Rosenthal. Barnert Temple Archives.

Groundbreaking ceremony for Derrom Avenue temple, November 17, 1963. *Left to right:* Rabbi Martin Freedman, Samuel Wolff, George Rosenthal, Barnert President Norman Lappin, Frank Stave, Campaign Chairman Samuel Schwartz, Maurice Glasgall, Visbeen Engineer Theodore Ruser. Barnert Temple Archives.

The trustees purchased the old Wall-Carroll estate on Derrom Avenue, across from Eastside Park, for immediate use as a school and temple annex, and later as the location of the new Barnert Memorial Temple.

In the summer of 1959, the mansion, which had been built in 1914, and the acreage surrounding it were secured for $125,000. The east side of Paterson had long been the residential center for Paterson Jewry. The Barnert Memorial Hospital, Temple Emanuel, Yavneh Academy, Temple Beth-El, and Congregation Ohav Shalom were all within walking distance of the new temple annex in the mansion.

> There were a lot of Jewish people on the east side of Paterson. The Eastside was a very close-knit community. We used to walk all the way down to 42nd Street. We had a walking patrolman named Spike Hennessey, and every night, at about five o'clock, he'd look at us and say, "All right, kids, come on." And he'd drag us all home. It was a wonderful, warm, homey situation in Paterson then.
>
> —William Lee,
> oral history

By the fall of 1959, the annex had opened, housing the temple school, the youth program, the nursery school, the Hebrew school, and the Institute of Jewish Studies, a stimulating and challenging program of lectures and seminars for adults.

In 1960, internationally renowned architect Percival Goodman, chairman of the department of architecture at Columbia University, whose work was inspired by the depth of his perception of the Jewish culture, was engaged to design the new synagogue. His plan for the new temple, completed in 1962, called for a modern brick structure to be constructed at a total cost of $575,000.

The building was to be dominated by the large peaked roof of the sanctuary that would rise over seventy-five feet across from Eastside Park. It was to be built adjacent to the old mansion, which would be retained for an interim period as the religious school. The new Barnert Temple would consist of a sanctuary seating over 600 people, a social hall–theater, a sculpture garden and terrace, administrative offices; and a youth lounge, kitchen, and lobby.

On November 17, 1963, groundbreaking ceremonies took place for the new temple on Wall Avenue and Derrom Avenue. Sale of the old temple awaited the completion of the new one, as the terms of Nathan Barnert's bequest provided that the old temple could not be disposed of until a new temple was built, ensuring the continuity of this historic congregation.

On May 3, 1964, the laying of the date stone for the new temple, which had been under construction since November of the previous year, was held in conjunction with the 117th annual meeting of the congregation.

Despite financial problems, the deterioration of the Byzantine-style building, and the steady exodus of its congregants to the suburbs, the last years of the first Barnert Memorial Temple at Broadway and Straight were rich in ambitious programs for its members and the community at large.

Topics for sermons at Friday evening services included: "A New Spirit in American Jewish Life," with guest speaker Rabbi David L. Davis, director of the New York Federation of Reform Synagogues; "Religious Differences under Doctrines of God," by guest speaker Rev. William L. Griffin Jr., rector of St. Paul's Episcopal Church; and "A Scholar's Heritage," a special service in honor of Rabbi Max Raisin.

"A Policeman's Service" was held, followed by a dinner tendered by the Shomrim Society, for the police officers of the city of Paterson. A cantata about the history and observance of the Sabbath was written by Rabbi Opher and Cantor Posner and presented by the children's chorus of the religious school (the children also read the liturgy, sang the hymns, blessed the candles and the Torah, and delivered the sermonette). And Ernest Bloch's *Sacred Service* was presented by the Barnert Temple Quartet and a choir of thirty voices from the Calvary Methodist Church of Dumont, New Jersey.

Other events during this period included a Brotherhood Night held by the temple's Men's Club. Rev. Dr. Sheldon Bishop, head of the psychiatric clinic in Harlem, New York City, was the guest speaker; the Westminster Choir rendered selections and the Men's Club of St. Augustine also participated. The Men's Club also presented an amateur revue and dance each year, "*Mischa Gaas*," (Yiddish for silliness) an evening of camaraderie, fun, and fundraising for temple programs.

The Sisterhood meeting on October 7, 1957 had as guest speaker the Rev. Nancy Forsberg, whose topic was "Israel from a Christian's Point of View." The Sisterhood also sponsored a yearly Strawberry Festival and the Barnert Temple Cabaret Nite (a yearly revue and fundraiser in Fellerman Hall), as well as the many religious school programs it supported. Bazaars were held and income from them and the gift shop was dedicated to the children's programs.

The shows we used to have were fun, and they were wonderful. Way before the last show, "Moving On," which everyone remembers, we used to have shows. Tippy Krugman and I used to be in all of them, and were also writing a lot of them.... We used to have a great time. My brother Bob [Joelson] didn't do much in the beginning, but did later on.

—Norma Joelson Hayman
oral history

In 1958, the pupils of the temple school adopted a nine-year-old Korean orphan, Yang Yoo Sik, through the Foster Parents Plan. A letter from the youngster, written by his brother, said in part: "Your foster child is so happy to know all of you as his foster parents. Your foster child studies harder in these days owing to your love and care."

Groundbreaking Ceremony for Derrom Avenue temple, November 17, 1963. *Left to right:* Congressman Charles Joelson, Cantor Joseph Posner, unidentified, Frank Stave, Campaign Chairman Samuel Schwartz, Samuel Wolff, President Norman Lappin, Adrian M. Visbeen Jr., Maurice Glasgall, George Rosenthal, Paterson Mayor Frank Graves, unidentified, Adrian M. Visbeen Sr., Rabbi Martin Freedman. Barnert Temple Archives.

CONGREGATION B'NAI JESHURUN
NATHAN BARNERT MEMORIAL TEMPLE

The Oldest Jewish Congregation in the State of New Jersey
. . Founded In 1847 . .

takes pride in announcing the opening of its

TEMPLE SCHOOL ANNEX

Located on a magnificent two-and-a-half acre estate
at 152 DERROM AVENUE, PATERSON, N. J.

IN THE FALL OF 1959 THE FOLLOWING FACILITIES WILL OPEN AT THE
TEMPLE SCHOOL ANNEX

THE TEMPLE SCHOOL — A Congregational Sunday morning school program (9:30 to 12:00) for boys and girls, which leads to Confirmation; from the First through the Ninth Grades. A program of Studies including Jewish History, Hebrew, Ethics, Customs and Ceremonies, Jewish Music and Dance are taught by a creative staff of teachers under the supervision of Dr. Herbert J. Lipsitz, Principal, and Rabbi Martin Freedman, Director.

The first class session will take place on Sunday morning, September 20th, 1959, in the new Temple School Annex with its excellent classroom and playground facilities.

YOUTH PROGRAM — A meaningful post-Confirmation teen-age youth program in affiliation with the National Federation of Temple Youth will begin in September, 1959. A special Teen-Town Lounge and Social Hall are being provided for young people. A professional Youth Director will carry on the national program of the NFTY in the Temple Youth Group.

NURSERY SCHOOL — A week-day Nursery School open five mornings a week (9:00 to 12:15) limited to an enrollment of thirty children will open in September, 1959. An excellent teaching staff will develop an exciting and creative pre-school program with Jewish content. The superb physical facilities will provide a separate classroom and playroom location and a spacious and beautiful outdoor playground.

HEBREW SCHOOL — A weekly Hebrew language program designed to develop a comprehension and facility in modern Hebrew as well as Liturgy.

INSTITUTE OF JEWISH STUDIES — A stimulating and challenging program of lectures and seminars for adults. Courses in Modern Hebrew, Jewish History, Religion and Contemporary Jewish Events will begin in October, 1959. A special Lecture-Forum involving noted Jewish scholars, writers and artists will take place once a month beginning in October, 1959.

YOUR INQUIRIES ARE INVITED — REGISTER YOUR CHILD NOW!

Congregation B'nai Jeshurun
A Reform Jewish Temple
208 Broadway, Paterson 1, N. J.
MU. 4-4744

MEMBERSHIP IS OPEN to all who are convinced that and preservation of our faith.

Application forms for membership are available at the voted upon at the next Board meeting. A membership privileges and to participation in all the numerous activ man Hall rental and cemetery plot costs are substantially

Each membership includes two reserved seats in the Tem membership affords the satisfaction of having joined your and a faith preserving and enriching Judaism's past glori

Announcement of opening of temple school annex. Barnert Temple Archives.

Barnert Memorial Temple To Be Dedicated Tonight

TEMPLE DEDICATED — Six past presidents of Congregation B'nai Jeshurun, oldest congregation in New Jersey, hold Torahs at dedication of new Barnert Nathan Memorial Temple in Paterson. From left are past presidents Daniel P. Lieblich, Barnet D. Zalon, Louis Sorkin, Warren Bauer, Frank Stave and Raymond Kramer.   (Staff photo.)

Paterson Morning Call, April 9, 1956.
Barnert Temple Archives.

A Friday Luncheon Club was formed to provide an hour of comradeship for the temple members, their friends, and the community each week. The lunch was usually followed by a lecture/discussion led by Rabbi Freedman.

A nursery school program was started, an Institute on Judaism held, and Purim parties and confirmations continued each year.

Confirmands in 1949 were: Henry Abrash, John Abrams, Robert S. Berliner, Emily Carlin, Sara Doblin, Albert Gladstone, Ruth Karpes, Barbara Kreiger, Carole Ann Levine, Lynda Shampanier, Sherman Stark, and Harmon Zacune. In 1958: Alan Harris Adler, Ronald Finn, Elizabeth Kramer, Michael Stephen Kramer, Susan Lee, Mireille Lipsitz, Susan Shinefield, and Stephanie M. Schneider.

In 1959, temple members and the community were invited to an open house to view the new site of Congregation B'nai Jeshurun on Derrom Avenue. Members were informed that the temple school, the Hebrew school, the nursery school, the youth program, and the offices of the temple would be situated at the new annex.

The sanctuary of the nineteenth-century Barnert Temple would be used for services and life-cycle needs, and Fellerman Hall for larger events, until the new Barnert Temple was built.

The last services were held at the beautiful original Barnert Memorial Temple sanctuary on May 17, 1964. Fittingly enough, the occasion was a happy one, the Shavuot Confirmation service. Even though the congregation was excited about its beautiful new temple on Derrom Avenue, however, many members looked back with nostalgia over the preceding seventy years. It was difficult to leave their old synagogue behind. The first Barnert Temple was filled with memories of life-cycle events that the members would carry with them to their new home on Derrom Avenue.

I remember Sunday school, learning the sounds of the vowels—and spitballs. When we moved to Wall and Derrom, I had a wonderful year in a great class with Rabbi Freedman. We all sat around the large conference table learning about things Jewish and the like —"outside the pale," so to speak.

[In the old Barnert Temple] I remember the mystery of the doorway to the rabbi's office, the creaking of the wooden floor, the organ and all its glory. When we were smaller, we had Purim carnivals and folk dancing at Fellerman Hall. Our Confirmation class was held at the Broadway temple on May 28, 1963. It's wonderful to have our new temple in Franklin Lakes, but I will always have fond memories of our other beautiful temples.

—Gail Cohen White
letter to author

Exterior of Derrom Avenue temple, 1964.
Barnert Temple Archives.

Sanctuary of Derrom Avenue temple.
Barnert Temple Archives.

Sabbath worship was conducted in the temple annex throughout the summer of 1964. By September the interior of the new temple on Derrom Avenue was completed, and the first service was held in the new sanctuary on Rosh Hashanah 5725. There was a series of gala events in 1965 to commemorate the dedication of the new Barnert Temple, culminating on April 23, 1965, with a New Members' Sabbath, since the new location brought with it many new members.

Initially, B'nai Jeshurun's membership grew to more than 300 families, and Paterson witnessed a rebirth of New Jersey's oldest congregation. But during the next two decades, the quickening pace of urban decay and rising crime rates took their toll on the city of Paterson, as its citizens struggled to keep it a viable place in which to work, live and worship.

> *The temple was broken into periodically, although there was little to steal. My favorite experience was when Dorothy Levy [office administrator and secretary] called me to report that the police had just taken away a man found sleeping in the rabbi's chair. It seems he broke in and liked the sacramental wine and fell asleep after imbibing a half liter.*
>
> —Robert Gutenstein
> oral history

Bimah of Derrom Avenue temple.
Barnert Temple Archives.

> *I decry what has happened to Paterson. It used to be very flourishing. It was lovely. Downtown ... used to have wonderful shops, restaurants, movies, the Paradise Confectionery, where we always went for ice cream. The temple moved to Derrom Avenue, but the decay moved there too and it became apparent that the parents didn't want to send their children to Sunday school there. People were leaving Paterson in droves. The handwriting was on the wall—Derrom Avenue could not survive.*
>
> —Leonore Albert

Barnert Temple Archives

Barnert Temple Archives

Blessed with a facility on Paterson's east side that was beautiful, but rapidly deteriorating and saddled with a huge mortgage, the congregation's leadership was forced to resort to Monday night bingo to raise needed funds in the late 1960s. Membership slipped back down to between 180 and 200 families. The temple annex, which housed the religious school, became so run down that classes were moved to Wyckoff's Sicomac School in 1977.

The situation in Paterson was bad. Parents were reluctant to come into Paterson with their children because most of our membership was up what is called the Route 208 corridor and they didn't want [to spend] the time [traveling], they didn't like the ambiance of Paterson, the neighborhood.... The first thing that went was the school. The school was years ahead of the temple itself. The school moved initially to Wyckoff, where we held Sunday school and Monday school.

—Ted Lobsenz
oral history

Financially, we would creep from pillar to post. [Rabbi Freedman] didn't cash his check during the summer, and Mrs. Levy didn't cash her check, and there was a guy by the name of Nooky Greenblatt who provided the oil, and he would get paid about three months a year and we would be constantly stretching out the payments.

—Robert Gutenstein
oral history

Despite its struggles, the congregation always managed to find the time and resources for the Mitzvah Fund, introduced in 1977 to show the temple community's concern and compassion for congregants undergoing difficulties. Self-perpetuating, and not funded by the temple, the Mitzvah Fund sends food gifts in times of family stress or loss. The late Rip and Joan Marshall for many years administered the fund, which continues to this day.

And events such as Israel Expo in 1971, and Expo 200, celebrating the nation's 200th anniversary in 1976, helped raise additional funding and enjoyed the near-universal involvement of all members of the congregation.

Israel Expo, which was open to the public, was held on November 11–15, 1971, and celebrated the 125th anniversary of the Barnert Temple. Co-chaired by Alvin and Susan Sauer, with the full support of the congregation's members in its organization and preparation, Israel Expo explored Israel's products, economy, history, and future.

Nearly 20,000 members and non-members of the temple enjoyed, learned and experienced the best of the Israeli heritage through Israel Expo's food and wine booths, industrial displays, art show, and other cultural exhibitions. It was a huge success and provided a great bonding experience for the congregation.

It was a fabulous thing, just the sort of stuff for a small congregation, as we were in those days, and boy, did we do a job. And we did so because everybody—not <u>almost</u> everybody—in the congregation helped out, played a role, participated.

I took the job on the condition that everyone on the board become a chairman or at least serve on a committee. Much to my amazement, they agreed. So on that basis, we did the job, and it was a splendid event, and we really had a good time. It was the greatest thing for the congregation.

—Alvin Sauer
oral history

Rabbi Freedman came up with the idea for Israel Expo '71 as a way of raising money to get us out of the hole. It was a most fantastic thing for the temple, because the congregation was exhausted from building a new building and everyone was kind of worn out. Everyone in the temple was involved.

There were displays, exhibits, shops—we had stuff on consignment. We had food stuff, provided by Mike Blumenfield ... and the entire school building was full of Super Sol's Supermarket. The sukkah was covered over as a dining room which Leon Kramer ran, where we served knishes, hot dogs, sodas and what have you.

—Robert Gutenstein
oral history

Expo 200 was an equally ambitious project, also conceived by Rabbi Freedman, that ran daily from May 13 to May 18, 1976, from 11:00 a.m. to 11:30 p.m., except for Friday evening, when a combined Sabbath service and choir concert was held with Temple Emanuel, with rabbis and cantors from both temples participating. Admission at Expo 200 was $2.00 for adults and $1.50 for senior citizens and children under twelve.

A bicentennial exposition and fair, it was a joyous celebration of the 200th birthday of our nation and focused on honoring the achievements of American Jews. It was an ideal way for the oldest Jewish congregation in the state to express its love and admiration for a society built upon religious freedom.

Rabbi Freedman described Expo 200's meaning as follows: "It's meant to celebrate the joyful quality of patriotism and to offer thanks to God that we are in America and not living in Russia or some other country where Jews are not free."

Booths were provided for the demonstration and sale of such American crafts as hand weaving, pottery making, leather tooling, copper sculpture, and quilting. There were booths for the sale of American silver, porcelain, stamps, and coins.

Special display booths with replicas of eighteenth-century background walls were created by Alvin Greenbaum of Glen Rock for the display of American antiques lent to the temple. Works by such leading contemporary American Jewish artists as Jack Levine, Ben Shahn, Leonard Baskin, Abraham Rattner, and Stefan Martin were shown.

Films on the American Jewish experience were shown, including *Rendezvous with Freedom*, lent by the Anti-Defamation League; *New Jersey, Know Your State*; *Sons of Liberty*; *Gossamer Thread*; *The Greatest Jewish City in the World*; and *What It Means to Be a Man*, a multimedia presentation produced by the New Jersey Cultural Council.

Each evening, live performances were presented. Ramapo College professor Harold Lieberman's "Contributions to Jazz by Jews in America" celebrated the contribution of such Jewish composers, performers, and musicians as George Gershwin, Benny Goodman, Harold Arlen, Irving Berlin, Jerome Kern, Richard Rodgers, Frank Loesser, and Frederick Loewe to this distinctly American art form.

Tenor Joseph Bach's "The Magnificent Melting Pot" presented an intimate history of the Jews of the Lower East Side of New York in song, picture, and story. Ruth Chertoff's "L'Chaim America" was a moving American Jewish heritage experience revealing the mutual contribution of Jews to America and America to Jews.

And "American Sampler," with Ronald Rogers, accompanied by pianist Doris Montville, traced in song and narrative the building and development of America through the music of the time.

Exhibits, historical artifacts, and works of art for display were loaned by the State Museum in Trenton, the American Jewish Archives, the Hebrew Union College, the Paterson Museum, the Paterson Bicentennial Commission, and the American Jewish Committee.

"The entire spirit of Expo 200 was a joyous one," said Rabbi Freedman. "It was an heroic effort on the part of the Barnert congregation, united in its love and admiration for the American Jewish experience."

But despite the success of Israel Expo '71 and Expo 200, one thing was clear: the middle-class descendants of the immigrants who gave Paterson its workforce, its industry, and its vigor were fleeing the city for the calm of the suburbs. The temple's future was not on Derrom Avenue.

My mother, Augusta Dorfman Politinsky, lived in a nice apartment in Paterson when it started to go downhill. I tried to get her to move to Ridgewood but she was reluctant, until one night outside Barnert Temple someone stole her pocketbook. So she moved to Ridgewood.

—Harold Polton
oral history

This great, historic congregation had served the Paterson Jewish community and the Paterson community at large since 1847 from its small, early quarters to its glorious Broadway synagogue, the first Nathan Barnert Memorial Temple, and its award-winning second Nathan Barnert Memorial Temple. But it was now evident that for the congregation to survive, a move was imperative.

In 1975, Barnert Temple president Alvin Sauer appointed Judge Joseph Conn to chair a long-range planning committee that included Rabbi Martin Freedman, Marge Feinstein, Michael Glanz, Dr. Allan Gold, Dr. Seymour Jaslow, Theodore Lobsenz, George D. Rosenthal, Alvin Sauer, Donna Singer, and Ernest Weiner. In Judge Conn's first report to the congregation in 1976, he stated that the committee had agreed on the following:

1. The future direction of the Barnert Temple lies to the northwest in the Route 208 corridor,

2. Barnert Temple should actively move at once to form a satellite-outreach religious school located in the Wyckoff area,

3. Barnert Temple should determine whether merger with another congregation is possible.

In 1977, Barnert Temple president Robert Gutenstein appointed Philip Sarna to chair a committee that would recommend positive action to the temple board to permit survival and growth. This committee included the long-range planning committee members, as well as Ellen Gutenstein, Robert Gutenstein, William Lee, Ellis Rosenthal, Richard Robinson, Susan Sauer, and Samuel Schwartz. Their special report recommended that the school board chair be authorized to arrange rental space for classroom facilities in the Wyckoff–Franklin Lakes area. In the years that followed, planning and review of the options available to the congregation were pursued vigorously, including the possibility of merging with a near-by congregation. Exploratory discussions were held with several congregations, including temples in Fair Lawn and Wyckoff and groups in Waldwick, Ramsey, Oakland, Mahwah, and Paterson's Temple Emanuel. If a merger with Temple Emanuel became a possibility, the concept was to build a temple edifice that would accommodate both a Reform and a Conservative congregation. Serious consideration and exploration was given to all these options, and Rabbi Daniel Freelander of the Union of American Hebrew Congregations served as a consultant to the Barnert Temple during this period of deliberation.

Ultimately, the Barnert Temple board and congregation, recognizing that the historic Barnert congregation represented the spirit of Reform Judaism in our area of northern New Jersey, decided to search for a new site in the northwest Bergen County area along the Route 208 corridor. At a historic meeting on February 9, 1982, the congregation voted to move on. It was the 135th anniversary year of the Barnert Temple in Paterson.

The Barnert congregation began the year-long 135th anniversary celebration in February 1981, with events scheduled throughout the year, concluding with a special 135th anniversary service on Friday evening November 19, 1982, and the 135th congregational supper on Sunday evening November 21, 1982.

To begin the year, on January 5, 1981, a letter describing an upcoming musical revue had been sent to the congregation membership. The letter said, in part:

> Isn't it amazing? Here we are, a loosely knit group of American Jews, celebrating a milestone—the 135th year of Congregation B'nai Jeshurun!!
>
> We are held together by mutual concerns of Jewish survival, ethics, culture, and a sense of history. We are kept apart by a third diaspora, caused by local migrations and a changing community.
>
> The very achievement of our upward and outward mobility, may, in itself, prove to be the demise of our congregation, unless we pause to recognize where we are going as a congregation. A revue, even a light-hearted one, has a message that we cannot ignore. We may come together but a few times a year for services, yet our sense of family consciously keeps us united.
>
> United we can be during this 135th anniversary year of our temple by attending this musical revue. We hope that all of you get as much enjoyment and feeling of pride in watching the performance, as have all the individuals who have been connected with the production. We are one.

I conceived of the idea for the musical revue, and developed the original story line. The idea was to enlist a majority of the congregation in a creative, fun-filled, bonding experience that would make them aware of the need for a campaign to move the congregation to the Route 208 corridor. I was able to enlist two talented friends, neighbors, and temple members, Stephen Cohen, M.D. and Robert Joelson, M.D., who expanded and improved my original outline and wrote the marvelous book and lyrics for the revue.

Cipora called me one night and told me a little story. It was a story about how the Barnert Temple needed to develop some enthusiasm as an impetus to moving out of Paterson before its congregation was lost to competing temples and before the diaspora received another generation of Jews. Her idea was that the temple needed a rallying point about which to focus so that concerted effort could be made to move the temple while the moving was good. According to her there had to be an original show written about moving, one with humor and yet seriousness and one with parts for lots of members. She had no ears for refusals, and she was willing to produce the show and would hire a more professional director than the likes of us—us being me and Bob Joelson. What she needed from me, and from Bob Joelson, my dear friend and companion in these and other endeavors, was a script based on her concept. Bob and I had written shows before. We had written original lyrics to existing music in several revues and had written some simple story lines. This would be a bit different, but not so different that we couldn't do it, particularly since Bob was a very talented and experienced showman. And we never considered saying no to Cipora. We put together a simple story, one about moving a temple. It centered around temple life and activities and had songs about the board room, raising money, the Sisterhood, treasurer's report, the problems of merging dissimilar congregations, acquiring land, and several other subjects. It was glued together with a song called "We'll Be Here Tomorrow" and a lamed-vavnik concept (the holy 36). The director, Albert, did a great job. There were lots of parts and places for everyone to show off and have fun, but the main thing was that Cipora was right and it galvanized the congregation enough to make the temple's move possible.

—Stephen Cohen, M.D.
letter to the author

I was the producer. With my co-producer, the experienced and invaluable Jill Edelson, the revue attracted nearly 100 members and their children, who rehearsed under the capable professional team of a director-choreographer, a musical director–pianist, a lighting director, and a percussionist member of the congregation. Not only did this large group of congregants enjoy the process of creating an enjoyable revue with a serious theme, but the participants became an "extended family" who understood that the purpose of the show had as a goal "Moving On" to the Route 208 corridor. In February of 1981, the revue sold out, with three standing-room-only performances. Both the opening and the finale were the memorable song "We'll Be Here Tomorrow":

> We'll be here tomorrow, alive and well and thriving;
>
> We'll be here tomorrow, our talent is surviving;
>
> If some night we find our fragile world might crack
>
> We'll just have to try to put the pieces back.
>
> Then from beneath the rubble you'll hear a little voice say
>
> "Life is worth the trouble; have you a better choice?"
>
> So let the skeptics say we'll soon be dead and gone;
>
> We'll be back tomorrow, simply going on."

And even as B'nai Jeshurun prepared to leave Nathan Barnert's beloved Paterson, Barnert's great legacy as an American Jew continued to serve as a model for the congregation. The lyrics from another song in the revue included:

> "A contribution is what we need,
>
> so Nathan Barnert is the hope we've got,
>
> or our temple is an empty lot.
>
> So it's good old reliable Nathan, Nathan, Nathan, Nathan Barnert....
>
> If the goal we are seeking I have to describe,
>
> it's a big brick building with a rabbi inside.
>
> In a temple provided by Nathan,
>
> Learned men will meet and debate,
>
> in the oldest established permanent congregation in the state."

Ladies Benevolent Society Minstrel Show, April 23, 1910.
Barnert Temple Archives.

Musical Follies, December 6, 1933.
Barnert Temple Archives.

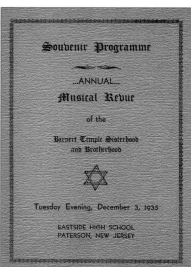

Musical Follies, December 3, 1935.
Barnert Temple Archives.

Barnert Temple Musical Follies cast, 1935. Private collection.

Mischagass rehearsal, 1946, women's chorus. Barnert Temple Archives.

Mischagass performance, 1949, male chorus. Barnert Temple Archives.

Mischagass performance, 1951. Barnert Temple Archives.

Moving On revue performance, February 7, 1981. Private collection.

Moving On revue in rehearsal, January 1981. *Left to right:* Robert Joelson, Stephen Cohen. Private collection.

135th ANNIVERSARY CELEBRATION

FEBRUARY 7 & 8, 1981

THE BARNERT MEMORIAL TEMPLE

presents

MOVING ON

A Musical Revue

Book and Lyrics by Stephen Cohen and Robert Joelson
Production conceived by Cipora O. Schwartz
Directed and Choreographed by Tom Panko

Music from Hoyt Axton, Belafonte-Attaway, Paul Clayton, George Gershwin, Jerry Herman, Karl Hoschna, Robert Joelson, Frank Loesser, Frederick Loewe, Amilcare Ponchielli, Rev. Lester C. Randolph, Richard Rogers, Allen Roth, Sholom Secunda.

Co-Producer . . . . Jill Edelson
Musical Director and Pianist . . . . Albert Zaranka
Percussion . . . . Stephen R. Schwartz
Lighting . . . . John Chenault
Lighting Assistant . . . . Lisa Grossman
Assistant to Mr. Panko . . . . Carole Davis

Moving On revue Program.
Private collection.

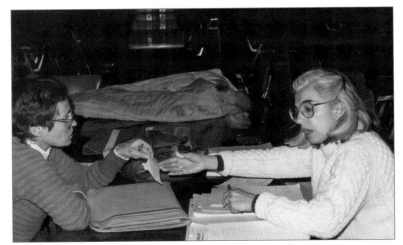

Rehearsal for *Moving On* revue, 1981. *Left to right:* Jill Edelson,
Cipora Schwartz. Private collection.

On April 24, 1982, the congregation continued the 135th anniversary celebration with a dinner dance and ad journal that enjoyed enormous membership support.

Our temple has had a long history of distinguished service here in the North Jersey area which has touched the lives of many, many, thousands of people in the course of our long institutional career of community service. It is important for a synagogue to periodically renew itself through a process of self-assessment and evaluation. Our temple, which will shortly be taking the preliminary steps of a move to relocate ourselves where our present membership lives, will be doing just that: namely, evaluating how we can serve the needs of the Jewish community in an ever-increasing way over the coming decades. A great deal of excitement is generated in such a dramatic step of relocation and renewal. It is through the dedicated labors of those who value the ideals and aspirations of our venerable congregation that we shall continue to grow from strength to strength.

—Edward Wexler
Barnert Temple president
1982 ad journal message

From June 11 to 13, 1982, the congregation held an anniversary weekend celebrating Rabbi Freedman's twenty-five years of devoted and distinguished service to our congregation, the Paterson community, our state, and the nation. The weekend included a special Shabbat service on Friday evening; a gala formal dinner dance honoring Rabbi Freedman on Saturday evening, with Paterson Mayor Lawrence "Pat" Kramer making the keynote address; and a reunion brunch on Sunday morning with special surprise guests for Rabbi Freedman—most of the young men and women he had named, bar and bat mitzvahed, confirmed, and married during those twenty-five years. The weekend was filled with affection, joy, warmth, and respect for our beloved Rabbi Freedman.

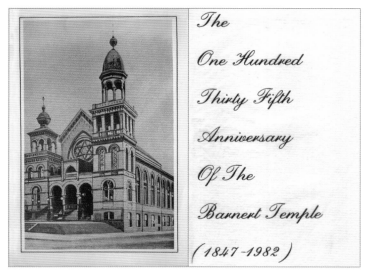

The One Hundred Thirty Fifth Anniversary Of The Barnert Temple

(1847-1982)

135th Anniversary booklet.
Barnert Temple Archives.

The conclusion of this memorable 135th anniversary year was a special Sabbath service held on Friday, November 19, 1982, which, in the tradition of this historic congregation, included the participation of religious and lay leaders from the Paterson community.

On Sunday evening, November 21, 1982, the 135th congregational supper was held and included, by request of the congregants, an abridged reprise of the musical revue "Moving On." The 135th anniversary booklet proudly included a list of the range of programs and services the congregation provided to its members and the community, including: religious, rabbinical, musical, study, community and social action, cemetery, social, Sisterhood–Men's Club–youth group, and ecumenical activities. A brief history of the congregation since 1847 was also included, with many historic photographs as illustrations. And the booklet included a list of the eighteen ways in which the congregation exemplified its traditional threefold mandate to be a house of worship, a house of study, and a house of assembly.

1. A beautiful sanctuary for prayer and mediation. The temple on Straight Street was a replica of the Central Synagogue built in New York City five years earlier. The Central Synagogue today is a national landmark. The temple on Derrom Avenue has won an international prize as one of the best community buildings in the United States built in the year 1964. Our architect, Percival Goodman, won an award for our temple as the most beautiful community building in the state of New Jersey in 1965.

2. A place of music and song in praise of God. Our congregation has had a tradition of cantor and choir going back to 1868. Cantor Joseph Posner, who passed away this year, was cantor of the temple for more than forty-one years.

3. A community building and center of Jewish learning. Over the years adult education programs (including an Institute of Jewish Studies) reflected the age-old injunction to study and learn all the days of one's life.

4. A reservoir of faith and repository of learning both ancient and new. The temple has stood as a beacon during good and bad times. After World War I, the congregation formally adopted a Polish Jewish orphan and brought her to the United States. During World War II the congregation supported all efforts to save the surviving remnants of the Jewish people.

5. A school to educate our young in the knowledge, piety, and richness of our Jewish heritage. The temple has always had a school for its young from kindergarten through tenth grade. The Barnert Temple has always observed the tradition of Confirmation Services and later, bar and bat mitzvah services (sons and daughters of the Commandments)

6. A physical link in the great chain of Jewish continuity.

7. A place to mark the rhythmic cycles of the festivals and holidays of the Jewish year.

8. An ark to house our holy Torahs and great literary heritage. The temple treasures seven beautiful Torah scrolls which have been gifts over the years. Three of the Torah scrolls are no longer usable because of their age, but are still preserved in our temple ark. The Jacob Cohen Memorial Library contains a collection of Judaica and contemporary Jewish literature.

9. A temple which provides and protects the sacred ground of Mount Nebo Cemetery, one of the most beautiful cemeteries in the metropolitan area. The temple originally shared a small cemetery in Hawthorne, N.J., and in 1847 acquired another small cemetery in Clifton, N.J. The Mount Nebo Cemetery in Totowa, N.J., was acquired in 1867.

10. A place for sharing our grief and expressing our sorrow in the loss of loved ones.

11. A center for celebrating the joyous cycle of life: child naming, consecration, bar and bat mitzvah, Confirmation and marriage. Thousand of men, women and children have marked such occasions over the past 135 years.

12. A forum for ideas of Jewish and general concern. Various community organizations have utilized the temple as a meeting place. It has often served as the rallying center for emergency needs of the Jewish community.

13. A meeting place for the Hebrew Ladies Benevolent Society, founded in 1883, which then became our temple Sisterhood; a meeting place for our Men's Club, youth groups and even the meeting place for the first Jewish Girl Scout troop of New Jersey.

14. A happy center for social activities, parties, dances and balls. The social aspects of the temple have always played a prominent role in binding the congregation together in a sense of family unity.

15. A community center for Jewish and general organizations supporting and enhancing the welfare of all people. Organizations such as the Barnert Hospital, the Daughters of Miriam, O.R.T., the Brandeis Women's Organization and Hadassah have regularly met in the temple.

16. A rallying place for community political and social concerns. The Men's Club, over the years, has held many pre-election forums for political candidates. Over the years organizations such as the Paterson Police Department and the Paterson Task Force for Community Action have held institutes and programs in the temple.

17. An instrumentality for raising funds for Jewish and charitable purposes. The United Jewish Appeal and the Bonds for Israel have regularly held many of their major affairs at the temple. In 1971, Rabbi Freedman was honored by a special Bonds for Israel dinner.

18. A meeting place for all faiths expressing the hope for unity and fellowship of all peoples. Many interfaith services have taken place in both the old and new buildings. The congregation has represented the highest aspirations of the American ideals of social justice and caring concern in the community of north Jersey.

The Barnert Temple has always been blessed by outstanding rabbis and teachers. Its pulpit has been occupied by twelve rabbis and ten religious functionaries. Our rabbi, Martin Freedman, is one of the outstanding leaders of higher education in the state of New Jersey. He has been appointed to positions of high influence in state, national and international organizations as a champion of human rights. He has been the recipient of many awards, including a Presidential Citation in 1968....

In keeping with his predecessors, he has been an active leader in Jewish causes, civil rights, Soviet Jewry, the arts and child welfare. He has been the rabbi of the congregation since 1957.

The number "18" stands for the Hebrew word "Chai"—LIFE!

These eighteen descriptions of our Congregation B'nai Jeshurun, the Barnert Memorial Temple, only begin to depict the *life* force of our historic congregation: 135 years young!

The mandate for Barnert Temple to survive was crystallized during this 135th year. It became clear that to survive, this oldest Jewish congregation in the state of New Jersey would have to move to where its congregants lived. The desire to serve the Jewish people was still alive and well at Barnert Temple, through life-cycle services, social action and outreach programs, religious services, and its school. There still remained the belief that our congregation, after 135 years, could continue to serve many generations to come in this great land where our religious freedoms were constitutionally guaranteed.

All this the Barnert congregation was committed to, and the congregation purchased ten acres of land on the Route 208 corridor in Franklin Lakes on August 15, 1985. It then began a "Survival Drive" campaign.

The difficulties of the Survival Drive appeared to be insurmountable. The congregation was small, with some of the members aged and ill, some retired to warmer climates, some residing in Passaic, Bergen, and other counties or in other states. The congregation was financially burdened with a huge mortgage on its Derrom Avenue building. However, the idealism and commitment of the congregants were astonishing. They remembered that the first-generation members in 1847 were shopkeepers, mill workers, menial workers; that the second and following generations became shop and mill owners, industrialists, and professionals; that the many moves of the congregation over the generations had not emerged in a vacuum, but were made possible by the sacrifices of the congregants and their vision. Our commitment was inherited from the generations that preceded ours; we built and built, again and again, responding to the needs of the current generation and anticipating the needs of tomorrow's. These late-twentieth-century American Jews respected the heritage of their first-generation blue-collar ancestors, with their melting pot aspirations for their children's education. These present congregants viewed themselves as the descendants of Jews who had sought and found in the dream of America the promise of opportunity, the potential for religious freedom, and the possibility for change that illuminated our lives as American Jews.

And so the Barnert congregation reaffirmed its confidence in its future as a congregation, and the Survival Drive campaign that would move the congregation from Paterson to Franklin Lakes began. The Survival Drive had a remarkable breadth of support from the membership. With Samuel Schwartz as honorary chair, Bertram I. Cohen as honorary vice-chair, and Robert Gutenstein and myself as co-chairs, and exemplary cooperation from the Barnert board, a campaign plan was formulated that resulted in the move. The campaign included a simple brochure, handouts, and pledge cards, printed in May 1984, that clearly and simply stated the urgency for survival of the congregation. Rabbi Freedman's message in the brochure stated:

> In this year 5744, we are the keepers of the flame! It is the duty of our generation to build this temple anew. It is at one and the same time both a sacred obligation and a grand privilege. As the oldest synagogue in New Jersey, we will move to a great new site where we shall once more construct a spiritual home of prayer, study and assembly. Through the leadership and generosity of some wonderful people who have shaped this building campaign, we are now reaching out to our whole congregation. Each of us must share the burden and the honor of building our temple. What we do now will form the pattern of Jewish life tomorrow. In our 140th year of existence we shall have "moved on" to our new and beautiful home where we shall rekindle the flame. There is no Jewish life possible without the synagogue for ourselves, our children and our future in this great land! Therefore, it is obvious that by giving now—we give for tomorrow, as well. Be generous! Open your hearts and hands! Be a Keeper of the **Flame**!

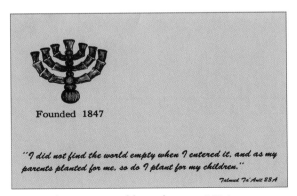

Founded 1847

"I did not find the world empty when I entered it, and as my parents planted for me, so do I plant for my children."

Talmud Ta'Anit 23A

"Survival Drive" pamphlet, February, 1984. Private collection.

Congregation B'nai Jeshurun ...
the oldest temple in New Jersey

"Survival Drive" brochure cover, May 1984.
Private collection.

Samuel S. Schwartz, honorary chairman of
"Survival Drive" campaign.
Private collection.

And the brochure text included these words:

> Congregation B'nai Jeshurun ... the youngest temple in New Jersey—When
> a group of Jews from Paterson organized the Congregation B'nai Jeshurun in
> 1847, they no doubt had never heard of "the Route 208 corridor." Nor we
> suspect had Nathan Barnert, the congregation's best known benefactor,
> when he attended the groundbreaking in 1892 for the temple on Broadway
> and Straight Street which bore his name. But they nevertheless would surely
> have approved of our congregation's decision to erect its seventh [known]
> and newest home on a spot which in their day must have been considered
> wilderness. They would have approved because they understood that where
> a congregation meets is important only in so far as it satisfies the needs of its
> members ... both present, and if it is to survive, future. Our congregants
> have, to a large extent, already moved to the area surrounding our planned
> home, helping to create a circle of Jewish life that will exist for generations
> to come. Our temple will be at the center of that circle, drawing its
> membership and its vitality from a broader area of Bergen and Passaic
> Counties than ever our forefathers dreamt possible. And in that way, New
> Jersey's oldest temple will indeed continue to flourish as New Jersey's
> youngest temple. Youngest at heart, that is.

The campaign's leadership was determined to minimize fundraising costs—the
total cost of the Survival Drive came to approximately 1 percent of the $2 million goal
(several volunteers worked nearly full-time to avoid hiring paid staff)—and the
campaign leaders committed to build only with the funds that were raised so not to
burden the next generation with debt. The effort was heroic, led by Rabbi Freedman's
vigorous and inspirational participation, which greatly motivated the solicitors. Rabbi
Freedman gave unstintingly of his precious time, and he was always available to
accompany any solicitation team. I made sixty-one personal solicitation visits to
members of the congregation, and Rabbi Freedman partnered with me on many of
these home visits, as he did with other Survival Drive campaign solicitors. He was a
dynamic motivator as a team member, and we are very grateful for his unwavering and
deeply meaningful support. A fair share of $10,000 per family unit was established as a
goal, recognizing that this was an averaged sum. The congregation's participation was
extraordinary—from the leadership gifts that made the move possible, to the small
symbolic gifts made by the poorest and oldest members of the congregation (some in
nursing homes). The heart, the impetus of the Survival Drive was the complete
cooperation of this dwindling congregation to survive, for more than 90 percent of the
congregants contributed to the campaign.

As the Survival Drive neared completion, it became clear that not enough money
was available to build the second floor of the religious school building. In anticipation
of a much larger student population and membership at the new Barnert Temple site
in Franklin Lakes, an additional mini-campaign was begun, and once again we went
to the congregants to explain the need. Samuel Schwartz, frail and ill at the 1986 Rosh
Hashanah services, made an impassioned, compelling appeal to the congregants to
participate in a two-for-one matching grant of $200,000 provided by four elders of the
congregation so that an enlarged religious school could be built. Again, a heroic stretch
was made by the congregants as the solicitors and donors were re-energized to

complete their vision for the future congregants, their children, and their children's children. We returned to the telephone calls, the personal visits, and the follow-ups, with the result that we raised a total of $2,270,000 and were able to build the religious school second floor—with no mortgage!

Concurrent with the fundraising activities was the planning for the new Barnert Temple in Franklin Lakes. Percival Goodman would once again be the designer-architect, adopting the successful floor plan of the award-winning Derrom Avenue building. Bergen County architect Raymond Wells would be the site architect, and Visbeen & Co. builders, also the builders of the Derrom Avenue building, rounded out the team. A clear vision for survival, integrity, teamwork, and the heroic stretch of this small Paterson congregation made the move possible. The new Franklin Lakes Barnert Temple was projected for completion in time for the High Holidays in September 1987.

Yet, as we prepared for the move to Franklin Lakes, we remembered Paterson and were determined to maintain our relationship with the community that had nurtured us. We made plans to care for our older congregants and to transport them to the new Barnert Temple Franklin Lakes. We would continue our support, through our social action committee members, for the various needs of the Paterson community. Paterson was home to our immigrant ancestors, and the city had welcomed the eighteenth-, nineteenth-, and early twentieth-century multi-national-cultural-religious families and given them the opportunity to become Americans. These immigrants and their children, grandchildren, and great-grandchildren became the middle-class Americans who served our nation in the Civil War, the Spanish-American War, World War I, World War II, Korea, and Vietnam to preserve our American freedoms.

During the mid-twentieth century in Paterson, as in many older urban cities, the now-educated middle class moved to the suburbs and to other American cities where they could more advantageously use their new skills and professional education.

In the 1960s, Paterson was faced with understanding ethnic diversity, as well as an exodus of many of its manufacturing companies. It was a dark period filled with urban decay and staleness, as it fought to remain a viable place to live and work. The 1970s and 1980s contributed to this neglect, as surrounding suburbs developed shopping malls, forcing the closure or relocation of many downtown retail businesses.

—Paul Harencak
chairman
Greater Paterson Chamber of Commerce

In the twenty-first century, however, Paterson would again welcome a diverse new population of immigrants and would be re-energized by their work ethic. The idea of the demise of the old cities was premature; along with the struggles, there are opportunities for these new Patersonians. There are programs today that would have been unthinkable for earlier immigrants. Federal and state government programs help develop job skills and training, provide medical care and health maintenance, and care for the elderly and handicapped through Medicare and Medicaid.

In the twenty-first century, Paterson benefits from excellent medical facilities at the Barnert Memorial Hospital Center and St. Joseph's Hospital and Medical Center, and excellent educational facilities such as nearby William Paterson University and Ramapo College, and in Paterson, the Passaic County Community College. The Greater Paterson Chamber of Commerce and the Paterson Economic Development Corporation are ready to help businesses and industries.

Paterson is also home to a number of cultural and arts institutions, including the Passaic County Historical Society at Lambert Castle, the Paterson Museum in the Rogers Locomotive building complex, the Great Falls Historic District, the Passaic Community College Art Galleries housed in the former Alexander Hamilton Club building, and the Paterson Free Public Library on Broadway, established in 1855 as New Jersey's first chartered public library.

Over the last 200 years, Paterson has had its share of successes and failures. What makes Paterson strong is a commitment from people who live and work within its borders, and who refuse to give up on its rich heritage. Today Paterson is teeming with activities in all sectors, private and public. The city can proudly boast of its accomplishments: a revitalized downtown shopping area, a rebuilt and preserved historic district, lower crime rates in local neighborhoods, and schools and businesses partnering resources to provide children and adults with a quality education. One of the most telling indicators of Paterson's resurgence is the lack of available industrial space for prospective tenants. The future is bright for Paterson. While there is still plenty of work to be done in all areas, there is a strong sense of involvement to ensure Paterson will regain its rightful reputation as an appealing community in which to live, work, and shop.

—Paul Harencak
chairman
Greater Paterson Chamber of Commerce

Once again, Paterson has become a more vibrant community, a base for the present population to thrive in positive new directions using the educational, industrial, medical, and artistic opportunities available to these new Americans.

Over the centuries poets have recorded their responses to and admiration for Paterson. From a 1923 anthology, *Poems of New Jersey*:

Joyce Kilmer, "**The Twelve-Forty-Five**"

Cities and Towns

Why, even strident Paterson
Rests quietly as any nun.
Her foolish warring children keep
The grateful armistice of sleep.

Ruth Guthrie Harding, "**The Old Wagon-Market**"

When came I first to Paterson,
(Full twenty years ago)
I hied me to its market-place,
With joy and wonder in my face,
To gaze upon the show.

Louis Ginsberg, "**The City-Park**"

A haven in a stormy sea,
A sweet oasis and a nook,
It nestles in the noisy streets,
A lyric in a prosy book.

David Maclure, "**The Founders**"

A city's glory is her citizens.
Remembering this, great may our city grow,
Each man a partner in prosperity,
Each man a brother to his fellow-man,
Sharing the gains of labor and of skill,
Rich in the spirit's fruits beyond all else,
Proud of his fellow-man, proud of himself,
Proud of his home, the city beautiful.

Washington Irving, **"The Falls of the Passaic"**

But the stranger still gazes with wondering eye,
On the rocks rudely torn, and groves mounted on high;
Still loves on the cliff's dizzy borders to roam,
Where the torrent leaps headlong, embosomed in foam.

Great Falls of the Passaic River, Paterson, 2005. Photo by author.
Private collection.

We, the congregants of the Franklin Lakes Barnert Temple, descendants of the nineteenth-century Patersonians and newer members, remember and continue our ties to Paterson, the community that nurtured us and our ancestors.

CHAPTER NINE

Rabbi Martin Freedman
The Renaissance Rabbi

Freedom Ride, August 6, 1964. Refusing to plead for mitigation of sentence, Leon County Jail, Tallahassee, Florida. *Seated, left to right:* Rev. Dr. Robert McAfee Brown, Rev. John W. Collier, Rabbi Martin Freedman. *Standing, left to right:* Rabbi Israel Dresner, Rev. Patty McKinney, Revs. Robert J. Stone, A. McRaven Warner, Arthur L. Hardge, and Wayne Hartmire. Barnert Temple Archives.

Rabbi Martin Freedman is an American, born in Newark, New Jersey, on November 13, 1926, to Rabbi Solomon Jacob Freedman and Yetta Tornheim Kahane Freedman. Both of his parents came from rabbinic families—on his mother's side for thirteen generations, and on his father's side, seven generations—and were born in Palestine while it was still part of the Ottoman Empire (his father, in fact, served as a water carrier in the Turkish army during World War I). Both parents, moreover, had first marriages that ended with the death of the other spouse. They met in this country after emigrating from Palestine and were married in the early 1920s. Their blended family consisted of eight children, and together they had two more, a daughter, now deceased, and Martin.

Solomon Freedman served as the rabbi of a congregation in Newark, New Jersey, and also owned a Jewish bookstore in Newark. Martin's brother David was a rabbi in Irvington, New Jersey, and was also active as a *mohel*. His brother Herman was a rabbi in Newark.

Martin's upbringing in Newark was deeply religious, and he was very much involved in his father's and brother's congregations. From early childhood, Martin would bring the challah to the synagogue for *seudah shlishit*, the "third meal" on the Sabbath, when the men were studying. At the age of six, Martin could sing Yiddish songs, and when he was only fourteen, he began teaching in his brother David's religious school, earning $6–8 per week (a princely sum at that time). One of his bar mitzvah students was Jerry Lewis, later to become famous as a comedian and actor.

As a teenager, while he was a freshman at New York University, World War II and the horrific events of the Holocaust had a profound effect upon young Martin Freedman.

The war and the Hitler period was very important. In my family, they were all deeply committed Zionists and very much deeply immersed in Jewish life, and the advent of Hitlerism, and fascism and Nazism was a terrible thing in its effect on my family.... although for the most part, 95 percent of my family was no longer European, but were living in Palestine and the United States, nevertheless it was something of great agitation and concern. In those days during the Second World War, you could no longer volunteer for the armed services ... you went in on your eighteenth birthday when you registered for the draft and you were inducted thirty days later into one or another of the armed forces. I was graduated from high school at the age of seventeen, so I went on to NYU, where I was a student for about a year before I entered into the army. I waived the thirty days, I wanted to go in to fight Nazis. I served in the United States Army in the 1st Infantry. I volunteered for overseas duty. This was just before the Battle of the Bulge in 1944. I ended up going to Germany, to the European theater. I came to the European theater in the end of February 1945. Landed in Le Havre. I was by then a corporal. My first experience was in Amberg, Germany, in the replacement depot. I was made corporal of the guard. Now this was the guard of a camp of SS officers. This is the first group of officers, this was the first stage before we were sent back further behind the lines, and I was on three hours and off six hours and I had a detachment of five soldiers under me, and through the course of the twenty-four-hour period it turned out that the next day at noon I was on duty. I'm coming up to check on my five men—I was all of eighteen years old—and I was checking on them and I see three German officers coming toward us. They had been taken out on a work detail and they're carrying something under their arms with their coats. And I said to this guy, "They could be carrying weapons in there," and he said, "Well, I don't know," and I said, "Halt," and in German tradition, they didn't put their coats down and [they] began to protest; I pulled out my '45, down came the coats. I kicked them open and there were two bottles of U.S. Army officer brandy liquor. And this was my third day in Europe, okay? I go to a field telephone and I call up a Sergeant Milkowski, who was the sergeant in charge of the detail, and I tell him I have some German officers with some booze. The next thing I knew, this Milkowski—before the jeep had even stopped—was out of the jeep, pounding the hell out of these three [German] officers and he says, "Corporal, you've done a terrific job," and disappears.

When the war ended, I was in the Third Army 48th Armored Field Artillery, which was, of all things, a New Jersey unit, originally. We carried guns, cannons on half-tracks and we were on our way to the Czechoslovakian border. We had come to the town of Schwabischalle, which was on the Czech border and in Patton's army. I ultimately ended up in a very cushy job for a nineteen-year-old kid. I became the acting sergeant major in the Third Army artillery [headquarters] in Heidelberg, Germany. And I was an acting sergeant major because at that point, the men were being shipped back to the United States and I was given the acting rank.

—*Rabbi Martin Freedman*
oral history

Martin Freedman had heard that Bad Kissingen, Germany, was the collection point for the last surviving children from the concentration camps. In charge of the children was the United Nations Relief and Rehabilitation Administration, manned mainly by a wonderful group of Norwegians who were taking care of these 600 children who were going to be safely transported to Palestine (now Israel) through various European countries.

I had the authority of assignment and reassignment of military officers—artillery officers. During this period, I kept getting letters from my father, in Yiddish, asking, "What are you doing, we hear terrible things, I hear the war is over now, can't you help, let us know what to do," etc. Eight of us soldiers were going to bring together a load of food, and PX material, chocolates, cigarettes to Bad Kissingen, where the children were. On the black market in those days, a carton of cigarettes sold for the equivalent of $800. I mean, it was just simply, utterly unbelievable. And the idea was we were going to take what we got together in the truck up to a camp we had learned about through the UNRRA—the last surviving Jewish children in all of Europe [were at a camp in] a place called Bad Kissingen, which is about 60 miles in the high mountains south of Berlin. And the agreement was that four of us were going to drive this truck up—-a three-quarter-ton truck—filled with the equivalent, in those days, of $100,000 worth of goods. On the Sunday morning I was the only one who showed up. Filled with sheer terror, I went with this truck at which we had posted a guard, and now—what [was] I going to do? Finally I screwed up my courage and I drove that truck up to Bad Kissingen. I never in my life before or since ever obeyed the traffic laws as carefully as I did for fear I would be stopped by the constabulary, and go explain, "What do you have there?" I came up the mountain to Bad Kissingen and there were about six hotels arranged around the square. I saw there were children seated on the porches and the verandas of the hotel and I pulled up to the center square, stopped the car in the center there, and waited for some of the children to come and help me. I threw open the back of the three-quarter-ton truck. And we started taking out cartons of Hershey candy bars and things for the children. I could hear the babble of Yiddish, and then, before I knew it, all of a sudden one group began to burst into a song, in Yiddish. And it completely laid me low, I mean I burst out crying. Of course I later discovered that that morning, Dr. Nahum Goldmann had visited the center and these children had put on a program for Dr. Goldmann of songs that they had learned, and what they were doing is they were simply welcoming me with a Yiddish song. I spent the day there, and that night, when I drove down that mountain, had there been any German on the road.... You know, this was the last group of 600 children from all of the death camps and all of the camps of Germany. Some of them were going to go on what was called the secret railroad, which it turned *out later on was run by a man who became a friend of mine, Rabbi Avram Klasner. The trains [went to Bari], Italy and from Italy, they would go onto little boats across to Palestine. It was a very emotional experience. It is indelibly part of me, something that I can never ever forget, and even as I tell it to you now, I feel … Whenever I tell it, I feel a kind of [unmitigated rage].*

—Rabbi Martin Freedman
oral history

Back in the United States after having served in the U.S. Army from 1944 to 1946, Martin Freedman returned to school, receiving a bachelor's degree from New York University in 1949 and a master's degree in 1952 from Columbia University, where he also taught Jewish studies and thought he would pursue an academic career. While at Columbia University, Freedman visited the Jewish Institute of Religion at the urging of his brother, Fred Kahan. That visit not only changed Freedman's career plans, but in future years, led to the revitalization and survival of the historic Barnert Temple in Paterson and Franklin Lakes.

This is 1949. My brother Fred had been speaking to me and was not very sympathetic to the idea of my having an academic career. He felt it was a kind of dead-end thing, even though it might be intellectually challenging, and he suggested that I go up and see Stephen Wise, or go up and see the Institute, the Jewish Institute of Religion. In December 1949, I went up to JIR and the place was in turmoil because they were merging with the school in Cincinnati, the Hebrew Union College. And all I did was come there for a catalogue to see what courses were being offered. The secretary there said to me, "Well, I'll make an appointment for you to come in to see somebody." And I said, "I don't want an appointment," and she said, "No no, it's the best way, since the catalogues are in a state of flux." And in January 1950, I was ushered into a room in which there were three people: one of them was Henry Slonimsky, the dean of the college; another one was Emanuel Green, a rabbi and professor of codes; and the third one was Rabbi Abram Granison, who was the associate dean of the college. Abram Granison later became the rabbi of the Barnert Temple. It was a very interesting interview. Slonimsky finally said to me, "Listen, the only way you'll ever know whether this is of interest to you in terms of a career is to take two courses—both of them are mine. Come in, we'll admit you in the middle of the year and you'll...." I never filled out an application, I never filled out a form, and I was in class in two weeks. Slonimsky was an incredible human being. At the end of four months, I was absolutely enchanted, more interested in the classes I attended there than all the classes I was taking at Columbia. The upshot of the matter is that by the following fall, I was a full-time student at JIR.

At JIR, I was a good student. I enjoyed what was happening in the school and learning there. And before I knew it, I ended up becoming an assistant student rabbi to a man called Joshua Trachtenberg, who was then the rabbi of a congregation in eastern Pennsylvania. Rabbi Trachtenberg was going blind. He was also a very, very powerful force of one period in my life, because he was also a brilliant, brilliant scholar and had written a number of very important books, two of which are still very important today— Jewish Magic and Superstition and Anti-Jewish Tradition in the Middle Ages in Church Law. He was a wonderful human being [and became my mentor]. [In the summer of]

1953, I came off a camping trip in the woods and there was a message [from JIR that] I have an appointment that evening in Elizabeth, New Jersey, with a group of people who want to talk to me. I quickly shaved, got dressed, jumped into my jalopy, drove out to Elizabeth and met a group of nine people who were starting a congregation. My name had been put forward by a representative of the UAHC. We talked.... And [by the following weekend] I was a student rabbi of a congregation of about fifteen families. And by the end of a year, I was the rabbi of a congregation of 200 families. I mean, that's a full-time position and here I was a student. I was in the congregation (Temple Beth El) in Elizabeth when I was ordained in 1955. It was by then a congregation of about 250, 280 families [and I was their rabbi]. [It was] a very young, dynamic congregation..... I [was there] for a year past my ordination when one day, I got a phone call. This was a phone call from a man, I didn't know him, named Mendon Morrill. He said he'd like to take me out to lunch at Bamberger's and I asked, "What's this all about?" and he said, "Well, we're looking for a rabbi up in Paterson, New Jersey." I said, "I'm not interested, my congregation is a new congregation, I started it, I'm happy with it." He said, "Listen, how old are you?" I said, "I'm twenty-eight." He said, "I'm going to give you a bit of advice: If anybody ever offers you a job, never refuse to listen to the offer. Even though you're not going to accept it, just listen to the offer." I said, "You've convinced me." I met him in Newark, and in those days Bamberger's had a restaurant up on the top floor, and we met there and he urged me to come and meet the congregation. And he described the congregation in the following terms, "It's a very old, decrepit congregation, which could limp along for many years now because, you know, there are people devoted enough to it, to still carry it through, but it's badly in need of a move and a new resurgence of life." I said, 'OK, I'll come up and see." I came up and met with, I think it was Lou Sorkin, then the president of the temple, and we sat and talked and I said, "I don't know why the temple is still downtown at Broadway and Straight Street ... I mean, there is no way it can survive." Sorkin said, "Well, you know, some people say it's a historic building and want to keep it." I said, "A congregation is not a building, a congregation is a living vital thing, an association of people." In any event, we had a series of meetings over a period of about three months and finally the person who was most influential at the meeting here was Mendon Morrill. ... the two of us became very close, fast, personal friends. I was ordained in '55. I served [in Elizabeth] through '56. I came [to Barnert Temple] in January '57 because they were absolutely dying to have a rabbi, they had been having temporary rabbis filling in now for a period of almost a year. And I made up my mind at the end of six months that if I did not move the congregation out of its location in downtown Paterson by the year 1960, I was leaving Paterson. I knew it had to be, you could read the handwriting on the wall—if the congregation didn't move, it would end up with forty families and just simply, slowly fade away.

[The temple officers] had been negotiating for years for a piece of property on Broadway and Derrom Avenue owned by a Mr. Carroll. In those days, there was no chance of moving out of Paterson because in those days, the congregation was Paterson and only Paterson, with a sprinkling of Fair Lawn and a tiny sprinkling of other communities. By '59, it was very clear that Carroll was not going to sell. And so the temple bought a piece of land on 20th Avenue and McLean Boulevard. And they bought a house, which

was on 42nd Street. And they said, you know, meanwhile, you might as well move into the house, it's a better house. And [from the house on 42nd Street] I thought it's a mistake; I would look out the back of that house and I would look at that 20th Avenue [and busy McLean Boulevard] and I knew that was not the place [for a new Barnert Temple]. So on a Monday morning—I had never met Mr. Carroll—I called up Frank Stave and I said, "Do you know Carroll?" and he said, "Yes," and I said, "Can you call him and make an appointment? Let's go up and see him." And he said, "Sure, I'll call him." We went up at eleven o'clock on a Monday morning and we spoke with Mr. Carroll. I said, "Mr. Carroll, you don't know me, I'm the new young rabbi of the congregation and I want you to know that we've purchased a piece of property on 20th Avenue and McLean Boulevard. In a period of two weeks, they're going to start construction of something.... I know that I have been told by Mr. Stave and by Mr. Peterson, whom I spoke to at the bank, that on two occasions you have agreed to sell the Derrom Avenue property and at the last minute, you decided that you weren't going to [sell]. The fact of the matter is, we have come to that absolute crossroad where, if we take this step one more week from now [it is irreversible]." I said, "Mr. Carroll, how much do you want for the property?" I knew that the negotiations for the property had been by our real estate people in the past. They were dealing with Carroll over these past negotiations like it was a real estate negotiation. It was no real estate negotiation [for Carroll]; he had to sell but he had a certain pride. I said, "$125,000?" and he said, "$125,000, that's what I want, that's what I've always wanted." I said, 'It's done, you'll hear from us this afternoon." That [afternoon] I went to see Sam Schwartz. I had not been with the congregation very long but I recognized that he was a natural for a position of leadership for this campaign. And I came to see Sam Schwartz and I made the case, and I said, "This is the problem that we have been dealing with—can we do it, can we get $125,000?"

[Sam] started telling me that the congregation is a peripheral interest of his, it's not a central interest, he doesn't function in the congregation in any specific role ... and I said, 'But you are the only person that I can turn to.... Excuse me." I turned to Esther and I said, 'You two are the only people I can turn to.' And she said, 'Well, I'll talk about it with him." The next day, I got a phone call from Sam Schwartz. "I'll support you." In the year 1959, $125,000 sounded like an insurmountable sum of money.

Shortly after the meeting with Sam and Esther Schwartz, a temple board meeting was convened. At that time the president of the temple was Norman Lappin. Norman was a wonderful person. We had the meeting and the agreement was that a number of people would make an immediate contribution to effect the purchase of the property and if it worked out, we would then have a building fund drive for the building of the temple. Sam and ten board members agreed each to put up, I think, $10,000 each, or $15,000 each, and it was the sum of $125,000. [The day after the board meeting, Norman Lappin, Frank Stave and I] met at the bank. Mr. Peterson was there and Carroll came in and we greeted each other, and by now I was his buddy. Carroll came across and he said, "Oh, my wife wants to meet you, she's anxious to meet you," and then he turned to Peterson and he said, "Where do I sign?" And that was it—we were now the proud owners of [the Derrom Avenue] property."

—Rabbi Martin Freedman
oral history

I went back to Sam and said, "Sam Schwartz, there's nobody else to head this [campaign]." He said, 'Well we're going to talk it over" —Esther was there— "we're going to talk it over again.' And the next day she presented me with a gift that I treasure very much. She gave me the gift of a rather rare edition [book] from 1709—the autobiography of the chief rabbi in Amsterdam, Rabbi Manasseh Ben Israel, and his appeal to Oliver Cromwell to allow the Jews to return to England. She said, "This is going to be the right start because we are going to make this work." [Sam, with Esther's urging, agreed to chair the building fund campaign.] But I think in the second time, he really did not want to head up the campaign, but he did. We had to raise $650,000.

That was an interesting [building] campaign because the campaign started and failed (fell short of its goal). We ended up raising $450,000—$250,000 and another $200,000. But by then, that extra $200,000 was absolutely the work of Sam Schwartz. He was the one who for three weeks, five times a day, I don't know how he conducted his business, but he was at it all the time. I'd get a call in the morning, "I just spoke to so and so, I got him to agree," but he was the one who really brought it in.

The architect, Percival Goodman, said it was the happiest building he had ever put up. As a matter of fact, the temple is, to this day, and I've been in it since the Muslims have taken it over, it is a great work of art. That building—people are really not aware of it—that building won the prize for the best public community building [built] in the state of New Jersey in the year of 1963. It won a money prize from a number of banks, which had put up the money to improve architecture in the state of New Jersey. [Architect] Percy Goodman won, I think, $1,500, and the temple won $2,500. The Barnert Temple was also cited in the magazine Le Arch, a French Jewish community magazine, as the most beautiful synagogue/community building in 1963. By the way [actual construction] for the Barnert Temple [began] on what date? November 22, 1963—the day Kennedy was assassinated. I went to the building site and I told the workers to stop. They said, "We just started." I said, "Stop. The president of the United States has just been assassinated."

As a matter of fact, we held services [in the new temple] before we had a certificate of occupancy. [The service was held] on the concrete floor, and we had it on folding chairs, and that weekend, we had a big ball and party on the concrete floor. It was a very exciting time.

—Rabbi Martin Freedman
oral history

The temple immediately experienced dramatic growth. It grew from 140 to 240 families. The school tripled in size. And the congregation re-established a nursery school, which was tremendously successful.

I was raised Reform and Alvin told me about Martin Freedman. [Alvin] told me [Martin] was 10 feet tall. [Martin] is very impressive from the bimah. I remember the first time [Alvin] took me to services there. He said, "Wait 'til you see this guy."

—Susan Sauer
oral history

November 22, 1963—John F. Kennedy, the president of the United States, was assassinated. Barnert Temple Archives.

The Derrom Avenue temple is now a Muslim Mosque. Photo by James D. Schwartz, 2005.

The 1894 Barnert Temple is now a White Castle restaurant. Photo by James D. Schwartz, 2005.

A Story Without End

Barnert Temple Pamphlet describing the programs and the move to Derrom Avenue, 1965. Barnert Temple Archives.

Everything was jumping and moving. The building itself was a building that gave us good use. We formed, I remember, a three-year Adult Institute of Jewish Education for certification, and I actually ended up with about nine people who got certified.

I also used to run a businessman's lunch-and-learn in downtown Paterson. I taught a group of people on a steady, ongoing basis in a hotel where these people come for lunch.

Bar mitzvahs.... When I was in the Barnert Temple on Broadway and Straight Street, I had one bar mitzvah every four–five months. All of a sudden, with the school growth we were having bar [and bat] mitzvahs [almost weekly] in the temple—it was a jumping and a happy kind of experience. In terms of the mortgage, it was heavy."

—Rabbi Martin Freedman
oral history

We joined Barnert Temple in 1968, mainly because it was Reform and because Martin Freedman was a very exciting rabbi.... Rabbi Freedman was quite an active fellow with a lot of ideas, and much to our pleasure, he came up with the Israel Expo in 1971 as a way of raising money [to help with the mortgage debt]. And the Israel Expo was a most fantastic thing for the temple ... because the temple had been exhausted from building a new building and everybody was kind of worn out. So Martin thought this up and everybody in the temple was involved.

Then Martin came up with "It's the Bicentennial." So in 1976, we did the American Bicentennial. And then after that, our fundraising went to action auctions, the Sisterhood ran Chinese auctions through 1985, '86. Every year, there were two or three serious fundraising activities, and we would creep from pillar to post.

The school building was a building that needed constant repair. In fact, Martin and I used to climb all over it, trying to figure out where the leaks were coming from or where plaster was falling from to prevent the children from being hurt.... And whenever anything went wrong, Martin would dash over from his home. He would fix the lights. He'd start the furnace. He'd change their air-conditioning filters, whatever. So, he was a hands-on, mechanical rabbi. Without him, there would have been no congregation.

Martin could tell you a whole lot about the relationships with different churches, and we'd have exchanges periodically for ecumenical purposes. They'd come for Passover. We'd go there for Christmas. I'd say, all in all, it was an excellent relationship with the community. The mayor was always cooperative regardless of who it was.

—Robert Gutenstein
oral history

Many years later, as rabbi emeritus, Martin Freedman was invited to speak to the Barnert Temple congregation on the subject of the historic civil rights movement and his participation in the Freedom Ride in 1961. It had been an important moment for our nation, as we were tested and our legal system was challenged to protect the freedoms of all Americans. Rabbi Freedman's experience and involvement vividly bring to life many of the core values of Congregation B'nai Jeshurun throughout its history: social activism, involvement in the community around us, and belief in the power of freedom.

The Freedom Riders of 1961 now, excepting for scholars and historians, is a nearly forgotten but important episode in the then ideological and political agenda of a small group of American activists for a legal solution to redress the then extant exclusionary civil rights laws in existence and to push the civil rights movement forward. These Freedom Riders with determination and unbelievable courage moved through the heart of the deep South, at a time when the Freedom Riders were looked upon with suspicion and hostility. It was a dangerous task with many potential personal perils. Against all adversity the Freedom Riders prevailed and we owe our own citizen—cleric, Rabbi Martin Freedman a great debt of gratitude for his actions.

*Within six months of the first Ride, travelers of all races were sitting side by side on buses and trains all across the nation without fear of arrest, the **white** and **colored** signs that had blighted the walls of Southern bus and train stations for decades were gone, the nation's major civil rights organizations had undergone significant transformations and the Justice Department had been pushed into a deepening engagement in civil rights matters.*

Raymond Arsenault
Freedom Riders: 1961 and the Struggle for Racial Justice

Let's go back some years.... I'm now talking about 1958, 1960. Important events had taken place in the United States. There was a sudden upsurge of interest and a movement for change in the area of civil rights. Part of it was led by the action of the Supreme Court of the United States in the famous decision of the public school system, the desegregation there. But it was also dramatically put before us in the action that took place in Birmingham, Alabama, when a middle-aged black lady by the name of Rosa Parks got on a bus, weary after having worked her day as a seamstress, and there were no seats in the back where the blacks were.... And the bus driver got upset to see her sit down in the front area and he said, "You've got to move, lady." And she said, "I'm not moving." He pulled the bus to a stop. The police were called. She was arrested. And thereby began an incredible series of events involving a young minister from Birmingham, Alabama, who came from a family of ministers, Rev. Dr. Martin Luther King Jr.

Reverend King ended up being arrested, and he wrote a famous "Letter from a Birmingham Jail." The letter had a profound effect upon me and upon many people, particularly clergymen—rabbis, ministers, and priests.

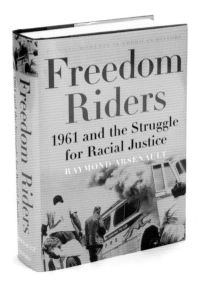

This book, by Raymond Arsenault, published in 2006, documents and reinforces the Freedom Riders' contribution to the struggle for racial justice.

I was, in those days, a very active anti-Communist, but at the same time, I was a deep believer in civil rights here in the United States. And [I was influenced by] a friend of mine named Bayard Rustin, who was active in a pacifist movement back in the 1940s, '50s and early '60s known as the Congress of Racial Equality (CORE). Bayard Rustin was someone that I looked up to, and I called him and asked him what could I do. He said, "Well, call the Congress of Racial Equality and I'm sure they'll come up with ideas." This is now January 1961. A few months earlier, the Supreme Court had ruled, in a decision known as the Boynton decision, that on all vehicles of transportation [and terminals], interstate, you could no longer discriminate. That meant interstate busing, interstate airplanes, anything that moved from one state to another, you could not have a separate section for blacks and a separate section for whites. This did not apply to intrastate facilities. There, the state had the right to embody discriminatory actions.

The head of the Congress of Racial Equality was a man named James Farmer. James Farmer was an impressive man. He was a giant of a man, physically and spiritually. He was a pacifist to the inner bones. He was a man who deeply believed in the nonviolent direct action way of making changes on the American scene. I was introduced to him and I said, "Mr. Farmer." He said, "Call me Jim." I said, "Jim, I'm interested in [serving the civil rights cause]." He said, "Get some freedom rides going. With the Boynton Decision, we have an opportunity to test facilities." And so I did some thinking about it and I came up with two ideas. One was an interracial, interreligious clergymen freedom ride, the first of its kind, made up of ministers, rabbis and priests. How to get a freedom ride going? I knew nothing about it. [CORE program director] Marvin Rich and Bayard Rustin gave me some clues, and I began to make some phone calls and sure enough, in short order, I had about five or six white Protestant ministers and four rabbis who were ready to participate, including myself, a couple of Roman Catholic priests, and there were about eight or nine black ministers.

What was the concept behind it all? The concept [of the freedom ride] was based upon a principle of nonviolent direct action, following the very, very carefully laid out form of political action of Mohandas K. Gandhi. If you will remember, Gandhi said under no circumstances would he engage in acts of violence, but he would participate in protests by placing his body, if need be, in a position for other people to commit violence on him with the hope that this would arouse their conscience.

Here in this country, the principle behind it all was that if you laid yourself on the line and you became an example in one way or another of right action on behalf of civil rights or whatever the cause was, if it was a righteous cause, in the end, it would arouse the conscience of the American people and they would respond accordingly. Therefore, make no mistake about it, you couldn't do it in a quiet way. You depended upon newspapers, publicity, early television, whatever it was to make your case known by your actions.

Back in the '40s and early '50s, there had been freedom rides organized by CORE. Nobody heard about them. Nobody knew they were going on. All it usually meant was that people were beaten close to death. I will never forget running into a man named Jim Peck who at one point said, "There is not one square inch of my body that doesn't show the nonviolent direct-action resistance that I made during the '40s and '50s."

Nobody knew about it. Nobody much cared. But by the mid-'50s and by the end of the '50s, this was a back-burner issue which was now on the front burner and before the American people.

The first group of trainees went down to Washington, D.C., in April of 1961. There were about five different freedom ride groups. One was made up of faculty and students from universities in America. Another included, of all things, the mother of the governor of Massachusetts, Mrs. Peabody, who was eighty years old. Eighty years old! And in our group, of course, were the eighteen of us, the Clergymen Freedom Riders. And we went through a training session which was based upon the principle of nonviolent direct action.

Well, the first thing you have to learn was that when someone threatens you with guns, you do not make a counter-threat of violence or even the appearance of violence. What did this mean? Well, when a mob appeared on the scene where you were and they threatened you and ultimately attacked you, you could not even lift your arms up to defend yourself for fear that that would be interpreted as a potentially violent act. You could, of course, cover yourself as best you could. The best thing was to fall to the ground, assume a fetal position, and cover yourself as best you could. Nobody could see that as a violent act.

We used the technique known as sociodrama, which means you acted out situations of southern sheriff, of being arrested, of going into jail, what it meant. We went through the whole spectrum of this thing, all of us, about eighty of us being trained for the freedom rides. I was very uncomfortable at the notion [of pacifism], but I accepted the discipline as a technique for political action.

We began the freedom rides in the beginning of May, through the month of May of 1961. The Interreligious, Interracial Clergymen Freedom Ride of May 18—by the way, each freedom ride was an independent democratic entity. It elected its own leaders. Our group left from Washington, D.C., and traveled to North Carolina. Our ultimate goal was going to be Tallahassee, Florida. Why Tallahassee, Florida? First of all, it was the capital of Florida. Secondly, it had a brand-new airport which had been subsidized by the federal government and therefore, planes that landed there made the airport and its facility [subject to] the Boynton Decision. And we were going to stop along the way in various cities and make demonstrations of integration [by desegregating interstate facilities].

When we left, where did the South really begin—Mason-Dixon line? Forget it. Where do you really get the feeling of a changeover? I can tell it to you exactly. It's when you cross from North Carolina to South Carolina. Oh, man, what a difference. We were on a public bus. We had integrated the bus. We were sitting all over the bus, black, white, together, etcetera. When the bus crossed from North Carolina to South Carolina, the bus driver, who was obviously in cahoots with the mob that was going to appear, started whistling ""Dixie." All of a sudden, two trucks pull up alongside of the bus and you could see a crowd of men in the back of each truck holding up whips, shotguns, baseball bats, and chains, and some guy had a cage of snakes. There was no question about it, this was the South that we were in.

We came to Sumter, South Carolina. That was going to be our stop. The bus stopped outside of Sumter at a motel and the bus driver said, "This is the stop," and Reverend

Perry, the leader of our group, said, "No, it's not. This isn't the bus terminal." [The driver] said, "Well, this is where this bus stops and from here, you'll be picked up by another bus and taken to the terminal." Perry said, "Unless you get this bus moving into the terminal, I'm going to report you." [The driver] said, "Get out, you got a rest stop here." We got out, as was our custom, and immediately went to desegregate the facilities. Where it said "blacks only," the whites went. Where it said "whites only," the blacks went; the bathrooms, right into the restaurant, serving blacks, whites, trying to get this whole ferment of integration going.

As we approached the restaurant, all of a sudden a mob encircles us. They came from behind the motel and behind the trees. That same mob was made up of those guys in those trucks waving whips, bats, chains, guns and snakes. We were completely encircled, the eighteen of us. And they would not let us into the restaurant. And Reverend Perry said, "We have every right based upon the Boynton decision," and they said, "You nigger lovers and you niggers are not getting in here. If you take one step across that lintel you are dead because we are aiming for your heads, not for your knees, with our bats and with our clubs and with our whips and with our chains. And some of you are going to get bitten by rattlesnakes which we've brought along. We hope you don't poison them." The principle of the group and its leadership was that under moments of [stress], there was only one person who could make the decision and that was the leader of the group. And Reverend Perry said, "Okay, let's get back on the bus."

We got back on the bus. The bus rode into town and now took us to the bus terminal. We proceeded immediately to integrate the facilities there, and then we were taken [by local leaders in their cars] to the black section of town to a black church. We were going to spend the night in the black section of town. It was safe there.

Now, for the next two days, we came down through Alabama, and the day after we made it along the northern tier of Florida, and I'll mention the name of a town called Lakeville, Florida. It's on the way to Tallahassee along the northern tier. The bus pulled in to a stop and we immediately got out, integrating the black and white water fountains. And I go into the restaurant and I have a black minister with me and I said to the waitress, "Would you give me that?" and I pointed to things that could be quickly given to me, didn't have to be prepared; potato chips, stuff like that in packages. And she looked startled by my voice, with my stentorian tone, "I'll have that. I'll have that, that," she was startled and served me. And I said, "What about him?" the black minister next to me, and she started serving him. So that was the act we were looking for. [The black minister] began to see the cook coming out and he began to get out of his seat to head for the bus. I grabbed his hand and I said, "Don't move." He [later said he] didn't know whether he was frightened more by me or by the cook. But he didn't move, and both of us sat there, chomping away on those idiotic potato chips.

Finally we get to Tallahassee. We get to the station there—big crowds, about a thousand people. We integrate, running around the bathrooms, restaurants, everything. We get into the cars and we're driven out to the airport, and as we approach the airport, you could see that chrome and glass, brand-new airport. And as we pulled up and opened up the doors to go into the waiting room of the airport, across the way, we could see behind they were hastily locking the doors to the restaurant. And they had a sign up,

"Closed for Cleaning." We integrated the bathrooms, the facilities, but there we stood in front of the closed restaurant. We looked in there and they looked at us, and the doors were locked. They knew that we were scheduled to be on an airplane at three o'clock that afternoon. This took place at about 12:30 p.m. Finally we were sitting in the lobby, the group of us, and I said, "Rabbi Israel Dresner and I have discussed the matter and we're not leaving. We're going to stay here until they open up that restaurant." Ten of us decided we were going to stay, eight decided they were going to leave [for New York on the 3 p.m. flight].

A reporter—the reporters were all over he place, the photographers, Time, Life, etc. —but a reporter for CBS News came up to me and he began to talk. And he said, "You know, rabbi, I'm from the South and I've brought my fourteen-year-old son here because I want him to see and to learn what is the right way. And I want to tell you we are very happy, both of us, that you are here, all of you, and [that you] are going to stay for that restaurant to open. But at the same time, I must tell you we're very worried for your safety because we've heard rumors that there is a mob going to be appearing this afternoon of KKK from across the state line from Georgia." Tallahassee is a hop, skip, and a jump from Georgia.

Well, we were sitting there and waiting for the restaurant to open—it never opened, naturally. Three o'clock went by, four o'clock, five o'clock, six o'clock. It began to get slightly dark, but we saw police around, local police were in the station. We'd been urged a number of times by the police chief why don't we consider our job done and leave. We said we're not leaving. And about seven o'clock in the evening, all of a sudden, the police disappeared. And outside in the parking lot came a parade of automobiles with horns blowing. There had to be at least fifty cars—they filled the whole parking lot. And we saw people getting out of that parking lot that were big, hulking, tough, southern— what do you call them—rednecks. And this reporter said to me, "Rabbi, they're here. I hope you don't mind, but my son and I are going to move back with the photographers. We are not part of the group, although we are with you in sympathy."

First of all, they surrounded the glass walls, and they began to make threatening gestures to us. And a couple of them came in and one guy started shouting, "I'm the head of the Ku Klux Klan from Macon, Georgia, and we're here to take care of you." I'm not using the exact language that he used. At that point, we were convinced this was the moment, that if anything happens, fall to the ground, cover yourself, and hope for the best. Just as they began to press through the doors from the back, two lone state troopers appeared. Not local police, two—only two—state troopers appeared. The moment they appeared that whole mass that had pushed through the door started pushing back. It was very clear that with the local police there was some deal, but with the state troopers, there was no deal. And the state troopers came in there with big shotguns. They pressed outside the door and just camped around the facility. By about ten o'clock, the manager of the airport said, "We close the airport until 6:00 a.m." Then the local black leadership came and took us by car to a church, and we stayed in the church. I slept on a bench. I didn't sleep; I rolled around on a bench. I didn't roll around; I sort of stretched out on the bench.

At six in the morning, we were back at the airport. There was no mob. Everyone was gone and it was very clear two lone state troopers were able to stave off this whole thing. At around noon, a whole entourage appeared of police officers and the mayor of the town. The mayor of the town comes in and he says, "I've got a piece of paper here that says you people are disturbing the peace and I hereby order you to leave these facilities immediately or you'll be arrested for disturbing the peace on the order of the City of Tallahassee." [Rev. John Collier, our newly elected leader,] stood up and said, "Mayor, I want to thank you for enlightening us about that statement, but I think you ought to know we are not disturbing the peace. We are travelers. We hold valid tickets in this airport and we're waiting to leave after we've had something to eat." [The mayor] said, "God damn it, man, I'm giving you an order!" [Reverend Collier] said, "I'm sorry, Mr. Mayor, we're not going to accept the order," with which immediately, each of us was surrounded by two police officers who grabbed us, manacled us and we were on our way to the police station.

We came to the police station and were fingerprinted and photographed. And now something important developed because in our training, we were told that before the arrest, the people who were at greatest risk were the blacks in our group, but after the arrest, the people who were at the greatest risk were the whites. Why? Because the jails were segregated. The blacks went into the black section of the jail and they were hailed as heroes. However, the whites went into that section of the jail where if those guys had been out of jail, they would be been in the mob, and that's the moment of greatest threat.

I ended up being the first one, fingerprinted and photographed, and I'm led to the jail. [I thought] "Oh my God, this is it." There's the block and I look inside and what was a jail block designed for twenty-four men had about forty. One set of doors open up, I step in, it closes. The second set of doors opens up and now I just did what the training said I should do. I walked in and said, "Hello, my name is Martin Freedman. How are you?" And the mob closed in. Rabbi Dresner, who was the next in line, was sure that I was being beaten to a pulp. But there I was, "Hello, hello," trying to personalize. And these guys were so shocked that I'm sticking out my hand. And it worked. The training worked.

In short order, we were in the crowded jail. They had to leave one cell open so that those of us who were sleeping out in the lobby could use the bathroom facilities. Rabbi Dresner and I and several others made the decision we're going on a hunger strike. The sheriff couldn't understand what was going on. He was convinced that the two rabbis who were going on a hunger strike were going on a hunger strike because we wanted to eat kosher food. I told them, "You can bring in the best hot pastrami that you can find in Tallahassee, kosher, I'm not eating it, period."

That night, I slept on a table out in the front section and I heard [three prisoners] saying, "Let's get that fat nigger lover." I was the only fat one there. I waited. Naturally I didn't fall asleep and about midnight, I saw three figures creeping out of the cell in stocking feet. They obviously were planning on beating me up on the table. And just as they got to me, I sat up and said, "What are you men doing here?" Oh, boom, they disappeared into the cell. The next day it was very easy to identify them.

We insisted upon being treated just like every other prisoner. We wanted no special privileges. Bail was set for us. We were released. Two days later, the trial took place. I have a whole transcript of the trial. In the trial, one amusing incident was that Tobias Simon, who was one of our lawyers from the ACLU, asked me the question, 'Rabbi Freedman, where are you employed?" I said, "Well, my major source of employment is Congregation B'nai Jeshurun in Paterson, New Jersey, the Barnert Temple, but I also receive some income from another subsidiary position. " The prosecutor said, "Rabbi, did I hear you say you have a subsidiary income?" I said, "Yes, I do." "Do you mean you get paid money by someone else that you have not revealed to us?" I said, "Yes, that's the case." "Rabbi, before this court, having taken an oath to tell the truth, I ask you in clear, unequivocal language, who gives you subsidiary income?" I said, "I'm part-time chaplain of the Paterson Police Department. I get $250 a year."

The trial was over. We were sentenced to six months in jail and a $500 fine. We appealed and bail was paid and we now went back to our various homes, wherever we came from. A few years later, of course, was the march on Selma. I participated in that, and in numerous other civil rights demonstrations, but around 1963, the middle of 1963, I get a call from Tobias Simon that the Supreme Court has not rejected our appeal, but has indicated that the appeal bypassed some of the state courts. We went directly to the federal court, and we had to go back and go through the proper chain of appeal. But in the interim, we had been called now to serve our term, and that we had to appear in Tallahassee, Florida, on Monday morning at nine o'clock. Of the original ten of us, nine of us showed up and were there. It was a big public arrest. We were taken to the jail and this time, we had a private cell block all to ourselves, and as a matter of fact, they were going to not even put us on a work detail or anything. The sheriff couldn't care less. He didn't care about anything. He just wanted peace—the same sheriff, by the way.

We insisted that we be taken out on work details, just like any other prisoner. They used to sneak us out from the basement of the jail, out to work chopping and cutting grass. Meanwhile, our attorneys were making a direct appeal on a writ which was undergoing very important scrutiny and change, the writ of habeas corpus, directly to the Supreme Court of the United States. And our attorney was in the Fifth Circuit Court of Appeals in Louisiana making that appeal. After three days in jail, that evening the sheriff comes in and says, "The mayor of the town and the prosecutor and the judge want to see you all. So let's go." We go out of the jail. He didn't bother manacling us or anything.

We get into a van. We're taken to City Hall. We're brought into a courtroom and there is the mayor, the judge, the prosecutor. The mayor says, "We've decided that if you make an appeal for clemency, I will release you on the spot." We said, "Our attorney is not here. Our attorney is in Louisiana. " He said, "I don't care whether you've got an attorney." [Rev. John Collier] said, "No, we don't act without an attorney." [The mayor] said, "Well, there's some Jew lawyer here," and there was, as a matter of fact, a young lawyer who was not with the ACLU but the NAACP. And we huddled together with him. And he said, "Listen, I can't advise you what to do. If you make the plea of clemency and are released from jail, the whole case is moot. It's over and done with. But if you don't accept it, the case is still on the burner." And he said, "But I can't tell you what

Freedom Riders, August 7, 1963—leaving Tallahassee after release from prison.
Left to right: Rev. Dr. Robert McAfee Brown, Rabbi Israel Dresner, Rabbi Martin Freedman, Rev. A. McRaven Warner, Rev. Rohn W. Collier, Rev. Robert J. Stone, Rev. Wayne Hartmire. Barnert Temple Archives.

to do. I can only explain to you the consequences." We came back in and John [Collier] said, "Mayor, our group has analyzed the situation carefully, and examined your offer and we respectfully wish to inform you that we reject it and we make no appeal for clemency." That mayor grew red. The red rose in his face and he said, "God damn it. I put you in jail and I'm throwing you out of jail." The next thing I knew, we were standing on the street. All of my personal belongings were back in the jail, but there we were on the street in Tallahassee. We had not made an appeal [for clemency], so the case was still appealable. Ultimately our case did go the Supreme Court, and along with thousands of others it was thrown out. We were reminded of Martin Luther King Jr.'s statement, "Injustice anywhere is a threat to justice everywhere."

In August 1996, we had a dinner in New York City, a thirty-five-year reunion of the ten of us. One was dead, one could not make it, so eight appeared. It was a very dramatic coming together. Marvin Rich came. Jack Greenberg, who was now dean of Columbia Law School, who had then been head of the legal defense committee, was there. In our group, by the way, there were some distinguished people. I'm excluding myself. The Rev. Dr. Robert MacAfee Brown, one of the important Christian theologians in America and ultimately professor of religion and philosophy at Stanford University; Rev. Robert Stone, who is head of the Presbyterian Commission on Race. Ralph Lord Roy, the author of "Apostles of Discord," a very important book about anti-Semitism in the church in the 1950s. It was a very dramatic coming together. It brought tears to the eyes of many of us.

How did my congregation, how did Barnert Temple [congregants feel about the freedom ride and the arrest]? I did not ask the board of this temple for permission to do what I was going to do. By the time the story hit the New York Times, and the Herald Tribune, it had a big photograph of us, and by then the Paterson Evening News already had a headline, "Rabbi Freedman, Freedom March," uh-oh, and I was wondering what was going on back in Paterson.

When I came back, I had a special service in the temple on Broadway and Straight Street. It was like Yom Kippur. I'd never seen so many members [and non-members] of our temple show up. And I spoke about my experiences and took questions from the audience. There were two members of the temple who resigned.

The congregation certainly supported my right to act in this regard. Insofar as the Paterson community is concerned, I received about 200 letters, of which fifty were extremely hostile and 150 were supportive. And interestingly there were some people—Jewish leaders in Paterson—from whom I never would have expected to have gotten such support who came out and openly wrote to me. But in the main, I have no qualms in saying that I am grateful that I had the opportunity to act on my own conscience and my own volition and not face the repercussions.

—Rabbi Martin Freedman
oral history

Martin Freedman was a great social activist rabbi during the '60s and '70s. The congregation supported that activism. I think that there was an unarticulated reason why, because the members of the congregation, of course, knew of the Holocaust, thoroughly. If they had no family there, they were aware of the horror, the calamity, the devastation. They knew that we needed to have complete religious, political, and legal venues for the freedom of every citizen in the United States, because if we had had that in Europe, we would not have had the Holocaust. And therefore, Martin Freedman was just as busy outside of the congregation as he was inside the congregation. And we knew all of the things that he did, and there was real admiration for what he was doing. His Friday night sermons were what attracted many, many people to the congregation in the last ten years in Paterson. It was his name, his reputation, his oratory skills, and his social activism that kept that place going during that last decade in Paterson.

—*Cipora Schwartz*
oral history

On November 23, 1997, during the celebratory sesquicentennial year of the Barnert Temple, the Men's Club sponsored a 150th anniversary event, open to the entire congregation and their guests, featuring Rabbi Emeritus Martin Freedman. The many new members of the Men's Club were interested in the history of the Barnert Congregation and its consistent record of social and political activism and its quest for religious freedom as represented by the early rabbis and by Rabbi Freedman. Introductory remarks were made by Joel Bauer, event chairman

There are times in our temple's 150 years when our history was coincident with that of the larger world. And this morning, we are going to hear about one of those times. I remember in 1961 hearing on a car radio that Rabbi Martin Freedman had been arrested. But I remember only a few occasions later on when he told the story of his Freedom Ride experiences, and almost none in the past fifteen years. It seems to me that stories are very important. They are a way that we, particularly as Jews, pass down our values from one generation to the next. Over time, stories become history.

The Freedom Rides were part of a large movement to end racial segregation in America. Today, as our temple celebrates our 150th anniversary, it is most appropriate that we hear the story of the part that the rabbi of this congregation played in this movement, an effort of American society to overcome past prejudices and to move towards a future of civil rights for all.

Rabbi Elyse Frishman then said:

Years ago, when I was a student, the professors at the college would speak about different colleagues in the field, about people that we could learn from. And Rabbi Martin Freedman was one of those names and individuals that were mentioned quite often. There were two reasons. One was for his speaking style, the way in which he could engage a community in whatever topic he was interested in offering. But beyond that, it was the nature of what he would offer based on his own life experiences. It was not just about what we say, but what we do, but how we live our lives too. And Rabbi Freedman, during so much of this time with our congregation, was committed to causes of social justice. This morning you will have the opportunity in particular to hear about one of those most challenging times in his years and in our lives, how he responded, the courage that he demonstrated to the occasion, and the ways in which he continues, simply by telling the stories, to inspire us to perhaps live our lives a little differently, on a higher level.

Rabbi Freedman's insights on the freedom rides and the civil rights movement, and his participation during that time in our ongoing American search for justice for all citizens, was an important reminder during the 150th anniversary year of our ancestors' struggles and the religious and civil freedoms they enjoyed in the United States.

I had the distinction, when I was chairman of the board of William Paterson College, of having the doors nailed shut during the student revolutionary periods of the late '60s and '70s and I, as chairman, being nailed into a room where I had to end up talking with some students about civil rights. But basically, when it came to the matters of civil rights, I've always had a very strong, deeply held feeling that one of the greatest injustices on the American scene in the past and still even in some respects in certain areas today, was the whole role of the black community and the suppression and repression that had been effectively utilized. Most of you will not recall—some of you will—the long history of riots that took place in the United States. During the Second World War, there were riots. The important figure, the seminal figure making the change and turnabout was, in fact, President Harry Truman. People don't remember this. But with the stroke of a pen, with one signature, Harry Truman desegregated the United States Armed Forces. The memory of that incredible act which took great courage was an extraordinary act that began the transformation.

—Rabbi Martin Freedman
oral history

Other temple members recall that they joined the congregation in the 1960s and 1970s because of Rabbi Freedman's reputation as a welcoming spiritual leader, as well as a great orator and activist. American religious freedoms made possible a broad-based, heterogeneous, and outreach-oriented congregation. The Barnert Temple Congregation, from its earliest days in the 19th century, viewed participation in the life of Paterson's citizens, our nation, and our world as a commitment based on our religious concepts of caring for others. This view has been a constant, and verified by Barnert Temple's Rabbis and congregants over the centuries by their activism and actions in behalf of humanities needs.

I have not been a member of Congregation B'nai Jeshurun long enough to have significant recollections from the past, or have stories about family ancestors who played roles in Barnert Temple's history. I can, however, say that from my first exposure to Barnert, when Laura, Daniel, and I would come for High Holiday services even before we were members, I felt a special feeling of being at home in the beautiful sanctuary where we are sitting without question or qualification. And that meant a lot to me, because I felt very ill at ease in many synagogues that I had tried to go to for various reasons. We enjoyed the sensation of unobtrusive welcome with which we were received, and we bathed in Rabbi Freedman's gloriously mellifluous and erudite oratory.

—Elliot Richmond
letter to the author

The predominant rabbi in my life was Martin Freedman—he was there for a long time, more than thirty-eight years. He is an unusual person. This man could weave a sermon that was absolutely spellbinding. You sat there and your mouth kind of dropped because he was so erudite and so well informed. His voice was almost hypnotic at times, because he could go on for thirty, forty minutes. Yes, he could do this, and he did it well, without a note, without referring to anything. He would usually pick on something that was contemporary, and it was good to hear somebody's opinion; you may not necessarily have shared it, but it was nice to hear. He wove, almost like a lawyer. It was logical, the progression of his thinking. And I miss that. I miss him dreadfully.

—Leonore Albert
oral history

Within a generation, it became evident that the survival of the congregation depended on relocating to where the congregants lived; where the Barnert Temple could become a regional religious, social, and cultural community to serve its members, potential members, and their children.

We were struggling. I think today that nobody really understands how we struggled to earn money. We really lived from hand to mouth. I don't think the young people today understand how difficult it was for us. We hadn't paid our [heating] bill. We really struggled. Martin Freedman didn't take his paycheck lots of times because there wasn't money to pay him. This was a very hard time.

—Susan Sauer
oral history

In a discussion I had with Joe Conn in 1974, I said there is no question about it that we have to begin to think about the need to move on. And by then, we had already gotten in a plateau; our new membership was not increasing. And as a matter of fact, our school was now declining from 135 now down to 110 and going down, and that was a sure sign that young people were not coming.

Then we had a board meeting—a famous board meeting in which I made the presentation that the temple … has to begin to think of a new building [and move on]. There was not much of an argument about it. The fact of the matter is when I looked at that board, there were only five families on that board that were still in Paterson; everybody else [had left] Paterson. Then there was the "Moving On" revue, setting that very dramatic instance in which we really indicated that the time has come to move on.

The board finally appointed a committee, a very important committee to look at the situation. At my urging, they appointed Judge Joseph Conn [to chair the committee]. What we decided, the best way to do it, was we got a big map of the Passaic–Bergen County area and wherever and however we knew there was a Jewish family, we put a little sticker, a little ball with a pin into that map. We got reports from real estate people, we got reports from the YMHA, the New Jewish Community Organization of Wyckoff, and we began to punch in.... And it was absolutely clear by the end of three months—you saw clumps of pins moving up Route 208. And that was absolutely the case, that we had to consider the move in that direction, and that a move anywhere else would have been a mistake, and frankly at that point, we had enough members in the temple who lived in those areas to give us the [incentive] to move there. At the time, the problem was: find a place. Well, we did find a place, a marvelous place.

—Rabbi Martin Freedman
oral history

I feel they did the right thing when they moved there. They had to because the nucleus of the congregation was then moving into Bergen County and it was a natural thing for them to do. And I went along with it. First thing, I had a warm feeling for Martin Freedman and my family had ties to the temple.

—Lewis Epstein
oral history

Phil Sarna [and Dr. Martin Hochberg] knew [real estate developer] Nevins McBride. And I spoke with Phil and he said, "There's this one piece of land which is not all usable, but it's ten acres. There's some deep gorges in back that you can't really access for building." We went to see Nevins McBride and it was late in the afternoon, about four o'clock, and Phil and I walked in and I met Nevins McBride and we made the presentation that we were interested in the lands and he said he was very interested in selling and he would very much welcome a Jewish congregation there. When the interview was over and the discussion was over, he said to me, "Tell me, Rabbi, do you lay on hands?" And I said, "What?" and he said, "Are you a healer?" and I said, "What's wrong?" And he said, "Well, I have stomach trouble and it's been bothering me very much." And I tell him, "Whatever healing power I've got, I don't know what it is, I'm giving to you. And I run over and he says, "Put your hand on my stomach." And I put my hand on his stomach and I said, "Heal." And that was the beginning of the purchase.

—Rabbi Martin Freedman
oral history

What sets Martin Freedman apart is the breadth and scope of his interests and activities, both within and outside of the Jewish community while leading his congregation for nearly forty years. Rabbi Freedman's belief in education was connected to his understanding that American religious and social freedoms were inseparably tied to the education of our population.

Rabbi Freedman was here for some thirty-eight years and still is the rabbi emeritus, and is well known in the entire state, having been a member of the state Board of Education, state medical school and other municipal and state commissions. I go once in awhile when Rabbi Freedman is speaking to the Men's Club. I always was attracted to his sermons, especially when they dealt with political affairs. I felt that it was informative. I always felt that he had a wonderful grasp of world affairs. He graduated from the point of having been a part of the marches in the South in the early civil rights controversies to the present.

—Lewis Epstein
oral history

While ministering to the spiritual needs of over 2,500 families over that time, leading the Barnert Temple through two significant moves, the last to its present location in Franklin Lakes, he still found the energy and inspiration to play an active leadership role in the educational system of the state of New Jersey and in Jewish education and activism.

A past chairman of the board of directors of William Paterson University (from which he received an honorary doctorate of humane letters in 1979) and the Council of State Colleges of New Jersey, Rabbi Freedman's involvement in higher education also included membership on the Board of Higher Education of the State of New Jersey and the board of trustees of the University of Medicine and Dentistry of New Jersey, where he was directly responsible for the establishment of a school of nursing.

Rabbi Freedman also received an honorary doctorate of divinity from Hebrew Union College–Jewish Institute of Religion in New York City in 1980. Among other citations for his championship of human rights, he was awarded a special commendation from the NAACP in 1961 and a Presidential Citation for Outstanding Citizenship in 1968.

My interest in education has been from the beginning. I was embarked in a career as a teacher; I turned down the law in '48. Both my dear friend Stefan Mengelberg and I were accepted to Harvard Law School and we both decided not to go—I ended up in graduate school [at Columbia University] and I was moving toward an academic career. I was approached by the new chancellor of the New Jersey schools in the end of 1966. Would I be interested in becoming a part of the board of William Paterson College? All of [the schools of higher education] were now undergoing a radical revision from teacher colleges into multipurpose liberal arts institutions. This was Chancellor Ralph Dungan, [who was appointed by] Governor Richard Hughes, a marvelous human being and a very rare and special person. On recommendation of the chancellor I was appointed to the board of William Paterson College. It is today called William Paterson University.... In the beginning of 1968, I became a member of the first board of trustees for the new function of the college as a multipurpose liberal arts campus. I became the second chairman of the board in 1970, and I served during its period of largest growth, from 1970 to 1973. It experienced an explosion of growth in those three years....

I served on [the Board of Higher Education of New Jersey] until 1977. Then, I was approached by Ralph Dungan, the chancellor, to become a member of the board of the College of Medicine and Dentistry of the State of New Jersey. The reason for that was he felt they did not have someone who was conversant with the governance of a college. This was a graduate school for the most part, but also, it was a multipurpose institution that not only trained physicians and dentists, it awarded doctorates in biology and graduate degrees in the allied health fields. In 1977, I was appointed by Goverernor. Hughes, a Democrat, and Governor Cahill, a Republican. I served on the board of the University of Medicine and Dentistry until 1995. I was a senior member, and I was appointed by five governors of the state of New Jersey to academic positions. I was personally involved and directly responsible for arguing the case for a school of nursing, which we won over great opposition from the state. Governor Christine Todd Whitman did not reappoint me ... because I fought the governor on her intent to dissolve the Board of Higher Education, which she ultimately did. And I went public on the issue along with a number of other people, and it was resented, and I was therefore not reappointed. [All was forgiven, though, as Governor Whitman sat on the bimah and helped us celebrate the temple's 150th anniversary.] It's just as well, because around that time, I became ill and could not have really functioned, and I'd been on that board eighteen years—enough. I am the first on that board of trustees, as a trustee, who was given an honorary doctorate.

I was also very much involved in Jewish affairs. In the Reform rabbinate, I was appointed the chairman of the Commission on Social Justice by the Central Conference of American Rabbis. I later became the chairman of the Committee on Soviet Jewry. I was very active in the Jewish Federation of North Jersey. I was chairman a number of times of the Committee on Social Action and various other committees of the Federation. I was active in Jewish Family Service [for twenty-five years] and also president of the New Jersey region of the American Jewish Congress. I also served on the governing council of the National American Jewish Congress. I ran a radio program for the Reconstructionist Foundation [in the 1960s] and was involved as an editor for a number of magazines, primarily the Reconstructionist magazine.

Well, my life in the Jewish world still continues. I'm [a board member of] NAORRR, which is the National Association of Retired Reform Rabbis. I'm still on call all the time.

—Rabbi Martin Freedman
oral history

When Rabbi Freedman became ill, it was clear to him that he needed to consider retirement.

I had been very seriously ill. I came down with myasthenia gravis, and I came down with it in an extreme form. I suffered nearly total paralysis, so the only things that I could move were the ends of my fingers. I was informed right from the beginning that it was a treatable illness and that I would come out of it, but I didn't believe it. I was convinced, for the first moment in my life, that my wife and my children and my doctors were lying to me, that they were trying to give me some sort of encouragement, but that I was now doomed to be paralyzed. And finally when I did come out of it, I came out of it like a skyrocket. I ultimately left [the University of Medicine and Dentistry hospital in Newark] after twenty-six days in critical care, intensive care. I left [the hospital] for the Kessler Institute in the Oranges to learn how to walk all over again. I came there on a stretcher on a Monday morning. On Tuesday morning, I was walking slowly with a walker. Tuesday afternoon on a walker with wheels. Wednesday morning with crutches. Wednesday afternoon with canes and Wednesday night, I walked the halls of Kessler Institute slowly—the whole night, I could not stop walking, I was so absolutely ... overcome. I've ... gone out of remission here and there, and I do take medicine, medical care continues in this area, but fortunately, I've come out of it.

—Rabbi Martin Freedman
oral history

We joined as the Steiger family and Rabbi Martin Freedman was the rabbi and we fell in love with him. He was our rabbi; Martin was part of our family. He was the third person I called when I was diagnosed with cancer. When I told him, he came over to bless me. He placed his hands on my head to give the blessing, and he and Joel are crying. I said to Martin, " What kind of help are you giving me when you are crying?" We have a deep affection for each other that continues to this day. He visited me at the hospital and at home on a weekly basis, sometimes more often during my illness. We have a personal ongoing relationship that is very precious.

—Carole Ann Steiger,
interview with the author

(A few years later, when Carole Ann learned that Martin Freedman was gravely ill at Valley Hospital, suffering with myasthenia gravis, she wrote to him: "Dear Martin, As soon as you are able to come home, I'll come to your house to give you a blessing!")

When Rabbi Freedman advised the congregation's leadership of his decision to retire, a retirement committee was appointed to develop celebratory events to honor him during the last year of his tenure at our synagogue.

There had been many celebrations over the years. Rabbi Freedman's thirty years of service to the congregation had been celebrated in 1987, and in 1992 a celebratory weekend honoring his thirty-five years as spiritual leader included a program in which messages of caring, love, and admiration reflected the congregation's feelings for Rabbi Freedman.

While no words could adequately reflect the deep love, respect and affection that is felt for him, this celebration is our way of recognizing how truly fortunate we have been. On behalf of those generations of congregants who have benefited from his efforts to help us find new meaning and answers in our lives and in our religion, we say, thank you.

—Nardyne Cattani
Barnert Temple president
35th anniversary celebration program

Dear Marty: Mazel tov on the forthcoming celebration of your 35th anniversary as spiritual leader of Barnert Temple. You have served Barnert Temple with unstinting dedication and have given of yourself with a full heart. The special service planned in your honor bespeaks the admiration, esteem and affection in which you are held by your congregants and the community.

—Rabbi Alexander M. Schindler
Union of American Hebrew Congregations

The committee charged with planning the year's celebratory retirement events was appointed by Barnert President Alvin Sauer, and included Gerald Batt, Joseph Dunn, Kenneth Edelson, Robert Gutenstein, Barbara Haubenstock, Harold Polton, Arnold Reiter, Dorothy Starr, Carole Ann Steiger, Valerie Tritt, Stephen Wener, and myself as chair. We were dedicated to making Rabbi Freedman's last year as the Barnert Temple's rabbi a year of celebration and gratitude for his tenure and his legacy. Rabbi Freedman's retirement celebratory events began on March 19, 1995, with a brunch, sponsored by the Sisterhood and Men's Club, honoring him and his wife, Shirley Freedman. (Rabbi Freedman is married to Shirley Shacknai Freedman and has an adopted daughter Francesca, two stepsons, David and Daniel Shacknai, and four wonderful grandchildren.)

This was a warm and loving way to begin the year's honors. We all sang "All the World Will Come to Serve Thee" (Rabbi Freedman's favorite song) at the program's end, with tears in our eyes. On May 3, 1995, witness to the Holocaust and Nobel Peace Prize winner Elie Wiesel spoke to our congregation. On May 5, a Sabbath service of celebration was held during which the love, affection and high regard the congregation held for Rabbi Freedman was expressed by myself, as retirement committee chair.

Thirty-nine years ago, our search committee, mostly first-generation Americans, selected you, Martin, to lead the oldest congregation in the state. They hoped they had found in you not just a religious leader, but someone as committed to the principles of social justice and freedom as the early members of this unique congregation were and we still are. Someone who understood and embraced the concept, as did Moses Aaron Dropsie in 1890, the "the perpetuation of liberty demands eternal vigilance." Someone who would protect and nurture our historic and cultural existence in this great land of religious freedom. Someone whose outlook was not simply Jewish, but American; not provincial, but national and international in scope.

They, and thus we, got all of that, and so much more. You have, above all, been our religious leader. You gave us spiritual sanctuary for all of our life-cycle needs. You named our infants; bar and bat mitzvahed and married our sons and daughters; buried our loved ones. You shared our joys and consoled us during our times of sorrow. You have been a rock, a shoulder to lean on, an understanding heart.

You have always understood the heterogeneous nature of our congregation and the range of religious backgrounds of its members. You have respected and accommodated our often differing needs. You have always made all of us feel welcome and wanted.

You, Martin, have been—and I know you will continue to be—a fighter for social justice. Your understanding of the Jewish historical past as a freedom loving people has been the basis for the social and educational activism which consumed so much of your energy. With you as our leader, we participated with pride in the social revolutions of the '60s and '70s.

You have been our historian. I will always treasure the memories of our trip with you to Israel. On that brief voyage, you made our ancestral home come alive historically, culturally and politically.

Your great subject has always been the nature of the Jewish experience and how to apply spiritual ends to the development of personal character and social justice. Through the consistency of your vision—a critical assessment of democratic values and our effort to revitalize political culture—you have made a difference. You contributed to the way we think about protest and freedom.

You, Martin, have been the driving force behind the construction of not one, but two temples, where we built not just edifices, but homes for our historic and cultural existence; havens for our co-religionists to pursue their beliefs as one, extended family.

You have been our most eloquent spokesman. The raw power of your oratory has commanded our attention to the larger issues of the day. With any single sentence, you are likely to veer into a sometimes humorous or profound back alley of history before emerging with a vast cosmic statement about human morality.

Nor has your oratory been confined to the pulpit. Your performance as the alms-seeking pauper in our musical production, "Moving On," while not a threat to Olivier, was nonetheless honest and convincing, influenced no doubt, by your vast experience as a fund-raiser for new building projects. And once built, even those buildings have benefited from your wisdom and talents because you have also been our plumber, and on occasion, electrician. Only you have been able to master the intricacies of the air-conditioning systems in two different temples, built a generation apart. Talk about the renaissance man!

And you have been a loving husband and father. Who can forget the image of you and Shirley dancing together at one of our temple festivities, in love with life and with each other? Your happiness made us all feel better about ourselves.

But most important of all, Martin—and Shirley—you have been our friends, and like all good friends, have always been there when we needed you. We know that you always will be, as we will be there for you. We love you both.

Martin Freedman—an American rabbi, an American citizen, committed to advancing the religious, educational, and legal freedoms of all Americans. Nearly forty years serving the Barnert Temple congregation, educating the children and the adults, performing life-cycle events with care, compassion and devotion. Rabbi Freedman twice rescued a diminished congregation, and with energy, vision, and dedication, when we moved to Franklin Lakes, he bound us into a single community of members although the members resided in many geographic communities and states. Rabbi Freedman's legacy is assured as we see our Barnert community thrive and grow for many, many more generations. An American rabbi, whose commitment to religious and legal freedoms we can be proud of. Rabbi Freedman leaves us a remarkable legacy.

The price of liberty is eternal vigilance.

—*Thomas Jefferson*

Rabbi Martin Freedman, composer-organist William Smith, Cantor Joseph Posner, Barnert Temple Broadway, 1958. Barnert Temple Archives.

Barnert Temple 120th anniversary celebration, Derrom Avenue, 1967. *Left to right:* George Rosenthal, Vivian Hoffman, Selma Zalen, Rabbi Martin Freedman. Barnert Temple Archives.

Barnert Temple trip to Israel with Rabbi Martin Freedman, December, 1978 to January, 1979. *Standing, left to right:* Harold Brown, Robert Meyers, Adam Meyers, Eugene Rosensweet, Robert Gutenstein, Michael Gutenstein, Rabbi Martin Freedman, Shirley Freedman, Roberta Meyers, Jack Birnberg, Louise Birnberg, Lori Solomon, Marilyn Solomon, Morton Solomon, Karen Solomon, Debrah Rosensweet, Ellen Gutenstein, Lisa Gutenstein, Cipora Schwartz, Martin Rosensweet. *Sitting, middle row, left to right:* Carolyn Brown, Julian Hirshfield, Lucille Hirshfield, Michael Birnberg, Professor David and Mrs. Karp, Naomi Rothstein, Yetta Alperowitz, Ben Alperowitz, John Birnberg, Joyce Solomon. *Seated floor, left to right:* Timothy Schwartz, Howard Gutenstein, Steven Birnberg, Jeffrey Birnberg, Ellen Rosensweet, Fran Rosensweet, Jennifer Meyers, David Meyers. Private collection.

Invitation to 25th anniversary celebration,1982. Barnert Temple Archives.

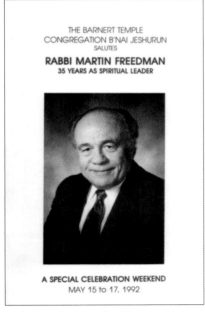

35th Anniversary of Rabbi Martin Freedman, 1992. Private collection.

Honoring temple benefactors, Franklin Lakes. *Left to right:* Rabbi Martin Freedman, Samuel S. Schwartz, I. Bertram Cohen, April 27, 1990. Private collection.

Officiating at Franklin Lakes temple, Rabbi Martin Freedman, 1991. Private collection.

Children's Purim service, Broadway temple, 1954. Barnert Temple Archives.

Children's Purim service, Franklin Lakes temple, 1992. Barnert Temple Archives.

Social Action programs expanded in Franklin Lakes under Rabbi Freedman's Leadership. Photo by author, 1992. Private collection

The Franklin Lakes preschool opened with six children in 1989. Rabbi Freedman hired educator Sarah Losch. In 2006 there were 84 children in the preschool. Author photo, 1993. Private collection.

Charcoal drawing by Barnert Temple member
Lou Lever in honor of Rabbi Martin Freeman's
retirement celebration, 1995.
Barnert Temple Collection.

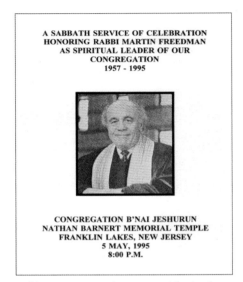

Rabbi Martin Freedman, A Sabbath of
Celebration, 1957–1995.
Barnert Temple Archives.

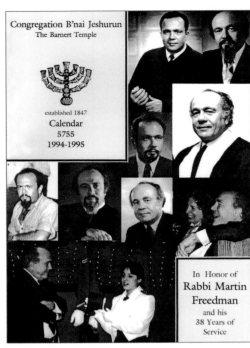

Calendar in honor of Rabbi Martin Freedman's
38 years of service, 1995.
Barnert Temple Archives.

Rabbi Martin Freedman's retirement committee, 1995. *Left to right:*
Barbara Haubenstock, Carole Ann Steiger, Cipora O. Schwartz, chair.

Rabbi Martin Freedman's retirement service, 1995. *Left to right:*
B. Irving Cohen ,Rabbi Martin Freedman, Steven Roth.

CHAPTER TEN

Moving On

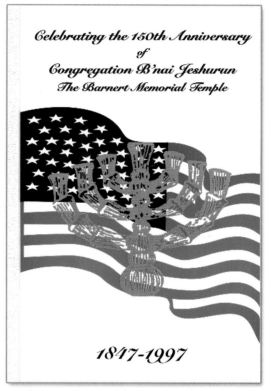

150th Anniversary celebratory booklet.
Barnert Temple Archives.

Moving on was a physical act and more. Why did we move from Barnert Temple–Paterson, the home of our ancestors? What were our most valuable assets and aspirations as we prepared the physical move from Barnert Temple–Paterson to Barnert Temple–Franklin Lakes? Again, we drew on our ancestral roots, our heritage, our commitment as American Jews, the beneficiaries of the religious and civil liberties all Americans inherit from our constitutional guarantees. We would move from Paterson to Barnert Temple united as a congregation, committed to our congregational extended family, to the community at large in Franklin Lakes, to our historic home in Paterson, to our blessed America, and to the world. We would continue to work on behalf of the common good and to remember the impact that our American religious freedom has had on all the peoples of the United States.

Groundbreaking ceremony for Franklin Lakes temple, June 1, 1986. *Seated, back, left to right:* Joel Steiger, Steven Wener, Cipora Schwartz, Philip Schwartz. *Seated, front, left to right:* Samuel S. Schwartz, B. Irving Cohen, Stephen Schwartz. Barnert Temple Archives.

Groundbreaking cememony for Franklin Lakes temple, June 1, 1986.
Barnert Temple Archives.

Groundbreaking for Franklin Lakes temple. Worn Torah scrolls ceremony, June 1, 1986.
Barnert Temple Archives.

An announcement in the May 1986 Barnert Temple bulletin invited the congregation and the general public to attend the groundbreaking ceremony for the new Barnert Temple in Franklin Lakes on June 1, 1986. The ceremony was an emotional temple family gathering of nearly 300 members and friends, representing many generations of the Barnert congregation's family as we all convened with joyous anticipation of a renewed, united, enlarged congregation.

The oldest congregation in New Jersey broke ground for a new temple June 1. After 140 years in Paterson, Barnert Memorial Temple (Congregation B'nai Jeshurun) is moving to ... Franklin Lakes. At the official ceremony, two worn, unusable Torah scrolls were buried at the site where the new ark will stand. A Torah scroll contains Jewish religious law; it is considered a living object and cannot be destroyed but must be buried in a holy place. Past and present temple leaders formed two chains, passing the scrolls from hand to hand before interment. Rabbi Martin Freedman kissed the scrolls before lowering them.... The temple is expected to be completed within a year.

—The Week Ahead
June 7, 1986

It was not the brilliant sunshine that had faces radiant at last Sunday's groundbreaking ceremony for the new home of Congregation B'nai Jeshurun, more commonly called Nathan Barnert Memorial Temple. Nor was it the natural topography of the beautiful ten-acre site located on 208 South in Franklin Lakes, nor the vision of the anticipated building designed to afford a view of both the mountains and the New York City skyline that produced the inner glow every bit as evident as the obvious external shine. Rather, it was a combination of reverence for their future and "burst your buttons" pride at their congregation's willingness and ability to adapt and survive that gave temple members and friends that unique blend of inner peace and unbridle excitement....

—Janet Finke,
letter to the author

In a short welcome to the temple, [Franklin Lakes] Mayor [William] Vichiconti captured the philosophical essence of the day. "It is a pleasure for me to welcome this temple here," the mayor commented. " New Jersey's oldest temple now becomes Franklin Lakes' first temple. May God bring you good fortune, health, happiness and prosperity." Temple President Susan Sauer ... [said], "Today marks the beginning of a wonderful relationship between one of the oldest institutions in the state of New Jersey and one of the oldest settled communities in our area of northern New Jersey. I am sure Mayor Vichiconti will agree that the borough officials of Franklin Lakes have long operated on the premise that they are dedicated to the health and welfare of the people in this great community. Barnert Temple has no less a standard and no less a goal. It too is dedicated to the health and welfare of the community in which it resides as well as to the biblical admonition which we have been taught through the ages. That is: brotherhood, peace and love.

—Wyckoff News,
June 5, 1986

While the new Barnert Temple was under construction in Franklin Lakes, Rabbi Martin Freedman, Cantor Sheila Pearl, religious school director Dr. Sheldon Shuch, and the Barnert Temple leadership prepared for the move, giving special attention to the educational programs of the religious school, the ongoing adult-educational needs, and the social and social action programs. All these programs would be expanded as the anticipated needs of a much larger congregational membership were being analyzed and planned for.

Practical matters regarding the new temple building also required attention. Since building the second floor of the religious school to accommodate a much larger anticipated student body was a foremost priority, and the commitment not to burden the congregation with a mortgage had become policy, there were no funds available for the completion of the building's interior and decorative needs. Those needs would have to be underwritten privately in the future, because this small congregation was exhausted from its heroic fundraising effort.

Fortunately, the generations of Barnert Temple–Paterson donors were very concerned about the completion and appearance of the building's interior. Aesthetic considerations were given a high priority in how spiritual communication is perceived. How to incorporate the honorial and memorial plaques from the Straight Street and Broadway and Derrom Avenue buildings in Paterson, as well as the other religious, historic, and artistic objects, some dating from the nineteenth century, was given great thought. A letter was sent to the congregants requesting their input and participation in the process. The committee, Daryl Roth, Carole Ann Steiger, Alvin Greenbaum, and myself, consulted with architect Percival Goodman about possible cost-effective solutions that could be implemented in the near future, after the move, and with the cost underwritten by Barnert Temple–Paterson donors.

We were moving on. The front page of the May 1987 Barnert bulletin was devoted to the dedication-weekend events with an announcement that on Friday, May 15, at 8:00 p.m. at Barnert Temple–Paterson there would be a special Shabbat service dedicated to the temple's 140 years in Paterson; Saturday, May 16, at 10:00 a.m. in Paterson, there would be a farewell Torah service; and at 7:30 p.m. in Paterson a Havdalah service followed by a Lower East Side block party and dinner. On Sunday, May 17, the Torah processional would begin at Barnert Temple–Paterson at 10:00 a.m., with the dedication ceremony at Barnert Temple–Franklin Lakes at 2:30 p.m.

The morning sun was shining as temple members of all ages removed the Torah scrolls from the ark of the Paterson synagogue to begin the procession to their new home in Franklin Lakes. The parade's route and timing had been planned for months by Leon Finke.... He had spoken with municipal and county officials for permission to walk on the streets and roads along the way and had been assured of their help to ensure the safety of the marchers.

Rabbi Martin Freedman, blowing a shofar, led the group a short distance to Temple Emanuel of Paterson, where it was welcomed by representatives of the congregation. The stop denoted a nostalgic leave-taking from our long-time neighbors and friends across Broadway. The procession then went across the bridge to Fair Lawn, with members passing the Torahs to one another as they walked, some briskly, others slowly, some joyfully, others a little sadly. People from other congregations turned out to cheer the Barnert group; some joined the march and even carried scrolls.

Procession leaving Paterson temple to bring Torah scrolls to new Franklin Lakes temple, May 17, 1987. Rabbi Martin Freedman blowing the shofar. Private collection.

Torah processional walking from Paterson to Franklin Lakes temple. Private collection.

Torah processional from Paterson arriving at Franklin Lakes temple, May 17, 1987. *Front, left to right, carrying Torah scrolls:* Robert Gutenstein, Susan Sauer, Leon Finke (former Barnert presidents). Private collection.

Dedication Journal for new Barnert Temple, Franklin Lakes, May 17, 1987, Barnert Temple Archives.

When it became unsafe to walk in traffic, the Torahs were taken by car to the foot of the road leading up to the temple in Franklin Lakes, where the entire congregation was eagerly awaiting their arrival. Accompanied by music and happy shouts, Rabbi Freedman and officers of the congregation strode up the hill to the entrance door, where [Rabbi Freedman] affixed a handsome mezuzah and dedicated the building. Everyone then moved into the sanctuary, their footsteps echoing on the bare concrete floor. There may have been no carpeting, but the pews were the very ones from the Paterson building.

Following the opening prayer led by Rabbi Daniel Freelander of the [Union of American Hebrew Congregations, now the Union for Reform Judaism], there were greetings from State Senator Henry McNamara and ... State Senator Matthew Feldman. ... Rabbi Freedman welcomed members of the family of Nathan Barnert and praised their ancestor's foresight in organizing the original congregation....

Other speakers were Congressman Robert Roe and Rodney Remie, representing the mayor of Franklin Lakes. Architect Percival Goodman and contractor Albert Visbeen, who had been involved with both the old and new temples, beamed from the podium....

As the emotional day ended, there was a realization that the long-planned and hoped-for goal had been achieved. Although there was still much to be done in the new building, the move had been made and Congregation B'nai Jeshurun was facing the future confidently.

—Janet Finke,
letter to the author

Dedication Tablet, Franklin Lakes, May 17, 1987. Barnert Temple Collection.

We moved on May 17, 1987. The planning, the transition, the synergy of the Paterson congregation, the moment and the message of survival—all now a reality. Much would be accomplished in the first three years in our new home, and various 1990 Barnert bulletins describe programs that were in place by then:

- In a Friday night sermon, Rabbi Martin Freedman spoke about religious and civil freedoms and reminded the congregation to remember significant dates in twentieth-century Jewish history. First, the "Kingdom of Night" (the Holocaust) and the "Republic of Birth" (Israel's modern history as an independent nation), then "Operation Exodus," when more than 1 million Soviet Jews migrated to Israel in search of civil and religious freedoms.

- Cantor Sheila Pearl reported that for the spring Jewish music season, Ernest Bloch's Sacred Service, "Sephardic Music in the Synagogue and Home," and the annual Cantor Joseph Posner Memorial Program would be presented. The Barnert Youth Singers were an integral part of these programs.

- Religious school principal Dr. Sheldon Shuch wrote about various programs in the religious school that also had a social action component. One example was visits to the Daughters of Miriam Center for the Aged, where the lower grades (K–3) would offer songs, companionship, and cheer to the residents. The children were accompanied by their teachers and Cantor Pearl. Dr. Shuch also reported that the religious school was including environmental studies in the curriculum, because many holidays such as Tu BiShvat, have strong nature themes.

- Sara Losch, director of the new [1988] Barnert Temple Preschool and Family Center, wrote about a program held on March 27, 1990, on the subject of "Parenting." An intergenerational discussion focused on parenting, the changes that have occurred, and how parents and grandparents can share their feelings and experiences to better communicate about their children and grandchildren.

- A "Learn with the Rabbi" series, open to the entire community, took place in April and May [of 1990]. Rabbi Freedman's topics: "Women in Jewish Tradition," "Women in the Bible," "Women in Rabbinic Judaism," "Modern Jewish Women."

- Co-presidents Kathy Press and Dorothy Starr announced that on April 7, 1990, there would be a dinner dance to honor four families for their many decades of leadership and devotion to Barnert Temple: Ellen and Robert Gutenstein, Susan and Richard Lane, Susan and Alvin Sauer, and myself and my husband, Philip Schwartz. A six-foot-tall, nine-branch (Chanukah) menorah would be presented to the congregation in honor of the four families.

- On Friday, April 27, 1990, a special service and Oneg Shabbat honored benefactors B. Irving Cohen and Samuel S. Schwartz for their many decades of service to the Barnert Temple congregation. These two men spearheaded the Survival Drive campaign to build the Barnert Temple–Franklin Lakes. The B. Irving Cohen and Family Sanctuary and the Esther and Samuel Schwartz Religious School are symbols of their personal commitment to the Survival Drive and to the survival of our Barnert congregation.

- A Sephardic Torah tik (holder) was presented to the congregation in honor of B. Irving Cohen and Samuel Schwartz. The tik (and the new Torah scroll it would later hold) was subscribed by congregants. The splendid Sephardic tik was hand-wrought in Portugal in chased silver and gold. Worked into its design are the three great edifices constructed in the history of the Barnert Temple: the first in Paterson on Broadway and Straight Street (1892–1965), the second Paterson building on Derrom Avenue (1965–1988), and our present building in Franklin Lakes. Also engraved on the tik is a seven-branched menorah, symbol of the ancient Temple in Jerusalem and the symbol that is on our temple's bronze tablets, which is used as a Barnert Temple logo. An inscription at the top of the tik in Hebrew reads, Etz chayim hee lamachazikim ba; the translation, inscribed at the bottom, reads, "It is a Tree of Life to them that hold fast to it." The silver and gold crown of the tik is a symbolic representation of the twelve tribes of Israel. When the tik is opened for the reading of the Torah, the dedications inscribed on the inside can be seen. They read: "In honor of the great benefactors of the Barnert Temple, Bertram Irving Cohen and Samuel S. Schwartz."

I think that the congregation has been extraordinarily lucky in terms of its benefactors. I'm talking specifically about B. I[rving] Cohen and Sam Schwartz, who made the move possible to Franklin Lakes.... And I'm hoping that that tradition will continue.

—Dorothy Starr
oral history

Tik honoring benefactors Samuel S. Schwartz and B. Irving Cohen, April 27, 1990. Barnert Temple collection.

Exterior of Franklin Lakes sanctuary.
Photo by Karen Galinko. Private collection.

Exterior of Franklin Lakes sanctuary with commandment symbols, 1987.
Photo by Karen Galinko. Private collection.

Succoth Garden, Franklin Lakes temple, 1987.
Photo by Karen Galinko. Private collection.

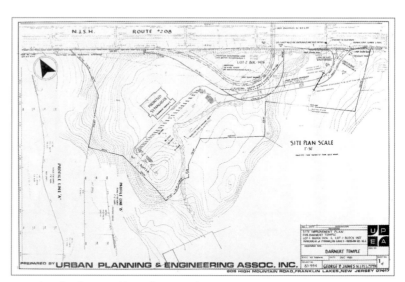

Site plan for the Franklin Lakes temple, 1987.

Cornerstone from Derrom Avenue temple, 1964—1987, installed in Franklin Lakes temple. Photo by Karen Galinko.

Memorial Alcove—Franklin Lakes temple, includes plaques and Eternal Light installed from Paterson temples since the 19th century. Private collection.

Rabbi Moshe Klein writing the Barnert
Temple Sefer Torah, Franklin Lakes, 1991.
Barnert Temple Archives.

Collage of honorial and memorial designations,
1987, Franklin Lakes temple.
Barnert Temple Archives.

Holocaust Memorial Entrance, "Am Yisrael
Chai—the People Israel Live." Franklin
Lakes temple. Photo by James D. Schwartz,
2005.

- Maimonides stated that every Jew is affirmatively commanded to write a Sefer Torah, and at the Simchat Torah service in October 1990, the Barnert Temple congregation began a Sefer Torah project, with the Torah completion scheduled for a May 12, 1991, dedication just before Shavuot, the celebration of the giving of the Ten Commandments at Mount Sinai.

  "Has your hand ever shaken so you make a mistake?" 11-year-old Bree Rosenfelt asked a bearded sofer, or Torah scribe, last week. The sofer, Rabbi Moshe Klein from Borough Park in Brooklyn, answered that yes, sometimes his hand shakes. If his hand shakes, he stops and takes a rest.

  Bree was one of some sixty Sunday school students who, along with a few dozen adults, gathered in the social hall of the Barnert Temple/Cong. B'nai Jeshurun here to hear Klein speak about the arduous and ancient process of writing a Torah. The congregation has hired Klein, a fourth generation sofer, to write a new sefer Torah.

  "It's a rare occasion that a congregation underwrites or starts a scroll.... It presents a great opportunity for education and coalescing," said congregant Janet Finke.

  "We expect it will have, spiritually and educationally, a unifying effect on the congregation," said Dorothy Starr, co-president of B'nai Jeshurun.

  Others involved with the Torah-writing project said they believed it would help unify old and new membership and various geographic [groups] in the synagogue....

  As part of the educational [program] of the synagogue's Torah project, Klein is expected to meet again with religious school students. Adult Torah study groups will also be coordinated.

  Klein made his first visit to the congregation's new site in 1987, when he helped bury two damaged Torah scrolls at the site where the congregation's new ark was later being built.

  —Jewish Standard,
  November 9, 1990

- The Holocaust Memorial Main Sanctuary entry was dedicated by the Elsie and Howard Kahan Memorial Fund, and proclaims, "Am Yisrael Chai—the People Israel Live." The strong colors of the stained-glass panels flanking the main entry doors are an expression of the fiery period of the Holocaust, a time of unspeakable horror and destruction. Six dark-gray slabs of rough slate are embedded into the brilliant stained glass to symbolize gravestones for the six million Jewish men, women, and children who were murdered during the Nazi Holocaust. The side panels of stained glass are linked to the upper panel by a great Hebrew letter shin. This shin has several meanings: it stands for shoah, the Hebrew word for "Holocaust"; it also stands for the sacred name of God— Shaddai, "Almighty." Inscribed across the two front doors are the words Ani ma'amin, "I believe." This statement urges us to believe in pursuing truth, justice, and peace and in performing righteous acts.

- The sanctuary ark doors, a gift from Daryl and Steven Roth, were commissioned and installed. The four tall oak panels of the doors represent four important

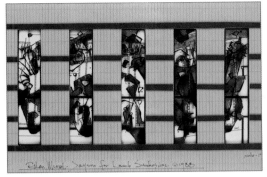

Stained-glass windows in Santuary of Franklin Lakes temple. The ten lancets are symbolic of the Ten Commandments. Barnert Temple Archives.

aspects of our Jewish faith: God, Torah, Israel, and the synagogue. The brass overlay Hebrew words state: L'dor va dor nagid gadlecha —"From generation to generation we shall proclaim Your greatness." These words are repeated in brass-on-brass lettering: "From generation to generation you shall transmit the teachings of the Torah."

- The stained-glass windows in the sanctuary were the result of the desire of the Paterson-generation congregants to have a spiritual-aesthetic statement in the sanctuary. When we moved to Franklin Lakes, the original windows had been covered with colored paper because of a lack of funds. Daryl Roth, Carole Ann Steiger, and I chaired an independent fundraising effort to underwrite the beautiful and meaningful new stained-glass windows.

Ark covers sewn by sisterhood members for Derrom Avenue temple, now rehung as wall hangings in Franklin Lakes Sanctuary. Author photo, 1992. Private collection.

The windows extol the commandments which were given to the people by God through Moses as described in Exodus. The ten lancets, themselves, are symbolic of the Ten Commandments. The windows speak of their relationship to the people.

To the left and right of the ark, the shofar blasts the message, bringing to mind that moment at Mt. Sinai.... To the left and lower areas, small groups of people are seen. They are families, the basic foundation of life, as the commandments are the basic foundation of law. The shofar is blasting the message of the commandments through the ages past.

People are bound together by laws and are like a fabric made whole by the threads that weave it. Jews are also bound together by ideas and traditions, which are like the human threads bound together through time forming the fabric of civilization....

To the right of the ark, the shofar is blasting this chain of tradition into the future. ... Two families below represent the present and the future. The large Torah is symbolic of the path to follow, of the laws which were given to the people so long ago. They remain so relevant today. The truth is and always will be relevant.

Each window has certain areas of clear glass. Seeing clearly through to the beauty of nature is a symbol for the gift of this beautiful earth....

Seeing through the windows is like entering into another world through prayer and meditation. Looking at the windows will remind one of the importance of their message.

—Ellen Miret-Jayson
artist statement

Interior of Franklin Lakes sanctuary. Photo by James D. Schwartz, 2005. Barnert Temple Archives.

We moved to Barnert Temple-Franklin Lakes in 1987, and we were truly at home there by 1990.

I remember the first year, the first Rosh Hashanah and Yom Kippur, and I looked around virtually with tears in my eyes, saying this is what I wanted when we built this building. Crowds of young people, children, activity, things happening, a spirit of "we can do wonderful things." And I think the Barnert Temple is off in a blaze of glory and everybody pulls together and keeps moving. The way they are, who knows what we can do.

—Robert Gutenstein
oral history

By 1991, membership had grown to over 300 families, with more than 200 members in attendance at any given Friday night service, vocally and spiritually expressing their enthusiastic involvement in the worship service. The highly praised preschool, started in 1988 with six children, now had a waiting list. Participation in synagogue programs by post-bar/bat mitzvah students was near 100 percent. A vibrant senior youth group had been formed to address the needs of post-Confirmation students.

The Academy of Jewish Studies, a two-year Confirmation program for teenagers designed to strengthen their Jewish identity and equip them with the ethical tools needed to establish an enriched life as a Jewish adult, was established.

What's also gratifying to me is the work that I do with children and with teenagers. ... By virtue of what we've done [at the Academy, we have kept] a significant and a growing number of our teenagers connected to their Jewish peers ... their Jewish roots, to Jewish learning, and to maintain their curiosity.

—Cantor Sheila Pearl
oral history

Within another few years, even more had been accomplished. A booklet written by member Leslie R. Cohen and edited by member Elliot Richman, Ph.D., was published in 1994, describing our congregation at the time. The booklet contained a short history of the Barnert congregation and its religious leadership, and included descriptions of Barnert Temple programs in 1994, excerpted here:

Our Prayerbook and Liturgy: We use Gates of Prayer and Gates of Repentance, the prayerbooks that were deeply rooted in both old and new Jewish traditions;

Men and Women Together: We continue the long tradition at Barnert Temple of equality of men and women in all aspects of ritual observance and lay leadership;

Liturgical Music: Organ, flute, cello, harp, piano, violin, synthesizer and guitar all meet to highlight new music while protecting the integrity of our traditional repertoire;

The Barnert Temple Choirs: We have both a professional choir and volunteer adult and junior choirs;

Affiliation with the Union of American Hebrew Congregations (UAHC) [now the Union for Reform Judaism (URJ)]: In Reform Judaism, creativity and progress are described as essential to our religious life, and each generation must seek contemporary expressions to the beliefs and practices of its religious traditions;

Who We Are: We are 350 families representing diverse backgrounds who have found a common spiritual refuge here at Barnert Temple as liberal Jews who share progressive religious beliefs and activist values;

Preschool and Family Center: We are committed to providing high-quality early childhood education for Jewish families in the region. The preschool opened in 1988 with six children registered, and now in 1994 the school serves more than 100 children with exceptional programs;

The Religious School: Its goal is to provide a substantive Reform Jewish education in the context of both traditional study and contemporary learning experiences. The curriculum includes preparation for reading Hebrew, music, art, biblical stories, holiday celebrations, Hebrew studies, Jewish history, Jews of the diaspora, the Jewish immigration experience in America, the founding of Israel, and the Holocaust. Social action activities are integrated in the religious school programs;

The Academy of Jewish Studies: This two-year Confirmation program's goal is "to strengthen the Jewish identity of our students and to equip them with the ethical and conceptual tools needed to establish an enriched life as an American Jewish adult";

For Our Children: The Barnert Temple Youth Group offers a wide range of cultural, community service and athletic activities;

Federation Youth Activities: Barnert Temple is a long-standing member of the New Jersey Federation of Temple Youth (JFTY) and its parent organization, the North American Federation of Temple Youth (NFTY). This national organization provides a varied array of cultural, social, and religious programs for all Reform youth in grades 9–12 in the United States and Canada;

Bar and Bat Mitzvah: This year of extensive work with the rabbi, cantor, and professional staff enables the students on their bar/bat mitzvah day to conduct most of the Shabbat worship service and chant from the Torah and Haftarah. The class work also includes discussions of basic concepts of mitzvah, and the process also involves the students' families;

Confirmation: Confirmations are a tradition at Barnert Temple since the nineteenth century. Today, educational programs that lead to the service of Confirmation on Shavuot remain an important milestone for Barnert confirmands;

Barnert Temple Sisterhood: The Sisterhood brings a diverse group of women together, helps build life-long friendships, and fosters an environment that enriches the spiritual and cultural experience of it members. The various Sisterhood year-round programs assist the entire Barnert community and the community at large;

Barnert Temple Men's Club: The Men's Club is committed to the spirit of friendship. The organization provides stimulating social activities and promotes cultural and educational programs for Barnert Temple members and the

Board of Trustees of B'nai Jeshurun, 1923.
Back row, from left, standing: D. J. Lefkowitz, Abram Klenert, M. H. Straus, Isidore Simon, M. I. Fuld, M. Weingaertner, H. Van Praagh. *Front row, seated:* B. Greenberg, H. D. Green, Jacob Rosen, Rabbi Marius Ranson, S. Boehm, A. L. Simon, Jacob Cohn. 1923–1924. Nathan Barnert Memorial Temple, Broadway.

Past presidents
Seated, left to right: Daniel Lieblich (1960–1961), Jack Gruber (1954–1956), Frank Stave (1943–1945, 1953–1957), Warren Bauer (1953–1954), Barnert Zalon (1958–1960). *Standing, left to right:* Rabbi Martin Freedman, Philip Sarna (1978–1981), Ernest Weiner (1971–1973), George Rosenthal (1965–1971), Alvin Sauer (1973–1976), Robert Gutenstein (1976–1978), Cantor Joseph Posner. Barnert Temple Derrom Avenue. Photo by Herman S. Paris, 1980. Barnert Temple Archives.

Board of trustees and Rabbi Martin Freedman, 1976. Barnert Temple Derrom Avenue.

Board of trustees and Rabbi Martin Freedman, 1984–1985. Barnert Temple Derrom Avenue.

Board of trustees and Rabbi Martin Freedman, 1988–1989. Barnert Temple Franklin Lakes.

New York Mayor Edward J. Koch with Alvin Sauer. Barnert Temple Speakers Forum, 1994. Private collection.

Nobel laureate Elie Wiesel with Cipora O. Schwartz and Philip Schwartz. Barnert Temple Speakers Forum, 1995. Private collection.

Opera singer and philanthropist Beverly Sills with Jill and Kenneth Edelson. Barnert Temple Speakers Forum, 1996. Private collection.

Left to right: Sherie Reiter, Alvin Sauer, Alan M. Dershowitz, Susan Sauer, and William Cohen. Barnert Temple Speakers Forum, 1997. Private collection.

community at large. Both the Sisterhood and the Men's Club are invaluable to the Barnert community as they assume countless responsibilities in the year-round needs of the congregation as committed volunteers;

Adult Enrichment: Amongst the ongoing offerings in Barnert Temple's adult education programs are the Sabbath and Festival Sermon (lectures), the eighteen-month Adult Bar/Bat Mitzvah training program, the Institute of Jewish Studies (which brings a noted scholar to the temple for an annual lecture series), and the annual Howard Kahan Memorial Holocaust Lecture. The synagogue also sponsors special community lectures, which have presented such notable speakers as Ambassador Abba Eban, New York City Mayor Edward I. Koch, author Leah Rabin, cultural leader and opera star Beverly Sills, and Nobel laureate Elie Wiesel. Members of the temple may also enroll in extensive programs sponsored by the New Jersey region of the UAHC [now URJ] and the education programs of the Hebrew Union College–Jewish Institute of Religion in the greater New York area;

Social Action: The commitment to programs of social action has always been a strong aspect of the Reform Jewish mandate. The support of programs and issues, including religious freedoms, church-state matters, food and sheltering agencies, civil rights, Soviet Jewry, anti-Semitism, and interfaith activities has, since the nineteenth century, always been an integral part of Barnert Temple's congregational life;

Social and Cultural Activities: A variety of ongoing and special events is presented by various arms of the congregation. The range is broad and has included appearances by the New Jersey String Quartet, the West Point Jewish Chapel Choir, a weekend presentation of a guest scholar-in-residence, square dances, progressive dinners, and at least three yearly special musical Shabbat programs, including the Cantor Joseph Posner Memorial Music Shabbat. The congregation also organizes an annual Food and Fun Heritage Festival, a book fair, a talent show that spotlights children (and some courageous adults), seminars on interfaith dating, trips to the Holocaust Museum in Washington, D.C., and occasional trips to Israel;

Mt. Nebo Cemetery: A cemetery is one of the most important and personal religious obligations of a synagogue. Our Mt. Nebo Cemetery, situated in Totowa, N.J., since 1886, is both beautiful and serene. The long-established Perpetual Care Fund guarantees the continuation of the cemetery's high quality maintenance program;

Congregational Organization: The congregation is governed by the officers and board of trustees. They are guided by the principles, procedures, and goals set forth by a formal constitution and set of by-laws. All members are encouraged to serve on the various boards.

The pamphlet summarized the state of the Barnert congregation's spiritual, educational, social, and operational activities in 1994. But with Rabbi Freedman's illness in 1993 and retirement in 1995, a new era of lay and religious leadership commenced that would assume responsibility for Barnert Temple for many future generations.

When we moved from Paterson to Franklin Lakes in 1987, the lay and religious leadership of the congregation continued from its Paterson base. From 1987 to 1995

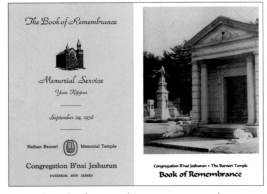

Annual Book of Rememberance Memorial Service with Mount Nebo Cemetery cover.
Barnert Temple Archives.

presidents Robert Gutenstein, Leon Finke, Kathy Press, Dorothy Starr, Nardyne Cattani, and Alvin Sauer continued to carry the responsibility of leadership while mentoring and encouraging the many new, younger members to become involved and assume the next generation of leadership.

> With the move to Franklin Lakes, the leadership and congregation can justly view with pride and good feelings a success which transcends anything in my memory of the prior years in Paterson.... Now there is a strong succession of leadership, which has inspired an active, vibrant congregation. Such was not the case in the late '60s.

> George Rosenthal had been president for five years. His vice president had been Ellis Rosenthal (Rabbi Raisin's son-in-law), who chose not to accept the presidency. At the time, I was president of the Men's Club. Rabbi Freedman and Artie Altschul approached me and urged me to become vice president for one year, after which (prepared or not) I became president (1970–71).

> Membership hovered between 180 and 200. That, of course, doesn't mean dues-paying members, because cash flow was always meager. It's not pleasant to recall this, but I had to resort to Monday night bingo, which added about $25,000 per year to our funds. Joe Conn was instrumental in getting this project going.

> You asked me to list the accomplishments of my years in office. They are only two: one, we (the Barnert Temple) survived during a difficult time in those last years in Paterson, a depressed, dying city ...; [and two,] as an augury for the future survival of the temple, by far my most important accomplishment was bringing in new, fresh leaders. I personally spanned the bridge from the old guard to the new. Alvin Sauer was vice president, Bob Gutenstein was treasurer. They represented the new, younger members from Ridgewood, Wyckoff, etc.

> —Ernest Weiner
> letter to the author

This continuity from Barnert Temple–Paterson to Barnert Temple–Franklin Lakes provided the congregation with a sense of pride in the temple's historic traditions, but also with clear direction that while the Paterson congregants were the link between past and present, the future of the Barnert congregation was the opportunity and responsibility of a new generation of leadership.

> Jacob Rosen, my grandfather, was born in 1863. He was very active in Barnert Temple. He was a young man of seventeen when he came here in 1880.... He joined Barnert Temple in 1885. He loved music and had a great voice. He formed the first choir at the temple. He was president of Barnert Temple for twelve years. He found Rabbi [Max] Raisin in Brooklyn and brought him to Paterson.... Rabbi Raisin coached me for my bar mitzvah at Straight Street in 1928. In our family, there were five Barnert Temple presidents: Grandpa Jacob Rosen, his oldest son Max Rosen, Raymond Kramer (through marriage to my cousin Selma Lieblich), Daniel Lieblich, my first cousin ..., and Louis Sorkin [related by marriage].

> —Julian E. Hirschfeld
> oral history

Barnert Temple presidents, Franklin Lakes.
Left to right: Robert Gutenstein (1976–1978),
(1987–1988), Kathie Williams (2001–2004),
Harry Plonskier (1995–1997), David Siegal
(2004 –), Dorothy Starr (1990–1991), Arnold
Reiter (1997–2001). Photo by Sherie Reiter, 2006.

The courage, passion, and resolve that motivated the Paterson congregants to survive and move to Franklin Lakes, that ancient impulse of survival, had understood and concluded that the precious religious and civil liberties they had inherited from their ancestors and our nation could only survive if a new generation of congregants would assume their responsibility as leaders.

The ultimate source for continuing to teach our children and for making sure that Judaism is a part of the American community is the synagogue. And so I became dedicated to it and that's why I worked for it. When I needed it [Barnert Temple] for my children to provide a Jewish education, someone had made sure that there was a synagogue there for me to attend, and my obligation in return was to make sure that it exists for future generations.

We have a lot of wonderful, dedicated people who continue at this time to give their energies and time to the temple in whatever capacity they can.... I'm also impressed with the dedication of some of the younger people who have stepped up now to take over some of the officer-ships and leadership.

—Dorothy Starr
oral history

As the twentieth century drew to a close, a new era of leadership was emerging that, together with the Paterson leadership, would respond to the needs of the Barnert congregation from the twenty-first century forward.

Congregation B'nai Jeshurun plays an essential role in each of our lives. We survive and thrive because our purpose is so vital. From generation to generation, we have had a leadership and membership devoted to that purpose. As a son of Holocaust survivors, whose grandmother settled in Paterson to find solace and security following her terrible ordeal, I am particularly appreciative of the rights and freedoms that are part of life in this great country and this wonderful state.

—Harry Plonskier
oral history

Since 1995, under the leadership of presidents Harry Plonskier, Arnold Reiter, Kathie Williams, and David Segal and our gifted Rabbi Elyse Frishman, Congregation B'nai Jeshurun, the Barnert Temple, has continued to expand the services and programs it offers both its congregants and the community. It has succeeded in the formidable task of retaining the interests and involvement of its long-established Paterson community members—especially those who had already gone through one or two moves—while attracting a whole new generation of members to continue in a sense of community in its new home.

Rabbi Elyse Frishman, ordained in 1981 by Hebrew Union College–Jewish Institute of Religion, had previously served for fourteen years as rabbi of The Reform Temple of Suffern, in Suffern, New York.

Our rabbi is nationally recognized as a writer, editor, and leader in transforming Reform Jewish worship. She is the author of *These Lights Are Holy: A Chanukah Home Prayerbook* and editor of *A Children's Haggadah, Gates of Prayer for Young People*, and *Gates of Prayer for Assemblies*. She is editing the new Reform prayerbook, *Mishkan T'filah*, a publication of the Central Conference of American Rabbis.

Rabbi Frishman has served on the URJ-CCAR Joint Commission on Religious Living and the CCAR Liturgy Committee, the Hebrew Union College–Jewish Institute of Religion Board of Alumni Overseers, and the Board of the CCAR. Rabbi Frishman is married to Rabbi Daniel Freelander, vice president of the URJ, and they are the proud parents of Adam, Jonah, and Devra.

On April 16, 2005, the Barnert congregation joined in a joyous celebration of Rabbi Frishman's tenth anniversary at Congregation B'nai Jeshurun, the Barnert Memorial Temple, with a dinner, Havdalah service, and special musical program. How blessed we all are to be the Barnert Temple family.

Celebration of 10th anniversary of Rabbi Frishman's tenure with her family, 2005. *Left to right:* Rabbi Daniel Freelander, Adam Freelander, Rabbi Elyse Frishman, Jonah Freelander, Devra Freelander. Barnert Temple Archives.

The Barnert Temple is like America. It's changed very dramatically. I'm thrilled that we're now once again imbued with a lot of people who are very committed and who are working endless hours to make the congregation grow, to be better and to be more responsive. We're again talking about the Barnert Temple family. We're again having functions going in every corner of the place. Growth has been incredible since the new rabbi, Elyse Frishman, came aboard. And the turnouts on Friday night and the turnouts for her various classes are marvelous. And hey, that's what we were there for.

—Robert Gutenstein
oral history

The congregation is very different today, as it should be. It's a different generation with different needs. And the new rabbi is sort of a Pied Piper for education. She's a magnificent educator. Her style is rather new to people of our generation. I hear it from friends and older members of the congregation. It's dramatic for some of us to see the changes. For some people it's more difficult to adjust to than for others....

I can only congratulate Rabbi Frishman and the people who have assumed leadership in the congregation. It is really their congregation now, and that, I think, speaks well for the future.

—Cipora Schwartz
oral history

By the end of the first year of the new millennium, the congregation's membership had soared to 492 families. Just as changes in the nineteenth century would reform the American Jewish congregation's style of worship (though not the content), so in the twenty-first century there is examination, evaluation, and evolution of the present-day and future needs of the American Jewish congregation. American constitutional, religious and civic freedoms enable all religions to adapt and reform according to current congregational needs without sacrificing principles.

It's all about relationships and spiritual growth. A corporate culture values titles; a spiritual culture values relationships. To sustain our temple, we must continue to cultivate leadership and greater volunteerism. The joy: watching people grasp the vision and feel terrific about being Jews.

—Rabbi Elyse Frishman
temple bulletin

The five-year Synagogue 2000 project provided an excellent path for the congregation to explore how to grow spiritually and become a kinder, gentler, more accessible congregation. Synagogue 2000 was a national, not-for-profit institute dedicated to revitalizing and re-energizing synagogue life in North America. Its mission was to be a catalyst for excellence, empowering congregations and communities to create synagogues that are sacred, vital centers of Jewish life. Rabbi Frishman was one of the original thirteen national fellows who guided the work of Synagogue 2000.

Synagogue 2000 envisions prayer where ritual rings true, prayer that is engaging, empowering and participatory. It accepts the challenge of spiritual renewal, where change is not a threat. It encompasses study, where learning runs deep for members of all ages and stages of life. It recognizes the importance of good deeds, where members matter and compassion counts. It reflects the welcoming, cooperative, supportive and nurturing ambiance of a synagogue suffused with spiritual searching. It represents a community where love and care are real and genuinely felt throughout. Congregation B'nai Jeshurun plays an essential role in each of our lives. We survive and thrive because our purpose is so vital. From generation to generation, we have had a leadership and membership devoted to that purpose.

—Harry Plonskier
oral history

In the year 2000, Rabbi Helga Newmark, the first woman Holocaust survivor to be ordained as a rabbi, came to our Barnert congregation as an assistant rabbi. She served with distinction until her retirement and continues to teach occasional classes.

I am pleased to announce that we have hired Rabbi Helga Newmark as our new assistant rabbi. In addition to Rabbi Newmark's profound teaching and spiritual skills, she is quite an extraordinary person. Her journey from the Holocaust to rabbinic ordination at age 67 is a story of perseverance, commitment and strength.

Rabbi Newmark brings to us a wealth of educational experience..... Prior to entering the seminary, Rabbi Newmark earned a master's degree in social work. Here at Barnert, Rabbi Newmark will focus her energies on adult and family education, teaching in the religious school, and participating in worship and life-cycle events.

—Arnold E. Reiter
August 10, 2000

Helga Newmark was 11 when she first heard the 23rd Psalm at the Theresienstadt concentration camp in Nazi-occupied Czechoslovakia. Each evening as she lay on her bunk, she listened to a woman's voice from the bed below.

"Yea, though I walk through the valley of the shadow of death, I will fear no evil; for thou art with me.... '"

Then she added, "Go to sleep, my beloved child."

The psalm brought her comfort then, Helga Newmark, now 67, recalls. But by the time she was liberated she had no use for a God that could allow a Holocaust, and no use for being a Jew.

Now, a half century later, at an age when others retire, Newmark has become the first woman Holocaust survivor to be ordained a rabbi....

She rarely mentions her own experience when talking to congregants in crisis. A shared pain, she says, can be communicated without words.

"It may be sufficient to get up from my chair and simply hold the person," she says. "Sometimes that's all that's needed to let a person know they're not alone and it's possible to survive."

—*New York Times*
June 5, 1994

The adult educational experiences for the congregants are varied and expanding. Some of the current ongoing classes include beginner's Yiddish, beginner's Hebrew, Saturday morning Torah study, "God Talk," weekly Torah study, the Melton Adult School, the Barnert Book Club, the Barnert Jewish Book Club, and Introduction to Kabbalah. There is a "350 Years of American Jewish History" seminar, an Israel Action committee, a Renaissance Group (for those over fifty-five), the Interfaith Outreach program, educational trips to New York City to visit the Lower East Side, the Jewish Heritage Museum, and the Jewish Museum, and occasional trips to Washington, D.C., and Israel.

How fortunate we are. There have been many celebrations since 1996 to remind us of service to our Barnert community and to other communities, and to mark milestones that define our Barnert family as a caring community.

- On May 15–17, 1996, the tenth anniversary celebration honoring Cantor Sheila Pearl for her excellent cantorial and educational contributions to our Barnert family included a special Shabbat service. Our own Tamara Freeman, musician, composer, and conductor, led the musical offering honoring Cantor Pearl at the Shabbat service.

It's hard to believe that since I was 8, the cantor has been part of my life.

The cantor's most effective impact on my life ... was after my bar mitzvah. I, along with six other students, became the first class to graduate from the temple's Academy program. The cantor revitalized the old Confirmation program into the Academy to make it more sensitive to students' interests, infusing discussions of values with video clips and setting prayers to contemporary music. Through the Academy and beyond, my study

150 Years
Congregation B'nai Jeshurun
The Nathan Barnert Memorial Temple
1847 - 1997

לְדוֹר וָדוֹר
L'dor va'dor

In Celebration
Erev Shabbat Chayei Sarah 5758
November 21, 1997

Program in celebration of the 150th anniversary of Congregation B'nai Jeshurhun, Barnert Temple, November 21, 1997. Barnert Temple Archives.

with the cantor built up my ethical base. Not only did she teach me about Jewish values, but she taught me how to practice them. Through many discussions comparing Judaism with other religions and Reform Judaism with other sects of Judaism, she helped me to find out what kind of Jew I am, and what kind of Jew I could be....

My most vivid memory of the cantor during the past ten years was not in the classroom, however. It was in the Valley Hospital emergency room three summers ago. Five minutes before I went to have surgery on my lung, the cantor came through the doors and gave me a big hug. She dropped everything just to comfort me for a minute. This is testimony to the undying compassion of Cantor Sheila Pearl.

—Jay D. Meisel
May 17, 1996

- In June 1996, religious school principal Dr. Sheldon Shuch was honored upon his retirement after eighteen years of exemplary educational leadership.

For the past ten years, I have worked with a colleague and friend.... Dr. Sheldon Shuch, who has been an integral part of the Barnert Temple because of his leadership of the religious school, is someone I will both personally and professionally miss. Dr. Shuch's unique calming style has created an atmosphere of ease and comfort for our teachers and our children.... For all that he has done for me and our generations of children, I express my gratitude and appreciation."

—Cantor Sheila Pearl
temple bulletin, June 1996

- On December 20, 1996, a special Shabbat service honored our own benefactor B. Irving Cohen on the occasion of his eightieth birthday, and we dedicated our new Allen organ on this Shabbat Shuvah 5757. The organ in honor of Mr. Cohen was a gift to the temple from his family and many congregants.

- The 150th anniversary year of our congregation was an opportunity for our Barnert family to celebrate our history, and to remind ourselves that making use of the past for the sake of the present and future could be a powerful history lesson, as well as a celebration of our Barnert community.

This year marks another interesting milestone in our temple's history. More than half of our current temple membership joined the temple subsequent to its move to Franklin Lakes nine years ago. This truly demonstrates the great wisdom of our temple leaders of a decade ago (1987) who had the vision and courage to understand changing demographics and migration and relocate from Paterson. We are proud of the new vitality and richness of Jewish life experienced in our new Franklin Lakes home.

The excellent and informative perspectives on the temple's history by Bob Gutenstein, Cipora Schwartz, Dorothy Starr, and Joel Bauer at January's joint Men's Club and Sisterhood Breakfast highlighted our temple's unique ability to adjust to changing times. Cipora stated that "the strength of the Barnert Temple is in its ability to adapt to the needs of its members." ... A new rabbi has afforded us the opportunity to re-examine, re-evaluate, and reaffirm our rituals and practices. Increasingly, the temple has placed the call for leadership from among its newer members, those who were not in Paterson and did not experience the unique challenges and successes of this temple.

—*Harry Plonskier*
oral history

150th Anniversary of Barnert Temple. Sabbath service celebration, November 20, 1996. *Left to right:* State Senator Henry McNamara, Susan Sauer, Harry Plonskier, Rabbi Emeritus Martin Freedman, Governor Christine Todd Whitman, Rabbi Elyse Frishman, Alvin Sauer, unknown, 1997. Barnert Temple Archives.

Remembering that our congregation was founded in Paterson on November 26, 1847, the day after Thanksgiving, we began our year-long 150th anniversary celebration, "In Thanksgiving," on November 20, 1996.

The "In Thanksgiving" program featured Governor Christine Todd Whitman as guest speaker. We began the program with the American flag salute and the Star-Spangled Banner," and we concluded with "God Bless America." The invocation was by Rabbi Elyse Frishman, the welcome by synagogue president Harry Plonskier, and the historical perspective was by Rabbi Emeritus Martin Freedman. A "Liturgy of Thanksgiving" musical presentation included the lines:

The dream of America:

land of diversity, land of possibility, land of hope.

The vision of our faith:

a world of harmony, of purpose, of peace....

With joy, we sing of America

With joy, we praise God for Torah

A special Shabbat of "Dedication and Rededication" was our next sesquicentennial event, held on Friday, December 6, 1996. The congregation was unified in its commitment to learn from and celebrate our history, as events were planned and completed for the culminating sesquicentennial celebrations in November 1997.

November 1997 will certainly be an incredibly exciting month for the extended family of the Barnert Temple. How fortunate for all of us to be part of the [150th anniversary] celebration.

As I reflect on this awesome notion of our 150th year, I often like to fantasize what it would have been like to be president of the temple in 1847, probably sitting in someone's living room or "sun parlor," as those rooms were called in those days, putting together an agenda for a meeting for the temple. Imagine what it would be like to organize such a meeting with no telephones, no faxes, no email and no typewritten minutes of any sort.... What could have been the issues of the day? Where was the worship? What discussions occurred concerning constructing a building? How were funds raised and how were dues assessed? What were the sermons of the day, and what issues did the rabbis in 1847 address from the human condition perspective that would be different from today?

Left to Right: B. Irving Cohen, Governor Christie Whitman, Warren Bauer. Barnert Temple Archives.

Moving On   145

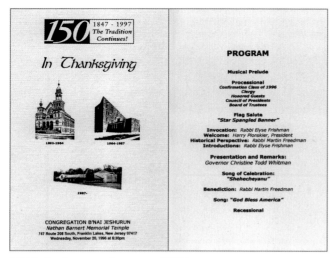

150th Anniversary Program, 1997.

Or flip-flop to today.… Imagine a member from 1847 hearing a discussion about a "web site." In 1847, a "web site" probably meant that you had a spider problem! Or a member from 1847 watching the agenda come magically to them by way of e-mail or a fax machine. Or being able to watch a video of a service or hearing the music of the congregation amplified by electronic equipment.

These contrasts from today to yesterday are extraordinary to comprehend. But the irony in this is that the basics of the service, emanating from the Torah, have remained a constant. The notion of a Torah portion each week commencing at the new year and ending at the next new year makes Judaism universally comprehendible in any era. And, I suppose that even the types of sermons that the rabbis do today vis-à-vis those from 1847 clearly focused on the basic human condition and lifecycle events—births, marriages, bar mitzvahs, weddings and deaths.…

Of most significance to us, as Jews, has been the development of the Jewish people in this 150-year time frame. The world in 1847 saw Jews as an oppressed minority. Anti-Semitism reigned and Jews, while a growing sect, were clearly discriminated against throughout the world. Since that time, many significant events have occurred, positive and negative in Jewish development: the oppression under czarist Russia; the development of Israel, culminating with the recognition of the State of Israel in 1948; in Israel, the ongoing development of activities—the Yom Kippur War, the peace process of Egypt and Israel,… the most recent peace initiative between the Palestinians and the country of Israel;… the Holocaust, and the horrible implications of that event that will live in the memories of Jews for eternity; and in the United States, the 'Golden Age' of American Jewry, symbolized by a growth in the number of Jews along with greater freedom of expression.

—Arnold Reiter
Barnert president
November 1997

On November 23, 1997, the *New York Times* featured an article entitled "A Jewish Congregation Marks a Journey of 150 Years" and interviewed Rabbi Elyse Frishman.

B'nai Jeshuran [sic], the oldest Jewish congregation in New Jersey, meets in a modern synagogue in northwest Bergen County. Its roots, though, are in 1847 Paterson. The congregation will celebrate its 150th anniversary this weekend under the leadership of Rabbi Elyse D. Frishman … who, since she was hired in 1995, has seen her congregation grow from 325 families to 470.

Q. Describe your congregation.

A. The congregation reflects the spectrum of Jewish observance, from interfaith couples to those coming from a more traditional background.…

Q. Have the needs of the congregation changed much over the years?

A. One of the greatest shifts is one that you see nationally in the realm of increasing desire for spiritual expression. For baby boomers there is a stronger spiritual need to worship regularly, to do that as a family, to learn more about what it is to be a Jew. The longer-standing members of the congregation had a great civic commitment. There was a great ecumenical spirit which came down through the generations. My job is easier and in some ways my job is harder trying to meet the needs of the current generation and at the same time trying to teach them about civic responsibility.

Q. What do you hope for the future of the congregation?

A. A decade ago there was much greater inclination to live Jewishly through the rabbi, for members to say, "O.K., rabbi, you go and do it." Now members say, "We'd like to learn more. Rabbi, help us do this." My dream is to be dispensable, to have a group that is so literate and so spiritual that they invite me to participate.

So the dream of America was celebrated during the sesquicentennial weekend events. On Friday, November 21, 1997, a remarkable Shabbat service took place, with Rabbi Eric Yoffie, president of the UAHC (now the URJ), giving the sermon, former Barnert Temple Rabbi Harry Blockman (1954–1956), Rabbi Emeritus Martin Freedman (1956–1995), Rabbi Elyse Frishman, and Cantor Sheila Pearl conducting the service, and a special music presentation. The printed program included a page listing our founders and builders, signers of the original charter in 1847, a list of recorded rabbis of the congregation since 1870, a list of the recorded presidents since 1912, and the names of the officers and the building committee on the tablet commemorating the dedication of the Barnert Temple building on Broadway and Straight Street dated September 17, 1894.

On Saturday, November 21, a 150th anniversary gala was held at the temple. A celebratory journal was distributed to all the attendees and mailed to the entire congregation. The journal included a brief history of our Barnert Temple and messages from President Bill Clinton, Vice President Al Gore, New Jersey Governor Christine Todd Whitman, U.S. Senator Robert Torricelli, State Senator Henry McNamara, State Assemblyman Nicholas R. Felice, and Mayor G. Thomas Donch of Franklin Lakes. The 150th anniversary journal continued a tradition begun at our centennial (1947), when the journal included a congratulatory letter dated October 19, 1947, from President Harry Truman, and the main address was given by Governor Alfred E. Driscoll.

The concluding sesquicentennial events on Sunday, November 23, included a Men's Club presentation, "Down Memory Lane," featuring Rabbi Emeritus Martin Freedman and many past Men's Club presidents. The religious school presented an educational Heritage Festival, and at noon a congregational reunion brunch featured recollections by members, memorabilia, photographs, and a 150-candle birthday cake. The entire sesquicentennial-year celebration was a journey for the present Barnert congregational family to remember and give thanks for our ancestors' visionary journey to our beloved United States of America.

THE WHITE HOUSE
WASHINGTON

October 1, 1997

Greetings to everyone gathered to celebrate the 150th anniversary of Congregation B'Nai Jeshurun/Nathan Barnert Memorial Temple of Franklin Lakes.

The anniversary of a place of worship is a testament to the lasting faith of a community. This faith is a covenant that binds members of a congregation together in a spirit of fellowship.

Our country was founded on a great tradition of religious liberty. This freedom helps to unite our nation of diverse faiths and creeds and gives us common ground for tolerance and understanding of others.

Your precious faith and freedom come with great responsibilities. This celebration is a reminder of the ways that God's gifts can be used to fulfill our obligation to help others.

Best wishes for a memorable ceremony and for great success in the future.

Bill Clinton

Letter from President Bill Clinton
150th anniversary, 1997
Barnert Temple Archives

STATE OF NEW JERSEY
OFFICE OF THE GOVERNOR
CN-001
TRENTON
08625
(609) 292-6000

CHRISTINE TODD WHITMAN
GOVERNOR

November 22, 1997

Dear Friends:

I am delighted to extend warm greetings and to offer my congratulations as you celebrate the 150th anniversary of the Congregation B'Nai Jeshurun\Barnert Temple.

As you celebrate this special occasion, it is fitting to reflect upon the rich history of the Congregation B'Nai Jeshurun/Barnert Temple. Generations of families in the Bergen County area have played a part in the vibrant life and tradition of Congregation B'Nai Jeshurun in service to the community. I join you in the hope that the congregation's energetic community involvement will continue for many generations to come.

Again, my congratulations, and my best wishes to all for an enjoyable celebration.

Sincerely yours,

Christine Todd Whitman
Governor

Letter from Governor Christie Whitman
150th anniversary, 1997
Barnert Temple Archives

891-0048

BOROUGH OF Franklin Lakes
DE KORTE DRIVE
FRANKLIN LAKES, NEW JERSEY 07417
COUNTY OF BERGEN

OFFICE OF THE MAYOR

September 30, 1997

Mr. Arnold E. Reiter, President
Congregation B'Nai Jeshurun
Nathan Barnert Memorial Temple
747 Route 208 South
Franklin Lakes, NJ 07417

Dear Mr. Reiter:

I would like to take a moment to reflect on the past. Barnert Temple can look back with pride and look forward to celebrating 150 years of serving its people.

At this time of the year, we all reflect on our blessings of fruitful fields and heartfelt thanks. Too often we forget from where these bounties come. So at the time of your celebration in November, we all will reflect and remember the last Thursday of November as a day of Thanksgiving. The Barnert Temple congregation will also, in its celebration, give thanks for the past and look forward to the future.

From my Office, the Council, and on behalf of all the residents of the Borough of Franklin Lakes, we wish you all the success and happiness during your celebration and in the years to come.

I congratulate you for all your accomplishments.

Sincerely,

G. Thomas Donch
Mayor

GTD/rmg

Letter from Franklin Lakes Mayor G. Thomas Donch
150th anniversary, 1997
Barnert Temple Archives

New Jersey Senate Resolution Certificate to Barnert Temple.
Barnert Temple collection.

State of New Jersey Proclamation in honor of Barnert Temple's
150th anniversary, Governor Christine T. Whitman, 1997.
Barnert Temple Archives.

County of Bergen, New Jersey, Certificate of Commendation on
150th anniversary of Barnert Temple.
Barnert Temple collection.

1999 Spring Gala
Congregation B'nai Jeshurun
Honoring Our Lifetime Trustees

Joel L. Bauer   **Cipora O. Schwartz**
Ellen Gutenstein   **Ted Lobsenz**

April 17, 1999

Honoring Lifetime Trustees, April 17, 1999.
Barnert Temple Archives.

Celebration of leadership to Barnert
congregation. *Left to right:* John Williams,
President Kathie Williams, Rabbi Elyse Frishman,
past president Arnold Reiter, 2004.
Barnert Temple Archives.

Other events celebrated during the end of the twentieth century and the beginning of the new millennium included a special service and Oneg Shabbat on May 14, 1999, honoring educator Sara Losch for ten years of excellence as our preschool director. A gala honoring lifetime trustees Joel Bauer, Ellen Gutenstein, Ted Lobsenz, and myself, held April 17, 1999, was a reminder of our Paterson legacy. Honoree Joel Bauer's family has been affiliated with Barnert Temple since the 1870s. Ellen Gutenstein's great-grandfather, Mangold Ellenbogen, and great-great-grandfather, Jacob Levy, were among the founders and builders of the Broadway and Straight Street Barnert Temple. Their names can be found on the marble dedication plaque dated September 17, 1894, displayed in the entrance to our current building. Ted Lobsenz's great-uncle was our beloved Rabbi Max Raisin. And the Schwartz family has provided leaders of the congregation for many generations, with Sam Schwartz (my father-in-law) chairing the building fund drives for not one but two congregational structures, to ensure the survival of our beloved congregation.

I have been privileged to know the four lifetime trustees of our temple for more than forty-two years. Joel Bauer, Ellen Gutenstein, Theodore Lobsenz, and Cipora Schwartz individually and collectively represent strong family traditions deeply rooted in our historic Kehillah Kedosha, the sanctified Congregation B'nai Jeshurun.

It is patently clear that in honoring these four lifetime trustees, we express our highest esteem for them and our gratitude for the blessing of their dedicated and glorious service to the temple....

I am profoundly thankful that in the almost forty years of my tenure as the tenth rabbi of our temple, I have been blessed with the wonderful opportunity to serve with such splendid congregants and trustees.

May we all grow from strength in the service to our Jewish community— and may their governance of the Barnert Temple be ever endowed with such outstanding life trustees. Kol Hakavod—all honor to our four lifetime trustees.

—Rabbi Martin Freedman
April 17, 1999

Judaism is based in covenant and relationship. The rich wisdom of our sacred tradition lies in its ethics. So it is that we deeply value personal contributions to life.

Cipora, Ellen, Joel, Ted: Each of your families has been connected with us for several generations.... We cannot imagine the Barnert Temple without the benefit of your contributions....

Thus, you honor us as our lifetime trustees. You are the guardians of our heritage and the champions of our future. You recognize the myriad needs and concerns of all our members, young and old, long-standing and newly joined, secular, classically Reform, traditional, newly Jewish. Your message to us has been clear: join not merely to fulfill the needs of your family or yourself, but to strengthen the entire community....

How clear and strong are your lights! May you continue to illumine our path as we journey together.

—Rabbi Elyse D. Frishman
April 17, 1999

On March 10, 2001, at a Purim ball, Arnold and Sherie Reiter were honored for their commitment and devotion to our congregational family. They represent a new generation of leadership that has deep dedication to our Barnert caring community. Arnie, Sherie, and their children, D.J. and Dara, were thanked for their unstinting service to our Barnert community.

And on November 23, 2003, the 155th anniversary of the congregation, a special Shabbat service was dedicated to reconnecting the 130 families that have been members of Barnert Temple since Paterson days. With Rabbi Elyse Frishman and Rabbi Emeritus Martin Freedman greeting the families, it was an evening of reminiscence and rededication to our congregation. The historic past and a new beginning were feted that evening, as a congregational cantorial concert took place welcoming to our Barnert family our new cantor, Regina Lambert-Hayut.

By the end of 2000, once again our temple was outgrowing its space, with membership at nearly 500 families from thirty-six surrounding communities, a huge preschool, religious school, b'nai mitzvah, and growing adult education programs. But this time, relocation was not the solution—rather, the expansion of the existing facility, from a religious school space to the Center for Jewish Education and Lifelong Learning.

The congregants understood that for the Jewish people to endure, religious education for all generations within the congregation was essential for us to transmit the heritage our forebears gave to us.

The expansion campaign, L'Dor Va Dor ("From Generation to Generation"), produced a brochure that quotes Rabbi Emeritus Martin Freedman, who thirty-five years earlier, when Barnert Temple–Paterson was moving from Broadway and Straight Street to Derrom Avenue, characterized the mission of the move. His statement was again applicable to the mission of expansion in Barnert Temple-Franklin Lakes:

> The responsibility is irrevocably ours, and it is a sacrosanct obligation which we must fulfill; for we are the trustees of Judaism, and only progress can perpetuate our culture and our creed. The great work which we have resolved to accomplish will impose a solemn duty upon each of us, but the dedication of our resources to this ennobling endeavor cannot be interpreted as an act of sacrifice. It is, in truth, a profound privilege, for the institution which we shall build will bring to our lives the reward of incalculable spiritual, social and cultural enrichment.

The Paterson generation and the new generation of members formed a formidable relationship of cooperation as they worked toward the goal of building the new education center. With campaign honorary chairs Bill Cohen, Steven Wener, Gail White, and myself, campaign co-chairs Robert Gutenstein and John Williams, and building committee co-chairs Andy Frankel and Ted Lobsenz, the enormous task of architectural plan development, fundraising, building, and renovating the older spaces culminated in a dedication ceremony on September 22, 2002, that gave hope and inspiration for the educational programs that would take place in this new Barnert Center for Jewish Education and Lifelong Learning.

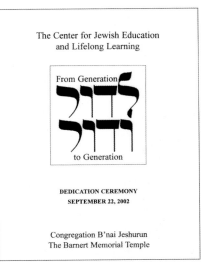

The Center for Jewish Education and Lifelong Learning

From Generation

לדור
דור

to Generation

DEDICATION CEREMONY
SEPTEMBER 22, 2002

Congregation B'nai Jeshurun
The Barnert Memorial Temple

Center for Jewish Education and Lifelong Learning. Dedication ceremony, September 22, 2002. Barnert Temple Archives.

Paterson Barnert members reunion on the 155th anniversary of the congregation, Nov. 23, 2003. *Left to right:* Rabbi Emeritus Martin Freedman, Ellis Rosenthal, Rabbi Elyse Frishman.

Members reunion on 155th anniversary of congregation, Nov. 23, 2003. *Seated, left to right:* Gail Cohen White, Ellen Gutenstein, Janet Finke, Dorothy Starr, *Standing, left to right:* Susan Sauer, Philip Schwartz, Cipora Schwartz, Robert Gutenstein, Harvey Starr.

Celebrating the harvest festival holiday of Sukkot took on added meaning Sunday for the congregation of Barnert Memorial Temple, the oldest Reform Jewish congregation in the state.

This year the congregation celebrated a different kind of harvest, one in which the community reaped the benefits of a 2-year fundraising campaign to build a new learning center.

It was the latest step in a long history of change and adaptation for a congregation that was founded more than 155 years ago, first serving European immigrants who worked in the Paterson textile mills, then following the suburban migration to Franklin Lakes.

With the congregation and its religious school enrollment continuing to grow, members of the temple Sunday dedicated their Center for Jewish Education and Lifelong Learning at its temple off Route 208....

The building includes religious school offices and nine classrooms that will serve the 375 children who attend classes three days a week, as well as the temple's full-time preschool....

Children will not be the only ones to benefit, according to [Rabbi Elyse] Frishman. Before the dedication she spoke of the growing popularity of adult religious education. "It runs the spectrum. We have adults who never had a Jewish education, who come back and say, 'We want to learn,' she says."

—Bergen Record
September 23, 2002

Following our tradition established centuries ago, we commemorate regional events with reverence and appreciation for their historical significance. For example, since Rev. Martin Luther King Jr.'s assassination in 1968, we remember each year, deeply and reflectively, Martin Luther King Day. As an interfaith shared experience with other neighboring religious institutions, we remember Dr. King's life and the concept of civil and religious rights. On January 23, 2000, Rabbi Martin Freedman spoke to our congregation and the community at large in celebration of the life of Martin Luther King Jr., on the topic of "Let Freedom Ring." And on January 21, 2002, Barnert Temple hosted a community-wide observance of Martin Luther King Jr. Day with guest speaker Rabbi Sy Dresner, freedom rider and personal friend of Dr. King.

The Reverend Martin Luther King Jr. was the giant for civil rights in America. He gave his life for the rights of hundreds of thousands of Americans. His dreams reminded Jews of our own vision: true freedom, and a life without discrimination.

One of our own understood this: Rabbi Martin Freedman. His freedom ride during the civil rights era changed the tide. He reminded Jews everywhere that our dream is the dream of all people, whatever religion or race or gender.

Let our community be strongest on Jan. 21.... We are committed to the pursuit of justice, and will not be swayed by human prejudice. The community's observance of Martin Luther King Day is testimony to our sincerity.

—Rabbi Elyse Frishman
temple bulletin, January 2002

There are also yearly commemorative remembrance services for the anniversary of the Warsaw ghetto uprising and Yom HaShoah, Holocaust Remembrance Day. The entire community is invited to these moving services.

In the unimaginable and horrific attacks on our nation on September 11, 2001, so many innocent people lost their lives—some were our friends, some were our neighbors. One was a Barnert Temple preschool child's father. On September 13, 2001, together with representatives of the Clergy Association of Franklin Lakes and Oakland and the Creative Living Counseling Center, we hosted an emotional and grief-filled memorial service, "Light in the Face of Darkness—A Community Offering of Prayer." Rev. Harold Lay of the Ponds Reformed Church of Oakland and president of the FLO Clergy Association, spoke to our collective grief through poetry, and Barnert's Rabbi Elyse Frishman offered soothing words: "We are gathered together in the shadow that has fallen on our lives. We raise our voices together in prayer asking for comfort and strength. We need light when gloom darkens our lives. To whom shall we look, if not the Creator of light?"

As did many other congregations, we provided in the following days, weeks and months counseling, special services, and opportunities for sharing feelings and experiences. We provided programs on how to speak with children about the 9/11 tragedy, and we quickly responded to requests for funds, new towels, blankets, bottled water, and non-perishable foods to assist local fire and police departments that were working on the 9/11 site.

Barnert Temple Bulletin, January 2000.
Barnert Temple Archives.

Like most of you, I have found no words to explain the unexplainable. It seems that this tragedy has brought out the best of our citizens including our congregation....

To try and describe Thursday evening's interfaith service is impossible. The 800 people who gathered together in our sanctuary again reminded us of the importance of coming together. The influence of Rabbi Frishman was clear to all of us who regularly pray with her. Rabbi Newmark's insights from her Holocaust experience could not have been more perfect. Our willingness and ability to host this service is another example of the special community we are.

The first Shabbat following the attack was so significant to many of us. This was another important time to be together and again we came together in large numbers. The service provided an additional opportunity for many of us to gain strength. On Sunday, a truckload of goods for the workers at Ground Zero left our temple. A week later, the rabbi organized a gathering of members who were witness to the tragedy to help support their needs. Finally, we should not forget our members who have been active in their other communities in supporting neighbors and friends.

—Kathie Williams
Barnert president
October 2001

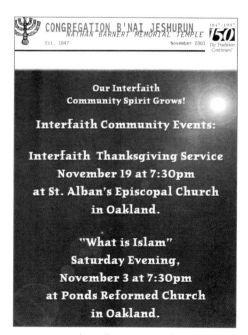

Barnert Temple Bulletin, November 2001.
Barnert Temple Archives.

1889				1889			
Ap. 7 By cash	✓	91	30	Ap 8 Fol 1 A. J. Rogers		75	
May 6 " "	✓	93	20	12 : 2 S. Goldsmith Secty	12	50	
June 2 " "	✓	80	00	May 2 . 3 Rev Hood Ap Salary	75	00	
June 22 " "	✓	20	55	" 2 4 H Bernstein Ap	8	33	
July 7 " "	✓	120	05	Ap 5 5 to poor Man		50	
Aug 4 " "	✓	103	80	May 6 7 to poor Man		50	
Sept 1 " "	✓	110	00	6 to Opel for Carpenter Work	4	70	
		618	60	10 Gas bill April	3	67	
Amount advanced —		165	76	15 Coal bill	18	40	
		784	36	31 Rev M. Hood May Sal.	75	00	
				31 H. Bernstein " "	8	33	
				16 Poor Man		50	
				June 7 H Bernstein Back Salary	18	68	
				10 May Gas	3	67	
				22 Printing Bill to B. Barnert	1	35	
				24 Water tax	3	00	
				24 Insurans to S Farrar	6	00	
				July 2 Rev M. Hood June Salary	75	00	
				2 H. Bernstein " "	8	33	
				9 Poor Man		50	
				10 June Gas	2	10	
				22 Ballens to Ex treasurer M. Cohen	100	49	
				30 Poor Man		25	
				31 Rev M. Hood July Sal	75	00	
				31 H. Bernstein "	8	33	
				Aug 5 Intress to David Megee Rev	75	00	
				8 Servis for Mrs A. Simon dec.	2	00	
				10 July Gas	1	92	
				22 Poor Man		50	
				28 Julius Schwaab for Insurans	18	00	
				Sept 2 Rev S. M. Hood Aug Salary	75	00	
				2 to Mr Bernstein Aug Salary	8	33	
				2 to Mr Bernstein Board for Chasen	1	25	
				2 to Secty Goldsmith Servis + Stationary	2	00	
				9 Aug Gas	3	15	
				23 Water tax	3	00	701.03
				Oct 1 Rev S. M. Hood Sept Sal.	75	00	
				" H. Bernstein	8	33	83.33
		165	76				784.36

Paterson Dec 12/89

We the undersigned Trustees
have examined the Secretaries and
Treasurers Books and found them
Correct

Simon Geet
Geo. Salen

Barnert Temple ledger, 1889. Recorded are the monthly charitable donations.
Hebrew Union College Archives, Cincinnati, Ohio

At this time of great national loss, we continued in our tradition of interfaith community participation. On November 3, we participated in an evening program to learn about "What Is Islam?" at Ponds Reformed Church in Oakland, and on November 19 we joined in an interfaith Thanksgiving service at St. Alban's Episcopal Church in Oakland.

Our heritage as American Jews, as it is of all religions in our nation, is assured by our constitutional guarantees of religious freedom. With all the blessings of America, how do American Jews, and specifically the Barnert Temple congregation, determine what is our most precious legacy from our 1847 ancestors to the present? The concepts of tikkun olam, "repairing the world," and tzedakah, "charity" or "righteousness," remain consistent themes in our congregation. We are a caring community. We make use of our historic past for the sake of the present and the future by aspiring to live a righteous life and to do good. In the American Jewish Archives of the Hebrew Union College–Jewish Institute of Religion in Cincinnati, there is a ledger of cash disbursements from Congregation B'nai Jeshurun of Paterson, New Jersey, covering May 1876 to April 1894. By this period the congregation had already established a culture of congregational and communal caring. In reviewing this document, we learn that in April–June 1877, Rev. M. Moll's monthly salary was $66.67, the monthly gas bill was $3.08, digging a grave cost $1.00, a ton of coal to heat the synagogue was $4.50, and cleaning the Mulberry Street synagogue cost $1.00. During the same three-month period we find twelve donations from the synagogue to "a poor man," "a poor woman," "Jerusalem men," and a named individual, totaling $13.50. Our benefactor Nathan Barnert, during his two terms as mayor of Paterson, donated his monthly salary to Paterson charities of all faiths.

We recall how in 1902, after the devastation of the great Paterson fire, Barnert Temple housed the Second Presbyterian congregation in our school and sanctuary for three years and accepted no remuneration of any kind. From the earliest Barnert Temple bulletins forward, in our archives we have recorded our rabbis and congregants working on behalf of congregational and community needs, welcoming speakers of all faiths, and participating in interfaith services over the centuries. Our American right of freedom of religion, and the gifts of our heritage and culture, become evident as elements that affect the direction and quality of our everyday lives in and outside our congregation today.

In the twenty-first century this heritage thrives at Barnert Temple as our 500-plus families follow in our founders' tradition of being a caring community.

Our social action activities are numerous and wide-ranging. In the 1980s, shortly after Barnert Temple moved to Franklin Lakes, two temple members, Susan Nashel and Judy Fromm, took a Community Action Program volunteer training session in Hackensack, because CAP needed volunteers for its overflow homeless shelter in churches and synagogues.

We asked Alvin Sauer, who was then president of the temple, if we could invite the director of CAP and representatives of other local social service agencies to speak to our board about the growing homeless population in Bergen County. Alvin readily agreed. The director of CAP, a representative of the Interreligious Fellowship, and the administrative chairperson for Eva's Kitchen in Paterson spoke to our board. Although it was not possible for our temple to become an overflow shelter, several temple members did volunteer in various capacities—some spent nights in one of the overflow homeless shelters in Ridgewood, Hackensack, or Woodcliff Lake, and others shopped and cooked for the family shelter at St. Cecilia's Church in Englewood. Judy and I worked at Eva's Kitchen once a week for about two years. There was a loose-knit group of individual temple members who responded to various needs in the community whenever they were asked to help.

In the mid-1990s Janet Finke met with Tracy Lind, the pastor of St. Paul's Episcopal Church in Paterson, to explore the possibility of Barnert Temple becoming involved with St. Paul's in an ongoing relationship. Since Barnert Temple's history began in Paterson and the need in the inner city was so great, Janet felt it would be a logical and meaningful match.

The result of the meeting was a proposal to the temple board of [trustees] to form a social action committee. Both Rabbi Frishman and the board were enthusiastic, and Janet and I became co-chairpersons. Members of the social action committee accepted the responsibility of providing a hot dinner and breakfast once a month for the forty to fifty residents of St. Paul's homeless shelter. That included shopping, cooking and serving dinner as well as stocking the pantry with breakfast provisions.

Additionally, the social action committee, in conjunction with the Community Blood Center, organized an annual blood drive in 1995. It has grown more successful each year, with more people donating blood and more people volunteering to set up and staff a canteen and organize the drive.

Susan and Richard Lane act as local coordinators [in Paterson] for a national program, Rolling Readers. A number of temple members read to Head Start classes and elementary school children in Paterson once a week. The volunteer readers donate books twice a year to 'their" classes....

Almost every group within the temple has a social action project that serves a need in our larger community.

—Susan Nashel
letter to the author

And this was only the beginning. Since then the Barnert social action committee has been actively interpreting and acting on the basic meaning of our religion and our ethical traditions. The social action committee supports and works at Eva's Village, Paterson; St. Paul's Episcopal Community Men's Shelter and Habitat for Humanity, both in Paterson; the Franklin Lakes Presbyterian Church Shelter Program; the Englewood Family Shelter; Van Dyck Nursing Home and the Valley Hospital, both in Ridgewood; Shelter Our Sisters; the Community Thrift Shop; the Center for Food Action in Mahwah; and the Social Service Association. Barnert Temple holds a special Thanksgiving food drive, as well as winter coat and sweater drives. We collect used cell phones that are refurbished to call 911 and distributed to victims of domestic violence. Our yearly blood drive is huge and benefits the Bergen Community Regional Blood Bank. We participate in the annual CROP (Community Response to Other's Poverty) walk, a project of the Church World Service, which has been addressing the issue of world hunger for fifty years. We also support the Ramapo-Bergen Animal Refuge and the Vietnam Veterans of America. Our participation enriches and expands us as a human family. The tragedy of genocide in Darfur is a high priority for the Barnert Congregation as it supports funding in on-going events, participates in the rally in Washington D.C. on April 5, 2006 and educates the congregants of this continuing 21st century tragedy.

Barnert Temple's Darfur Day raised $58,000 to be donated in support of Darfur relief efforts. The donations represented sponsorships of 150 adult congregants, teenagers, and children who volunteered to run and walk on treadmills, ride exercise bicycles or jump rope. Sponsors included numerous members of the wider community, in addition to congregants.

In addition to fundraising, the purpose of the day's events was to raise awareness of the situation in the Darfur region of Sudan. Lisa Margolis, Barnert Temple's social action co-chair explained that a presentation by Yah-ya Osman, from the Darfur Rehabilitation Project, who escaped from Darfur, educated scores of congregants and teenagers.

"He shared the story of his life in Darfur and the history of the situation in the region," she said. "His audience included Barnert's Religious School students in grades five and up who were held spell-bound by his moving and emotional story."

—The Village Times
May 26, 2006

Account of Darfur tragedy in Barnert Temple Bulletin, April 2006.

To All of the Members of the Congregation of Barnert Memorial Temple—

Thank you, from the heart, for all of your efforts in "stocking the pantry" at Social Service. Thank you for contributing, collecting, decorating, organizing and delivering. Thank you for caring and sharing so generously.

Currently, SSA is helping 270 local residents. Half of them are children, one-quarter are older Americans, one-fifth are disabled. All of them join me in saying: "We couldn't make it without you!"

—Barbara Swanson
for the board of Social Service
November 1996

Thanks to you and your generosity, we are able to continue to " feed the hungry, shelter the homeless, aid the addicted and give medical help to the sick." These words succinctly describe all that we do at Eva's, but they do not describe how vital your generosity is to us. I do not believe any words can!

Thank you for your gift of food that enables us to continue to care for those less fortunate. More than you know, we are grateful for your goodness to us.

—Eva's Village
December 2003

Students' program at the Renaissance One School of Humanities, Paterson, New Jersey, 2004. Private collection.

Paterson Renaissance School Exterior, 2004. Private collection.

On behalf of the board and staff of our agency, we appreciate the temple's most generous donation of fifteen baskets of Passover food and supplies....

The food baskets were distributed to recently arrived émigré families who are truly experiencing the meaning of freedom—and to frail elderly who smiled and realized that they are cared for and not forgotten.

Our heartfelt thanks to all donors for their thoughtfulness and kindness.

—Abraham Davis
Jewish Family & Children's Service of North Jersey
(May 2002)

Remembering our Paterson heritage, individual families at Barnert Temple support individual needs and such projects as the Paterson Public Library Fund, the Paterson Museum, and the Renaissance One School of Humanities.

Thank you so very much for supporting our school [Renaissance One] both financially and spiritually. You have made a difference in the lives of Paterson's children by exposing them to quality programs that build character, responsibility, respect, and caring. Both <u>Bully-Proof Your School</u> *and* <u>Through the Eyes of a Friend</u> *helped our students understand the need for all of us to stand up for what is right....*

Our sincere thanks in making these programs possible.... You have given a gift that will last a lifetime.

—Renaissance One School Principal Maria Lopez
May 20, 2004

Donations Needed to Help a Vietnamese Child

Arrangements have been made for plastic surgical repair of a cleft palate lesion in a 3-year-old girl who my wife and I met while touring Vietnam in February. Dr. Michael Grannick, chief of plastic surgery at UMDNJ/Newark, and the University Hospital administration, have offered to provide care pro bono. The family will stay in our home while in the United States.... What is needed now is funding to cover the cost of their trip to and from the United States.... Please make any donations payable to "Rabbi Frishman's Discretionary Fund," noting that the money is to be used for the Vietnamese child.... Thank you for any contribution towards this humanitarian gesture. Every donation, no matter how small, will help.

—Dr. Samuel A. Cassell
temple bulletin, September 2002

When the West Side Presbyterian Church in Ridgewood, New Jersey, suffered a devastating fire on January 8, 2002, many members of the Barnert Congregation called Rabbi Frishman that day to ask what they could do. Rabbi Frishman met with the leader of the church the following day to offer any help that would be useful. A century earlier, after the fire that destroyed the Presbyterian Church in Paterson, Barnert Temple had housed that congregation, its services, and school for over three years until the church was rebuilt. This is our legacy. Barnert Temple–Franklin Lakes was not large enough to accommodate the West Side Presbyterian Church, but their request that Barnert Temple replace all their destroyed hymnals and bibles was readily agreed to. We also offered to store the books at our synagogue until the church was ready to receive them. Our senior youth group undertook special fundraising projects on behalf of the church.

> *The generosity of your members and friends in sending a check for $8,000 to cover [the] cost of hymnals and bibles for our church leaves us groping for words with which to express our gratitude. As you can imagine, the loss of our sanctuary in the devastating fire of Jan. 8 has affected us deeply, but we have been heartened by the support and expressions of friendship we have received from friends.... We remember that you were among the early neighbors to reach out to us offering a helping hand.*
>
> *—Tom Delleart*
> *chair of the finance committee for*
> *rebuilding West Side Church, May 29, 2002*

Remembering the human voices and past deeds of our congregation, as well as the blessings of our American constitutional guarantees of religious and civil liberties, forms a collective memory for our congregation, a compass for the present and a clearer road map for a better future. We honor our past as we teach our future generations.

> *Warren Bauer, an esteemed member of our temple, died this month. I didn't know Warren personally. President of our temple for a year, he was, I've been told, caring, kind, considerate, thoughtful, and very proud of his Paterson roots. He was chairperson of the Free Will Campaign for years, helping bring needed funds into the temple.*
>
> *Warren has two children, Susan and Joel. Joel is married to Janet, and they have two daughters. Both girls worked, at different times, in our Summer Day Camp. And there is the connection that lives forever. Though Warren and I didn't meet, his support of the Barnert Temple laid the foundation for all of the programs that came after his presidency and his most active years. His connection to the temple fostered his children's and grandchildren's involvement after him.*
>
> *We have many other Patersonian families—the "renaissance" generation—whose grandchildren are joining us in preschool and religious school. They are slowly but steadily taking their place on committees and as leaders for their children. Olivia Low, Susan and Alvin Sauer's granddaughter, will be a preschooler next year. Both of her grandparents are past presidents....*
>
> *Our second graders took a tour of the temple building some weeks ago. On the walls they saw the names of those who came before us, whose generosity of time, money and spirit literally paved the road for us to continue to study as Jews as a community. Many of our students see the names of their parents and grandparents, even great-grandparents. The continuity, l'dor va dor ("from generation to generation"), is tangible at Barnert. You don't get that everywhere. It defines us, and we should never forget to be thrilled by it.*
>
> *—Sara Losch*
> *director of youth education*
> *February 2004*

In the year 2002, the Rabbi Emeritus Martin Freedman UAHC Camp Scholarship Fund was established. The fund enables a Barnert Temple student who could not otherwise afford it to attend a four-week summer session, either at the Union for Reform Judaism's Eisner Camp in Great Barrington, Massachusetts, or at Kutz Camp in Warwick, New York.

Dear Rabbi Freedman and Rabbi Frishman,

I am so honored that you picked me for your scholarship program to Camp Eisner. Judaism has increasingly become a top priority for me, and I know that Judaism will forever be an important part of my life. It is because I love the warmth of the temple, and everybody in it. I go to services nearly every Friday night, participate in the youth group, and contribute to many other temple happenings. Also, my goal for the future is to become a cantor....

Rabbi Frishman, you have affected me so much since my bat mitzvah. I am so glad that you noticed my interest in Judaism, and that you nominated me for this great opportunity at Camp Eisner.

—Thalia Halpert Rodis
September 2004

Our students respond with touching effectiveness and express themselves as the new generation of a caring community. In the January 2004 temple bulletin, fourth-grader Chelsea Abramowitz shared her experience volunteering at the Family Shelter in Englewood: "When I went to the homeless shelter I felt sad because the kids there have no home. They have to share one bed with their brothers and sisters. There were seven families living there. The kids were between 3 and 12 years old.... I went because I wanted to brighten their day and show that people care about them. I felt good because we made them happy. We had fun making turkey hands, decorating sugar cookies, and playing games. I played jump-rope with two boys and two girls. I hope I made a small difference in their lives, and I hope to go back again soon."

The Barnert Temple Youth Group (BARTY), amongst its many volunteer and fundraising projects, earmarks all proceeds from its Homecoming event to fund the Urban Mitzvah Corps, a project of the North American Federation of Temple Youth's New Jersey region. Mitzvah Corps is an intensive six-week summer program on social justice, during which teens live at the Rutgers University campus in New Brunswick, New Jersey, and spend their days volunteering with the mentally and physically challenged, the underprivileged and the elderly.

Another way our religious school transfers the idea of tikkun olam is a formal program that requires students to participate in a mitzvah project before they can become bar or bat mitzvah. Through the L'Dor Va Dor project, students are matched with seniors in the congregation. The project intends to expose the students to the idea of "the gift of giving" on a one-to-one basis.

My name is Simone Krame, and I am in the seventh grade. As most of you know, before someone can [become] bar or bat mitzvah, they have to do a mitzvah project. For my mitzvah project I chose to work with a man named Phil Schwartz. Phil is elderly and needs help around the house, so I volunteered. I started working with him in September, and most likely will continue up until June. I go to his house every other Wednesday. The biggest project we have worked on was his movie collection. I helped Phil alphabetize the whole thing (which is over 200 movies).... Working with Phil has been a delight. He is no longer just a person to me; he is an extremely close friend. I feel very happy to know that what I am doing can make such a big difference in someone's life. Phil has taught me the love of classical music, opera, as well as old-time movies. Another thing Phil taught me was to strive for success. I am having an experience of a lifetime by helping Phil.

—Simone Krame
February 2004

New and older generations at Barnert Temple Sabbath. *Left to right:* Simone Krame, Philip Schwartz. Barnert Temple Archives

The history of American Jewry and the Barnert Temple community is a long, glorious record of dedication and appreciation to a dual tradition—the sacred heritage of an ancient religion combined with the American ideals of freedom and democracy. As Americans and as Jews we are our history—history has brought us to the present.

Our Jewish forefathers and mothers, expelled from Brazil by the Inquisition, arrived in Dutch New Amsterdam (now Manhattan) on September 21, 1654—350 years ago.

On November 16, 1905, in celebration of the 250th anniversary of this first permanent Jewish settlement in North America, the American Jewish Historical Society held an anniversary dinner. A former president, Grover Cleveland, delivered the keynote speech, and the chairman of the celebration, Jacob H. Schiff, read a message from his friend President Theodore Roosevelt:

The celebration of the 250th anniversary of the settlement of the Jews in the United States properly emphasizes a series of historical facts of more than merely national significance. Even in our colonial period the Jews participated in the upbuilding of this country, acquired citizenship, and took an active part in the development of foreign and domestic commerce. During the Revolutionary period they aided the cause of liberty by serving in the Continental army and by substantial contributions to the empty treasury of the infant republic. During the Civil War thousands served in the armies and mingled their blood with the soil for which they fought. I am glad to be able to say, in addressing you on this occasion, that while the Jews of the United States, who now number more than a million, have remained loyal to their faith and their race traditions, they have become indissolubly incorporated in the great army of American citizenship, prepared to make all sacrifice for the country, either in war or peace, and striving for the perpetuation of good government and for the maintenance of the principles embodied in our Constitution.

In September 2004, the Library of Congress in Washington, D.C., opened a year-long exhibit, "From Haven to Home: A Library of Congress Exhibition Marking 350 Years of Jewish Life in America." This exhibition will travel throughout the United States. The material draws from several collections, including those of the Library of Congress, the National Archives, and the American Jewish Historical Society. One item in the exhibit is the original text of "The New Colossus" by Emma Lazarus, the famed 1883 ode to the Statue of Liberty.

Give me your tired, your poor,

Your huddled masses yearning to breathe free,

The wretched refuse of your teeming shore,

Send these, the homeless, tempest-tost to me,

I lift my lamp beside the golden door.

Just about everywhere you go in the Jewish world, you hear that this is the 350th year of the American Jewish experience....

The Jewish civilization has changed the course of human history. From contributions in every art and science to the foundation of societal ethics, Judaism has made a profound difference. And Judaism is: the Jewish people. The Jewish people is: you and I. How we live, how we enact our part in human history, matters. How we play out the real-life experience of America 2004 demonstrates the way all people might live. To be "a light to the nations" means to care about others, and to live according to the highest ethical values possible.

So the American Jewish experience isn't just about how we Jews live in America; it's about how Jews have influenced the course of the United States of America. Each of us must consider our place, not as famous individuals, but as influential neighbors and friends and advocates of social justice. The course of the world is changed by great leaders, but it is also influenced, according to the Jewish way of thinking, by you and I. Our lives matter.

As we enter this 350th year of being Jews in America, we also enter the Jewish New Year 5765. Let's use this year to reflect on our roles, you and I, in making a difference, and working to ensure another 350 years of glorious opportunity and contribution in our great nation.

—Rabbi Elyse Frishman,
September 2004

America's open accommodation to its emerging society was established as an ongoing process early in our national ethos. Our nation's founders anticipated not a perfect democracy, but a society that strives and responds to the ongoing civil and religious needs of its citizens.

New Jersey is one of four original states that never had an established or preferred religion, and the state has a recorded constitutional history that precedes our U.S. Constitution and continues to make state constitutional changes to this day.

That no Men nor number of Men upon Earth hath power or Authority to rule over mens consciences in religious matters....

—Concessions and Agreements
of the Proprietors, Freeholders and Inhabitants
of the Province of West New Jersey
March 3, 1676–1677

That liberty of Conscience in matters of faith and Worshipp towards God shall be granted to all people within the Province aforesaid who shall live peaceably and quietly therein, and that none of the Free people of the said Province shall be rendered incapable of Office in respect of their faith and Worshipp.

—Fundamental Agreement
of the Governor, Proprietor, Freeholders and Inhabitants
of the Province of West New Jersey
November 25, 1681

That no Person shall ever within this Colony be deprived of the inestimable Privilege of worshipping Almighty God in a Manner agreeable to the Dictates of his own Conscience....

That there shall be no Establishment of any one religious Sect in this Province in Preference to another....

—Constitution of the State of New Jersey, July 2, 1776

There shall be no establishment of one religious sect in preference to another; no religious or racial test shall be required as a qualification for any office or public trust.

Constitution of the State of New Jersey (as amended November 1961)
Article I

On the federal level, in 1791 the Bill of Rights became part of the U.S. Constitution, and the First Amendment guarantees freedom of religion. Since then U.S. Supreme Court decisions testing religious and civil rights cases have been an ongoing process of examination and review that affect all Americans and require our participation and vigilance in our democracy. Examples of this continuing process are such major Supreme Court cases as *Cantwell v. Connecticut* (1940), *Brown v. Board of Education of Topeka* (1955), *Engel v. Vitale* (1962), *Lemon v. Kurtzman* (1971), and *Wallace v. Jaffree* (1985). In the last decade of the twentieth century there continued to be great concern in both the legislative and judicial branches of the federal government over how best to protect our citizens' constitutional rights to freedom of religion, as in the Religious Freedom Restoration Act of 1993 and the case of *City of Boerne* (Tex.) *v. Flores* (1997) demonstrate, and in the *McCreary v. ACLU*(2005) decision Justice Sandra Day O'Connor defending the separation of church and state wrote, "Those who would renegotiate the boundries between church and state must therefore answer a difficult question. Why would we trade a system that has served us so well for one that has served others so poorly?"

> *Now, I say to you my friends, even though we face the difficulties of today and tomorrow, I still have a dream. It is a dream deeply rooted in the American dream.*
>
> —Rev. Dr. Martin Luther King Jr.
> August 28, 1963

Just as Barnert Temple's Rabbi Max Raisin, a son of immigrant parents, expressed his love for America, I, as a daughter of immigrant parents, am keenly aware of and deeply grateful for our American Jewish heritage. I understand the meaning of the words freedom, peace, liberty, and responsibility in a profound way. The educational goals at Barnert Temple include transmitting these moral and ethical values and responsibilities to our children and our children's children.

> *At the beginning of this month, we exercise our right to vote for the direction and soul of our great nation—participating in the process of electing a president and legislature who we pray will together lead our country responsibly and with integrity and insight. Toward the end of the month we will observe another joyful and important holiday, Thanksgiving. In the middle, on November 11, is Veterans' Day—less actively observed by many of us, but important in marking our gratitude to those men and women who fought to keep our country, and the world, a safer place....*
>
> *It seems that as American Jews, we are so blessed to have the opportunity to be both Americans and Jews and have the opportunity, in freedom, to participate in these seemingly not-Jewish rituals. However, in so many ways, these very rituals uphold some of our very dear and true values. We have responsibilities as both American and as Jews in participating in our democratic process. It is not about whether or not our candidate is elected; it is that we have a voice, a privilege that most of our ancestors simply did not have as they suffered under the tyranny of kingdoms and dictatorships of the past generations around the rest of the world. And so many of our fore-"fathers" were conscripted into armies that fought for leaders and countrymen who never cared for or attended to the basic needs of Jews in their land.... So, as we move through this month of November—from responsibility to remembrance to rejoicing—we should keep high on our agenda the counting of our blessings, not only on the one day each year set aside for "Thanksgiving," but every day.*
>
> —Cantor Regina Lambert-Hayut
> November 2004

We are called the People of the Book. Our Ten Commandments (Exodus, chap. 10) constitute an ethical and legal legacy for our American civilization. The values they embody have influenced Jews and non-Jews for generations, and have been the foundation of Roman law and many other legal systems.

Yet cherishing our past goes beyond any biblical or cultural mandate. History is especially important for diaspora communities because institutional memory, rather than territorial space, ultimately ensures our survival. All dreams are dreams, and aspirations may ultimately be found wanting by any individual or people. Yet, the American Jewish experience of religious and civil freedoms is evidence that the promise of America could be realized. Without the opportunities, freedoms, and openness of America, American Jews, indeed all other immigrant nationalities and religions, would not have been able to realize their talents, energies, and dreams to become what they are today.

But there are obligations that go along with the blessings of America. We at Barnert Temple teach our children the meaning of tzedakah: more than just "charity," it means "righteousness," an obligation to help and to give to those less fortunate. We also teach the meaning of tikkun olam: to repair the world, to heal the world. We, the Barnert adult community and our sons and daughters, strive to live those words through deeds, and as a caring community to look at the world at large as our world. There are no outsiders here—at Barnert Temple, everyone is an insider.

May God bless America; and for our community, our country, and all the world, we pray for peace.

> *Grant us peace, Your most precious gift, O Eternal Source of peace, and give us the will to proclaim its message to all the peoples of the earth. Bless our country, that it may always be a stronghold of peace, and its advocate among the nations. May contentment reign within its borders, health and happiness within its homes. Strengthen the bonds of friendship among the inhabitants of all lands. And may the love of Your name hallow every home and every heart. Blessed is the Eternal God, the Source of peace.*
>
> *—Union Prayer Book*

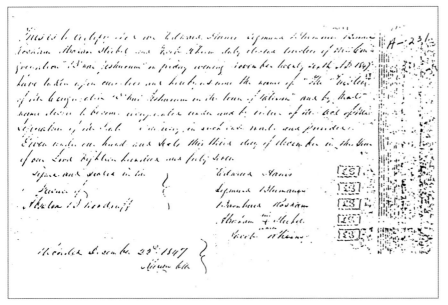

Certificate of Incorpation of Barnert Temple Paterson,
November 29, 1847.

Certificate of Incorporation

      This is to Certify that we, Edward Harris, Sigmund Blumauer,
Barnhard Roskam, Abraham Stiebel and Jacob Rheim, duly elected Trustees
of the Congregation Bnai Jeshurun, on Friday evening, November 26,
A.D. 1847 have taken upon ourselves and hereby assume the name of
"The Trustees of the Congregation Bnai Jeshurun in the Town of
Paterson", and by that name desire to become incorporated under and
by virtue of the act of the Legislature of the State of New Jersey in
such cases made and provided. Given under our hands and seals this
third day of December in the year of Our Lord 1847.

Signed and sealed in   s/Edward Harris _____ L.S.

the presence of   s/Sigmund Blumauer _____ L.S.

ABSALOM B. WOODRUFF   s/Barnhard Roskam _____ L.S.

     s/ Abraham Stiebel _____ L.S.

Recorded December   s/ Jacob Rheim _____ L.S.
22, 1847

KEENAN, Clk.

Book of Miscellaneous Documents

Register of Passaic County

A -231

Certificate of Incorpation of Barnert Temple Paterson,
recorded December 22, 1847.

Confirmation class 1884. *Seated, left to right:* Edward Cohen, Julia Levy, (niece of Nathan Barnert), Rabbi B. Newmark, Bertha Samuels, née Klein. *Standing, left to right:* Fannie Simon, Charles Katz, David Newman, Simon Feder, Max Goldsmith, Rachael Greene, (née Klenert) Abram Levy. Barnert Temple Archives.

Religious school, Barnert Temple, Broadway, June 4, 1911. Barnert Temple Archives.

Religious school certificate of honor for Helen Weiss. Cyril Barnert, teacher, 1901. Barnert Temple Archives.

Confirmation June 12, 1910. *Left to right:* Justin Basch, Rabbi Leo Mannheimer, Bessie Weingaertner, Joseph Brown. Barnert Temple Archives.

Confirmation service pamphlet, June 12, 1910. Rabbi Leo Manneheimer, Lewis Levi, president. Barnert Temple Archives.

Confirmation class 1915. *Seated, left to right:* Emma Friedberg, Adele Lefkowitz, Rabbi Marius Ransom, Berta Cohen. *Standing, left to right:* Grace Stam, Adelphia Basch, Helen Jacobus. Barnert Temple Archives.

Confirmation class, June 8, 1924. "For our dear Rabbi from Confirmation Class 1924" written in back of photograph. Rabbi Max Raisin and Confirmands. Barnert Temple Archives.

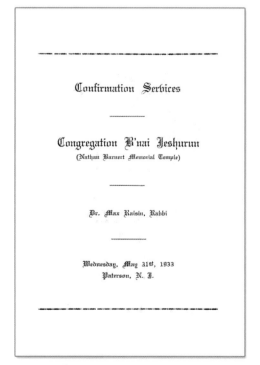

1933 confirmation service. Barnert Temple Archives.

Confirmation class, May 20, 1934. *Seated, left to right:* Sylvia Feinstein, Rabbi Max Raisin, Dorothy Sirota. *Standing, left to right:* Mangold Ellenbogen, Miriam Berliner, Barbara Glasgall, Leonore Raff, Allan Mikola. Barnert Temple Archives.

Confirmation class 1941. *Left to right:* Elizabeth Cole, Judith Glassgall, Lois Stave, Rabbi Max Raisin, Justine Stave, Ann Lynn Cohen, Barbara Polowe. Barnert Temple Archives.

Confirmation class 1952. *Left to right:* Paula Brown, Leah Jacobs, Janet Slater, Rabbi Aaron Opher, Peter Strauss, Linda Notkin, Peppi Gruber, Ruth Epstein. Barnert Temple Archives.

Confirmation program, 1963. Private collection.

Confirmation class 1964. *Front, left to right:* unidentified, Stephen Schwartz, Ellen Ephron, Rabbi Martin Freedman, Elizabeth Stein, unidentified. *Back, left to right:* Avrom Posner, Barry Nachimson, unidentified, unidentified. Private collection.

Confirmation class 1949. *Left to right:* Carole Ann Levine, Sarah Doblin. (*See page 78.*) Private collection.

Confirmation class 1977. *Seated, left to right:* Joanne Lobsenz, Fayth Gurman, Beth Schneider. Standing, left to right: Michael Birnberg, Tara Tandlich, Rabbi Martin Freedman, Lisa Gutenstein, Larry Spizer. Barnert Temple Archives.

Confirmation class 1981. *Left to right:* Peter Nashel, James Sarna, Valerie Feder, Stephanie Sauer, Rabbi Martin Freedman, Toby Cohen, Howard Gutenstein, James Lobsenz. Barnet Temple Archives.

Rabbi Martin Freedman and confirmands, 1991. Barnert Temple Archives.

Adult confirmation class 1988. *Left to right:* Cantor Sheila Pearl, past president Kathie Press, past president, Nardyne Cattani, confirmands, *and right end*, Rabbi Martin Freedman. Barnert Temple Archives.

Confirmation Class 2005. *Back row, left to right:* Nicole Harris, Jonathan Curran, Nicole Auerbach, Sam Segal, Jared Fischer, Matthew Kagan, Adam Lieberman. *Middle row, left to right:* Allison Filan, Noah Levine, Aaron Newman, Nadia Nimberger, Ilana Frechtman, Susan Paykin, Megan Hess, Janine Mascari, Laura Galinko. *Front row, left to right:* Sarah Sommer, Rebecca Cimino, Melissa Schwartz, Rabbi Elyse Frishman, Thalia Halpert-Rodis, Elana Chalmers, Madeline Eldridge. Photo by Karen Galinko. Barnert Temple Archives.

APPENDIX

[Specifically, Jack and Louise Birnberg were the chairmen,. Other chairmen included Jill Edelson and Cipora Schwartz General Program; Robert Gutenstein, Finance; Allan Marshall, Treasurer; Ed Wexler and Leon Kramer, Food Service; Susan Sauer and Joan Croland, General Exhibits; Heather Spitzer, Publicity; and John Spitzer, Advertising.

[Also, Ellen Gutenstein, Personnel; Martin Haubenstock, Gene Rosensweet and Rona Rosen, Journal and Program; Alvin Greenbaum, Decoration; Gil Rubin, Construction; Michael Glanz, Printing; Philip Sarna, Transportation; Janet Blauvelt, Group Sales; Lois Kramer, Jewel Page; Helen and Bill Lee, Raffle Book; Leon Weissberg, Youth Coordinator; and Nicole Stern and Gail Yamner, Tee Shirts.

[And Carol Cassell, Newsletter; Louis Lever, Floor Manager; Anita Sarna, Pre-Sponsor Ball; Charles Dorman, Photography;

Marilyn Solomon, Museum Exhibits; Paulyne Lever and Jackie Glanz, Dinner Dance; and Arlene Greenbaum and Ruth Greenberg, Art.

Expo 200 (1976) Bicentennial Leadership (Chapter 8)

RABBIS

(INCOMPLETE)

1867–1871:   Reverend Herman Blichrode

1871–1873:   Rabbi Jacob S. Jacobson, CCAR

1873–1875:   Reverend Solomon Bergman

1875–1876:

1876–1878:   Reverend A. Brasch

1878–1881:   Reverend Max Molle

1881–1884:   Reverend Moses Cohen

1884–1887:   Reverend B. Newmark

1887–1892:   Reverend Meyer Hood

1892–1893:   Reverend Solomon Rosenberg

1893–1894:   Reverend S. Eisenberg

1895–1896:

1896–1897:   Reverend William Muetter

1898–1906:   Rabbi Abraham S. Isaacs, CCAR

1906–1909:   Rabbi Elli Mayer, CCAR

1909–1915:   Reverend Leo Mannheimer

1915–1919:   Rabbi Marius Ransom, CCAR

1919–1920:   Rabbi Harry Richmond, CCAR

1920–1921:

1921–1946:   Rabbi Max Raisin, CCAR

1947–1953:   Rabbi Aaron Opher, CCAR

1953:   Rabbi Abram Granison, CCAR

1954–1956:   Rabbi Murray Blackman, CCAR

1956–1995:   Rabbi Martin Freedman, CCAR

1995–Present: Rabbi Elyse Frishman, CCAR

TEMPLE PRESIDENTS
(INCOMPLETE)

_ 1900 _: Nathan Barnert *(Total years of presidency unknown)*

_ 1913 _: Lewis Levi *(Total years of presidency unknown)*

_ 1920 _: Moe I. Fuld *(Total years of presidency unknown)*

1921–1943: Jacob Rosen

1943–1945: Frank Stave

1945–1949: Max Rosen

1949–1952: Raymond Kramer

1952–1953: Frank Stave

1953–1954: Warren G. Bauer

1954–1956: Jack Gruber

1956–1958: Louis Sorkin

1958–1960: Barnert Zalon

1960–1961: Daniel P. Lieblich

1961–1965: Norman Lappin

1965–1971: George D. Rosenthal

1971–1973: Ernest S. Weiner

1973–1976: Alvin H. Sauer

1976–1978: Robert Gutenstein

1978–1981: Philip E. Sarna

1981–1982: Edward Wexler

1982–1987: Susan Low Sauer

1987–1988: Robert Gutenstein

1988–1989: Leon Finke

1989–1990: Kathy Press

1990–1991: Dorothy Starr

1991–1992: Nardyne Cattani

1992–1995: Alvin Sauer

1995–1997: Harry Plonskier

1997–2001: Arnold Reiter

2001–2004: Kathie Williams

2004–Present: David Siegal

ORAL HISTORIES

DATE	SUBJECTS	INTERVIEWER
January 28, 1978	Samuel and Esther Schwartz	Delight Dodyk and Cipora Schwartz
January 12, 1982	Esther Schwartz	Jonah Sweig
August 18, 1986	Samuel Schwartz	Jonah Sweig
September 10, 1986	Esther Schwartz	unknown
August 18, 1986	Samuel Schwartz	unknown
November 20, 1997	George Sauer	Dr. David Roth
November 20, 1997	Dorothy Dublin	Dr. David Roth
November 23, 1997	Rabbi Martin Freedman	Barnert Temple Men's Club
December 1, 1997	Dr. Joseph Shapiro	Dr. David Roth
December 19–21, 1997	Rabbi Martin Freedman	Cipora Schwartz and Dr. David Roth
December 24–27, 1997	Alvin Sauer	Kenneth Edelson
October 1998	Robert Gutenstein	Janet Finke
January 19, 1998	Susan Sauer	Joel Bauer and Lenore Alpert
February 6, 1998	Bea and Walter Okker	Lenore Alpert
February 9, 1998	Theodore Lobenz	Dr. David Roth
March 1, 1998	Alan Kessler	Minna Greenberg
March 6, 1998	Dr. David Roth	Minna Greenberg
March 8, 1998	Warren Bauer	Dorothy Starr
March 9, 1998	Lenore Alpert	Minna Greenberg
April 15, 1998	Kathy and Harold Polton	Minna Greenberg
April 19, 1998	Daniel Lieblich	Kenneth Edelson
May 5, 1998	Norma Joelson Hayman	Kenneth Edelson
May 13, 1998	Lewis Epstein	Kenneth Edelson
November 10, 1998	Sarah Losch	Janet Finke
November 10, 1998	Rabbi Elyse Frishman	Janet Finke
February 1999	Cantor Shelia Pearl	Kenneth Edelson
March 4, 1999	Dorothy Starr	Kenneth Edelson
January 23, 2000	Rabbi Martin Freedman	Rabbi Elyse Frishman
February 6, 2001	Cipora Schwartz	Janet Finke

BIBLIOGRAPHY

Accounts Ledger of Barnert Memorial Temple, May 1876– February 1895. Cincinnati: American Jewish Archives.

American Jewish History 82, 1–4. Waltham, Mass.: American Jewish Historical Society, 1994.

Ard, Patricia M., and Michael Aaron Rockland. *The Jews of New Jersey: A Pictorial History*. New Brunswick, N.J.: Rutgers University Press, 2002.

Arsenault, Raymond. *Freedom Riders: 1961 and the Struggle for Racial Justice*. New York: Oxford University Press, 2006.

Barber, John, and Henry Howe. *Historical Collections of the State of New Jersey*. Newark, N.J.: Benjamin Olds, 1844.

Baron, Salo W., and Joseph L. Blau. *The Jews of the United States, 1790–1840: A Documentary History*. 3 vols. New York: Columbia University Press, 1963.

Baum, Michael T. *A Biography of Paterson's Most Useful Citizen: Nathan Barnert*. Paterson, N.J.: News Printing Co., 1914.

Berman, Howard Allen. "That I May Dwell Among Them." High school term paper, 1967. Available in Barnert Temple Archives.

Birmingham, Stephen. *Our Crowd: The Great Jewish Families of New York*. New York: Harper & Row, 1967.

Bloch, Joshua. *The People and the Book*. New York: New York Public Library, 1954.

Boyd, Andrew. *Boyd's Paterson and Passaic Directory*. Paterson, N.J., 1875.

Brockett, L. P. *The Silk Industry in America*. New York: George F. Nesbitt, 1876.

Brydon, Norman F. *The Passaic River: Past, Present, Future*. New Brunswick, N.J.: Rutgers University Press, 1974.

"Clifton Jubilee" Section. Herald News (Clifton/Passaic, N.J.), April 24, 1967.

Cohen, David Stern (ed.). *America, The Dream of My Life*. New Brunswick, N.J.: Rutgers University Press, 1990.

Cohen, Stephen, Robert Joelson, and Cipora Schwartz. *Moving On*. Story, music, and lyrics of revue presented in February 1981.

Cunningham, John T. *New Jersey: America's Main Road*. Garden City, N.Y.: Doubleday, 1976.

Dantowitz, Faith Joy. *Generations and Reflections*. Short Hills, N.J.: Congregation B'nai Jeshurun, 1998.

Eichhorn, David Max. *Jewish Folklore in America*. Middle Village, N.Y.: Jonathan David, 1996.

Elbogen, Ismar. *A Century of Jewish Life*. Philadelphia, PA.: The Jewish Publication of America, 1944.

Finkelstein, Louis. *Beliefs and Practices of Judaism*. New York: Devin-Adair, 1941.

Fitzgerald, Thomas F., and Louis C. Gossons. *Legislative Manual, State of New Jersey, 1885*. Trenton: Fitzgerald & Gosson, 1884.

Legislative Manual of the State of New Jersey, 1885. Trenton, N.J.: Legislative Register.

Foster, Geraldine S., Eleanor F. Horvitz, and Judith Weiss Cohen. *Jews of Rhode Island, 1658–1958*. Dover, N.H.: Arcadia Publishing, 1998.

Frazier, Nancy. *Jewish Museums of North America: A Guide to Collections, Artifacts and Memorabilia*. New York: John Wiley, 1992.

Furnas, J.C., *The Americans: A Social History of the United States, 1587–1914*. New York: Putnam, 1969.

Gazetteer of the State of New Jersey (1834). In John Barber and Henry Howe. *Historical Collections of the State of New Jersey*. Newark, N.J.: Benjamin Olds, 1844.

Goldowsky, Seebert J., and Judith Weiss Cohen. "History of the Rhode Island Jewish Historical Association." *Rhode Island Jewish Historical Notes* 12, no. 3 (November 1997).

Graetz, Heinrich. *Popular History of the Jews, with a supplementary volume of recent events by Dr. Max Raisin*. New York: Hebrew Publishing Co., 1919.

Grassl, Gary C. "Joseph Gans of Prague, the First Jew in English America." *American Jewish History* 86, no. 2 (June 1998).

Grinstein, Hyman M. *The Rise of the Jewish Community of New York, 1654–1860*. Philadelphia: Jewish Publication Society, 1945.

Gutstein, Linda. *History of the Jews in America*. Edison, N.J.: Chartwell Books, 1988.

Gutstein, Morris A. *To Bigotry No Sanction: A Jewish Shrine in America, 1658-1958*. New York: Bloch, 1958.

Hacker, Tina (ed.). *Shalom: The Heritage of Judaism in Selected Writings*. Kansas City, Mo.: Hallmark Editions, 1972.

Handbook and Guide for the City of Newark, New Jersey. Newark, N.J.: Newark Daily Advertiser Print., 1872.

Herbst, John A., and Catherine Keene. *Life and Times in Silk City*. Haledon, N.J.: American Labor Museum, 1984.

Hertzberg, Arthur. *The Jews in America: Four Centuries of an Uneasy Encounter*. New York: Simon & Schuster, 1989.

Hertzman, Rachael. *An American Rabbi: A Translation of Four Essays from Max Raisin's Dapim Mi Pinkaso shel Rabi.* (thesis for ordination, Hebrew Union College-Jewish Insititute of Religion), June 1985.

Hoobler, Dorothy and Thomas. *The Jewish American Family Album.* New York: Oxford University Press, 1995.

Howe, Irving, and Kenneth Libo. *We Lived There Too.* New York: St. Martin's/Marek, 1984.

Jick, Leon A. *The Americanization of the Synagogue, 1820–1870.* Hanover, N.H.: Brandeis University Press, 1976.

Joselit, Jenna Weissman. *The Wonders of America: Reinventing Jewish Culture, 1880–1950.* New York: Hill & Wang, 1994.

Kahn, Roger. *The Passionate People: What It Means to Be a Jew in America.* New York: William Morrow, 1968.

Kleeblatt, Norman L., and Gerald C. Wertkin (comps.). *The Jewish Heritage in American Folk Art.* New York: Universe Books, 1984.

Korn, Bertram W. *American Jewry and the Civil War.* Marietta, Ga.: R. Bemis Publishing, 1951.

Kurzweil, Arthur. *From Generation to Generation: How to Trace Your Jewish Genealogy and Family History.* New York: Harper Perennial, 1994.

Labaw, George Warne. *Preakness and the Preakness Reformed Church: A History, 1695–1902.* New York: Board of Publication of the Reformed Church in America, 1902.

Learsi, Rufus. *The Jews in America: A History.* Cleveland: World Publishing Co., 1954.

Lewis, Theodore. *Sermons at Touro Synagogue.* Brooklyn, N.Y.: Simcha-Graphics Associates, 1980.

Lindsay, James Elliott. *A Certain Splendid House: The Centennial History of the Washington Association of New Jersey.* Morristown, N.J.: Washington Association of New Jersey, 1974.

Lipset, Seymour Martin, and Earl Raab. *Jews and the New American Scene.* Cambridge, Mass.: Harvard University Press, 1995.

London, Hannah R. *Miniatures and Silhouettes of Early American Jews.* Rutland, Vt.: Charles E. Tuttle, 1970.

"Saint *Mémin* Portraits: Solomon Reuben Etting." *Antique Magazines,* July 1959.

Lurie, Maxine N. (ed.). *A New Jersey Anthology.* Newark: New Jersey Historical Society, 1994.

Miles, Ellen G. "Saint *Mémin* Mechanical Profiles in America." In *Saint-Mémin and the Neoclassical Profile Portrait in America,* edited by Dru Dowdy. Washington, D.C.: National Portrait Gallery and Smithsonian Press, 1994.

Mitchell, Martha. "Jewish Studies at Brown University a Century Ago." *Rhode Island Jewish Historical Notes* 12, no. 3 (1997).

Murphy, T. Palmer, and Margaret Murphy. *Paterson and Passaic County: An Illustrated History.* Northridge, Calif.: Windsor Publications, 1984.

Nelson, William, and Charles A. Shriner. *History of Paterson and Its Environs (the Silk City): Historical-Genealogical-Biographical.* New York: Lewis Historical Publishing Co., 1920.

Niemcewicz, Julian Ursyn. *Under Their Vine and Fig Tree: Travels Through America in 1797, 1799 and 1805.* Elizabeth, N.J.: Grassman Publishing Co.,1965.

Norwood, Christopher. About Paterson: *The Making and Unmaking of an American City.* New York: Saturday Review Press, 1974.

Our SNOA, 5497-5742: The 250th Anniversary of Synagogue Mikva Israel Curaçao. Curaçao: Congregation Mikva Israel, 1982

Panitz, Esther L. *The Alien in Their Midst: Images of Jews in English Literature.* Cranbury, N.J.: Associated Universities Presses, 1981.

Patt, Ruth Marcus, *Uncommon Lives: Eighteen Extraordinary Jews from New Jersey.* New York: Vintage Press, 1994.

Perera, Victor. *The Cross and the Pear Tree: A Sephardic Journey.* Berkeley: University of California Press, 1995.

Potter, M. D. Ed. D. *Fiber to Fabric.* New York: The Gregg Publishing Co., 1945.

Raisin, Max. *A History of the Jews in Modern Times.* New York: Hebrew Publishing Co., 1919.

Raisin, Max. *Great Jews I Have Known.* New York: Philosophical Library, 1952.

Raisin, Max. "My 50 Years as a Rabbi." Typescript, 1953. Biographies collection, American Jewish Archives, Cincinnati.

Sarna, Jonathan D. *American Judaism: A History.* Princeton, N.J.: Princeton University Press, 2004.

Schoener, Allon. *The American Jewish Album: From 1654 to the Present.* New York: Rizzoli, 1983.

Schwartz, Esther I. "Restoration of the Touro Synagogue." *Rhode Island Jewish Historical Notes* 3, no. 2 (October 1959): 106–31.

Scranton, Philip B. *Silk City: Studies on the Paterson Silk Industry, 1860–1990.* Newark: New Jersey Historical Society, 1985.

Shriner, Charles A. *Four Chapters of Paterson History.* Paterson, N.J.: Lont & Overkamp, 1919.

Shriner, Charles A. *Random Recollections.* Paterson, N.J.: Privately printed, 1941.

Silberman, Charles E. *A Certain People: American Jews and Their Lives Today.* New York: Summit Books, 1985.

Slater, Alpert H. *Who's Who in Passaic County.* Paterson: Evening News, 1917.

Slezkine, Yuri. *The Jewish Century.* New Jersey: Princeton University Press, 2004.

Somerville, Mollie. *Washington Historical Landmarks: Pillars of Patriotism.* Washington, D.C.: National Society, Daughters of the American Revolution, 1985.

Speizman, Morris. *The Jews of Charlotte: A Chronicle with Commentary and Conjectures.* Charlotte, N.C.: McNally & Loftin, 1978.

Teplitz, Saul I. (ed.). *Best Jewish Sermons of 5717–5718.* New York: Jonathan David, 1958.

Best Jewish Sermons of 5725-5726. New York: Jonathan David, 1966.

Topper, Frank, and Charles A. Wills. *A Historical Album of New Jersey.* Brookfield, Conn.: Millbrook Press, 1995.

Troy, Leo. *Organized Labor in New Jersey.* Princeton, N.J.: Van Nostrand, 1965.

Trumbull, L. R. *A History of Industrial Paterson*.
    Paterson, N.J.: Carleton M. Herrick, 1880.

Wallerstein, Jane, comp. *Voices from the Paterson
    Silk Mills*. Portsmouth, N.H.: Arcadia
    Publishing Co., 2000.

Walton, Perry. *The Story of Textiles*. Boston:
    Walton Advertising & Printing Co., 1912.

Who's Who in Passaic County, 1917. Paterson
    Evening News.

Wyckoff, William C. *The Silk Goods of America*.
    New York: Van Nostrand, 1879.

Yaffe, James. *The American Jews: Portrait of a Split
    Personality*. New York: Random House, 1968.

*Yearbook of Congregation B'nai Jeshurun,
    Diamond Jubilee 1847–1922*. Paterson, N.J.
    1923–1924.

INDEX

References to images are indicated by *f*.

Academy of Jewish Studies, 134, 135
Albert, Lenore, 45, 61, 63, 71, 79, 115
Alexander II, Czar, 5
Alexander III, Czar, 5
American Jewish Historical Society celebrations, 161–162
America's Cup race, 12

Baltimore Independent Blues, 2
Banner, on Rabbi Leo Mannheimer, 46
Barnert Center for Jewish Education and Lifelong Learning, 151–152
Barnert, Ida, 28*f*
Barnert Memorial Temple, Broadway at Straight Street, 20*f*, 41*f* (1894 Barnert Temple memorial tablet). *See also* Barnert Memorial Temple, Derrom Avenue; Barnert Memorial Temple, Franklin Lakes
   bulletins (*see* Barnert Temple Bulletins)
   children's Purim service, 123*f*
   civic organizations, 46 (*see also* Barnert Memorial Temple Sisterhood; Barnert Temple Men's Club; Barnert Temple Youth Group; Girl Scout Troop; Red Cross Ladies)
   construction of, 32, 39–41
   current occupants, 103*f*
   dedication of, 41–42
   87th anniversary celebration, 53*f*
   Fellerman Hall, 70–71
   Freedom Rides, response to, 112–113
   incorporation, certificate of, 166*f*
   last years, 76, 77–78
   ledger from 1889, 154*f*
   1920s, contemporary themes, 60–62
   120th anniversary celebration, 122*f*
   President William McKinley, visit by, 42–43
   relocation, need for, 73–75
   sanctuary at, 32*f*, 39*f*, 60

Second Presbyterian Church, Paterson, temporary home for, 43–44, 44*f*
   Touro Synagogue restoration, 3
Barnert Memorial Temple, Derrom Avenue, 79*f*. *See also* Barnert Memorial Temple, Broadway at Straight Street; Barnert Memorial Temple, Franklin Lakes
   bicentennial celebrations, 81–82
   construction of, 76, 76*f*, 77*f*
   current occupants, 103*f*
   dedication of, 79
   fundraising activities, 80–81
   Israel, trip to, 122*f*
   relocation, need for, 79–80, 82, 83, 115–116
Barnert Memorial Temple, Franklin Lakes. *See also* Barnert Memorial Temple, Broadway at Straight Street; Barnert Memorial Temple, Derrom Avenue
   benefactors, 129
   continuity in leadership, 138–139
   dedication-weekend events, 127–129, 127*f*
   design, 93, 130*f*-131*f*, 132*f*
   expansion plans, 151
   groundbreaking ceremony, 126, 126*f*
   Holocaust Memorial Main Entrance, 132–133, 132*f*, 133*f*
   presidents, 140, 140*f*
   programs at, 123*f*, 134–135, 138
   Sefer Torah project, 132, 132*f*
   Sephardic Torah tik, 129
   social action activities, 155–158
   Synagogue 2000 project, 142
   West Side Presbyterian Church, assistance to, 158–159
Barnert Memorial Temple Sisterhood, 46, 135, 138
   fundraising activities, 64, 69, 77
Barnert, Meyer, 28*f*
Barnert, Miriam, 30, 32*f*
   death and funeral of, 32, 33, 37*f*
   memorial projects, 32*f*, 33–35, 33*f*–35*f*

Barnert, Nathan
   Boyd's Directory, listed in, 23
   death and funeral of, 35–37, 37*f*
   early life, 27–28, 27*f*
   home of, 38, 38*f*
   marriage, 30 (*see also* Barnert, Miriam)
   mayor of Paterson, service as, 30–31
   mercantile life, 29
   philanthropy of, 33 (*see also* Barnert Memorial Temple, Broadway at Straight Street; Daughters of Miriam; Nathan and Miriam Barnert Hospital)
   portrait of, 38*f*, 43*f*
   statue of, 35, 35*f*, 36*f*
Barnert Silk Mill, 29
Barnert Temple Bulletins
   1920s records, 60–62
   Rabbi Max Raisin, activities of, 55
   World War II coverage, 66, 69
Barnert Temple Men's Club, 77, 135, 138
   150th congregation anniversary, 113
Barnert Temple Speakers Forum, 137*f*, 138
Barnert Temple Youth Group, 160
Bauer, Warren, 74, 159
Belarus, Jewish immigrants from, 5
Belle Vista Castle, 15
Benz, George, 44–45, 45*f*
Bill of Rights, 2
Boyd's Paterson Directory, 23
Boynton decision, 106
Brazil, Jewish immigrants expelled from, 1–2
Brown, Rev. Dr. Robert MacAfee, 112

Cadillac Textiles, Inc., 16
Call, The, Newspaper, 43
Carroll estate house, 75*f*, 76
   purchase of, 101–102
Catharine Radziwill, Princess, 60
Civil Rights activism, march on Selma, 111. *See also* Freedom Rides; King, Martin Luther, Jr.
Civil War, impact on Paterson, 29

Clinton, Governor DeWitt, 9

Clinton, President William, 148*f*

Cohen, B. Irving, 123*f*,,124, 129, 144

Cohen, Rev. Moses, 24

Cohen, Stephen, M.D., 84–85

Cohn, Morris M., 67*f*

Cohen, William, 137*f*

Cole, David, 4*f*

Collier, Rev. John, 110

Colt, Christopher, 11, 13, 14*f*

Colt, John, 10, 11, 12

Colt, Peter, 10, 12

Colt, Roswell, 11–12

Colt, Sarah, 11

Community Action Program, volunteer training sessions, 155

confirmation classes, 167*f*–171*f*

Congregation B'nai Israel, 26

Congregation B'nai Jeshurun

    benefactor (*see* Barnert, Nathan)

    bulletins (*see* Barnert Temple Bulletins)

    cantors, 61, 64–65, 65*f*

    centennial anniversary, 70

    choir, 45–46

    Constitution and by-laws, 21*f*, 22*f*

    early home, 9 Mulberry Street, 1860–1877, 23*f*

    early years, 22–23

    honoring of congregants, 150–151, 150*f*

    incorporation, 22

    mandate, threefold, 88–90

    military service by members, 66, 67*f*, 68*f*

    Mount Nebo cemetery, 24, 24*f*, 138, 138*f*

    musical programs, 61, 64–65, 84–85, 87*f*, 88

    1920s growth, 59

    150th anniversary, 144–148, 144*f*, 145*f*, 146*f*, 148*f*, 149*f*

    135th anniversary, 83–88, 87*f*, 88*f*

    organist, George Benz, 44–45, 45*f*

    reform Judaism, move toward, 24–26, 39–40, 62

    Second Presbyterian Church, Paterson, temporary home for, 43–44, 44*f*

    1905 letter, 44*f*

    synagogues (*see* Barnert Memorial Temple, Broadway at Straight Street; Barnert Memorial Temple, Derrom Avenue; Barnert Memorial Temple, Franklin Lakes)

    trustees, 136*f*

    World War II, activities during, 66, 69

Congregation Shearith Israel, 1–2

Congress of Racial Equality, 106

Conn, Judge Joseph, 68*f*, 83

Constitution of the United States, and religious freedom, 2

cotton industry, advances in manufacturing process, 12–13

Crawford, John, 10

Dagger Bobbin Mills, 23

Darfur Day, 157

Daughters of Miriam, 33

Declaration of Independence, 2

Dershowitz, Alan M., 137*f*

Dexter, Lambert, and Company, 15

Doblin, Dorothy, 42

Donch, G. Thomas, 148*f*

Dresner, Rabbi Israel, 109, 110, 111*f*

Dutch West India Company, 2

Eastern European Jews, emigration of, 57. *See also individual countries*

East Side Park, 30

Edelson, Jill and Kenneth, 137*f*

Edison Electric Illuminating Co., 17*f*

Epstein, Lewis, 116

Etting, Reuben, 2, 2*f*

Expo 200, 81–82

Fabian, Jacob, 45

Farmer, James, 106

Fellerman Hall, construction of, 70–71

First Amendment. *See* Constitution of the United States

Fisher, Rev. Samuel, 21

flags, silk, 13, 13*f*, 14*f*

Freedman, Rabbi Martin, 68*f*, 75, 88

    awards and recognitions, 117

    Carroll estate, purchase of, 101–102

    education system, involvement in, 116–118

    family, 97

    Freedom Rides, participation in (*see* Freedom Rides)

    Jewish Institute of Religion, education at, 100–101

    military service, 98–100

    myasthenia gravis, recovery from, 118

    outstanding rabbi, 90, 123*f*

    retirement celebrations, 119–121, 122*f*, 124*f*

    scholarship fund, 160

    Survival Drive campaign, role in, 91, 92

Freedom Riders: 1961 and the Struggle for Racial Justice (Arsenault), 105, 105*f*

Freedom Rides, 105

    Barnert Temple, commemoration at, 113–114

    Florida, in, 97*f*, 108–112, 111*f*

    Ku Klux Klan, opposition from, 109

    Mohandas K. Gandhi, influence of, 106

    reunion of 1996, 112

    South Carolina, in, 107–108

    training for, 107, 110

Freehof, Rabbi Solomon, 25–26

Frishman, Rabbi Elyse, 140–141, 141*f*, 142

    New York Times interview, 146–147

Fry, Varian, 65

Gandhi, Mohandas K., 106

Gans, Joachim, 1

Germany

    Bad Kissingen, children at, 99–100

    Jewish immigrants from, 3

    persecution of Jews, 65

Ginsberg, Louis, 95

Girl Scout Troop, 55*f*

Godwin, Captain Abraham, 9

Godwin, General Abraham, 9

Goodman, Charles, 69

Goodman, Percival, 76, 93

    award, 103

Greenberg, Jack, 112

Greenville, Sir Richard, 1

Guidice, Vincent Del, M.D., 38

Gutenstein, Robert, 68*f*, 79, 80, 81, 104, 134, 141

Haines, Harry, 45

Hamilton, Alexander, 7, 8

Harding, Ruth Guthrie, 95

Hayman, Norma Joelson, 5, 26, 63, 77

Hebrew Union College, Cincinnati, 49

    honorary doctorates, 54

Herman, Kenneth, 66, 68*f*

Hirschfeld, Julian E., 139

Hitler, prosecution of Jews, 65

Hood, Myer S., 24

intermarriage, Rabbi Max Raisin on, 52

Irving, Washington, 96

Isaacs, Rev. Dr. Abram, 41*f*, 42

Israel Expo, 80

Jastrow, Marcus, 42

Jewish immigrants

    first settlement, 1–2

    retail industry, influence on, 3–4

    textile industry, in, 4, 6

    origins (*see individual countries*)

Jewish Institute of Religion, 100

Jewish Standard

    Sefer Torah project, about, 162

Varian Fry, 65
Joelson, Morris, 5
John Ryle and Sons, 13
Juviler, Amy Herz, 4, 4f

Kassel, Moshe, 26
Katz Brothers Brewery, 16, 17f
Kennedy, President John F., 103f
Kessler, Alan, 16, 56, 71
Kilmer, Joyce, 95
King, Martin Luther, Jr., 105
    Martin Luther King Day celebrations, 152, 153f
Koch, Mayor Edward J., 137f
Koppell, Joseph, 61
Ku Klux Klan, conflict with Freedom Rides, 109

Lafayette, General, 9
Lambert Castle. See Belle Vista Castle
Lambert, Catholina, 15
Lappin, Norman, 102
L'Dor Va Dor ("From Generation to Generation")
    expansion campaign, 151
L'Enfant, Pierre, 10
Library of Congress, exhibits on Jewish life, 162
Lieblich, Daniel, 22, 46, 64, 71
Lieblich, J., 26f
Lind, Jenny, 12
Lithuania, status of Jews, 6
Lobsenz, Ted, 51, 80
Low, Nicholas, 9

The Machine Works, 16, 17f
Maclure, David, 95
Mannheimer, Rabbi Leo, 45, 46
Marshall, Rip and Joan, 80
Martin Luther King Day celebrations, 152, 153f.
    See also King, Martin Luther, Jr.
Mayer, Rev. Dr. Ely, 41f, 45
McKinley, President William, 42–43
Meyer Brothers' department store, 17f
militia regiments, 2
Miriam Barnert Dispensary Association, 33, 34f,
    35. See also Nathan and Miriam Barnert
    Hospital
Miriam Barnert Memorial Hebrew Free School,
    33, 33f
Mischagass performance, 86f
Mishkan T'filah, 141
Morgenthau, Henry, Jr., 54
Morning Call, on retirement of Rabbi Max Raisin,
    57
Mount Nebo cemetery, 24, 24f, 138, 138f
Moving On, revue, 84–85, 87f

Muetter, Rabbi William, 42
Murray, George, 13
music
    Benz, George (organist), 44–45, 45f
    Cantor Joseph Posner Memorial Music
        Shabat, 138
    Congregation B'nai Jeshurun choir, 45–46
    Koppell, Joseph (cantor), 61
    minstrel show of 1910, 86f
    Mischagass performance, 86f
    Pearl, Sheila (cantor) 143–144
    Posner, Joseph (cantor), 64–65, 65f, 122f
    revues, 84–85, 87f, 88
myasthenia gravis, 118
My Fifty Years as a Rabbi (Raisin), 48, 50, 51

Nathan and Miriam Barnert Hospital, 33–35, 34f,
    68f
Nazi Party, in Paterson, 52–53
Nazis, rescue of European Jews from, 65
"The New Colossus" (Lazarus), 162
New Jersey
    Ackquackanonk, 8
    constitutional history, 163
    Paterson (see Paterson, New Jersey)
    poetry on, 95–96
    Sunday school, first, 11
Newmark, Rabbi Helga, 142–143
Newmark, Rev. B., 24
New York Times, interview with Rabbi Frishman,
    146–147
Nieuw Amsterdam (New York), First Jewish
    congregation in, 1–2
9/11 tragedy, 153, 155
nonviolent direct action, principle of, 106–107
North Jersey Times, on Rabbi Max Raisin, 53

Oppen, Heike, 46, 46f
oral histories
    Albert, Lenore, 45, 61, 63, 71, 79, 115
    Bauer, Warren, 74
    Doblin, Dorothy, 42
    Epstein, Lewis, 116
    Freedman, Rabbi Martin (see Freedman,
        Rabbi Martin)
    Gutenstein, Robert, 79, 80, 81, 104, 134, 141
    Hayman, Norma Joelson, 5, 26, 63, 77
    Hirschfeld, Julian E., 139
    Kessler, Alan, 16, 56, 71
    Lieblich, Daniel, 22, 46, 64, 71
    Lobsenz, Ted, 51, 80
    Low, Nicholas, 9
    Plonskier, Harry, 140, 142

Polton, Harold, 74, 82
Sauer, Alvin, 3, 81
Sauer, George, 71
Sauer, Susan, 75, 115
Schwartz, Cipora O., 113, 141
Schwartz, Esther, 18
Schwartz, Samuel, 74
Shapiro, Joseph, 25, 29, 65
Starr, Dorothy, 65, 140

Paris Exhibition, of 1878, 17f
Passaic County Historical Society, 15
Passaic County Park Commission, 15
Passaic Hotel, 9, 9f
Passaic River, the Great Falls of, 7f, 8f, 9f, 96f
Paterson Daily Guardian
    Barnert Memorial Temple, groundbreaking
        ceremony, 40–41
    Barnert, Nathan, election as mayor, 31
Paterson Daily News, gender integration in
    synagogue, 25
Paterson Evening News
    Barnert Memorial Temple, groundbreaking
        ceremony, 40
    retirement of Rabbi Max Raisin, 57
    Second Presbyterian Church, housed at
        Barnert Memorial Temple, 43–44, 44f
Paterson Morning Call, dedication of Barnert
    Memorial Temple on Derrom Avenue, 78f
Paterson, New Jersey. See also New Jersey
    architecture, 17f, 18, 18f–20f
    Civil War, impact of, 29
    Colt family, influence of, 10–12
    East Side Park, 30
    founding of, 7, 8
    great fire of 1902, 43
    map, 11f
    mills, 11, 12
    nineteenth century, growth during, 16
    notable citizens, 4
    Passaic Hotel, 9, 9f
    poetry on, 95–96
    Society for Establishing Useful Manufactures,
        8–9
    suburban population shift, 73–74
    town charter, 10
    twenty-first century revival, 93–94
Paterson's Most Useful Citizen (Baum), 37
Paterson, William, 8
Patterson, Colonel John Henry, 60
Pearl, Sheila, 143–144
Phillips, Miriam. See Barnert, Miriam
Pilgrims, arrival of, 1

Pioneer Silk Company, 13
Plonskier, Harry, 140, 142
Poems of New Jersey, 95–96
Polton, Harold, 74, 82
Posner, Joseph, 64–65, 65*f*, 122*f*
Post, John H., 41

rabbi, changing roles of, 25
Rabbi Emeritus Martin Freedman UAHC Camp
    Scholarship Fund, 160
Radziwill, Princess Catharine, 60
Raisin, Rabbi Jacob, 49
Raisin, Rabbi Mordecai (Max) Ze'ev, 47*f*
    black Americans, support for, 50
    call to Congregation B'nai Jeshurun, 46, 50
    childhood in Russia, 47–48
    congregations prior to Paterson, 50
    defense of causes and freedom, 52–53
    honorary doctorate, 54, 54*f*
    House of Representatives, guest chaplain at,
        54–55, 54*f*
    intermarriage, on, 52
    literary works, 50, 50*f*, 51, 52, 56–57 (see also
        My Fifty Years as a Rabbi)
    Nathan Barnert, sermon after death of, 36
    1920s, activities during, 60
    parents, 47–48
    rabbi emeritus status, 70
    religious education of, 49
    retirement, 56–57
    Zionist cause, support for, 51–52
Raleigh, Sir Walter, 1
Ranson, Rabbi Marius, 45
Red Cross Ladies, 68*f*
redemptioners, 7
Reform Judaism, 24–26
    new prayerbook, 141
    Rabbi Max Raisin, views of, 51
    Union of American Hebrew Congregations, 62
    Union Prayerbook,1895, 40*f*
Reiter, Sherie, 127*f*
religious freedom, and Constitution of the United
    States, 2
Renaissance One School of Humanities, Paterson,
    158, 158*f*
retail industry, influence of Jewish immigrants,
    3–4
R.H. Addams and Company, 13
Rhode Island, 2, 2*f*, 3
Richmond, Rabbi, 46
    UAHC quota, on raising of, 62
Rogers Locomotive and Machine Works, 17*f*

Rosen, Jacob, 26*f*, 45–46, 45*f*, 139
Rosen, Max, 26*f*
Ross, Betsy, 14*f*
Roth, Steven, 124*f*
Rustin, Bayard, 106
Ryle, John, 13

Sabin, Dr. Albert, M.D., 4*f*
Sarna, Philip, 83
Sauer, Alvin, 3, 81, 137*f*
Sauer, George, 71
Sauer, Susan, 75, 115, 137*f*
Schuyler, General Philip, 9
Schwartz, Cipora O., 113, 127*f*, 137*f*, 141
    Moving On production, 84–85, 87*f*
Schwartz, Esther, 18, 102–103
Schwartz, Philip, 127*f*, 137*f*, 161, 161*f*
Schwartz, Samuel S., 74, 92, 92*f*, 123 *f*, 129
    construction of Barnert Memorial Temple,
        Derrom Avenue, 102–103
Second Presbyterian Church, temporary home
    for, 43–44, 44*f*
Sefer Torah project, 132, 132*f*
Shapiro, Joseph, 6, 25, 29, 65
Shavuot, 132
S. Hold and Sons, 13
Shuch, Dr. Sheldon, 144
Siddur Avodath Israel, 42
Sik, Yang Yoo, 77
silk industry, 13, 13*f*, 14*f*, 15, 16, 17*f*
    in Barnert, 29
Silk Industry of America, The (Brockett), 16
Sills, Beverly, 137, 137*f*
slaves, 7
Slonimsky, Henry, 100
Smith, William, 122*f*
Society for Establishing Useful Manufactures, 8–9
Starr, Dorothy, 65, 140
The Star Spangled Banner, 12
Steiger, Carole Ann, 119
Steinhardt, Florence, 50
Stern, Jack, 69
Stiles, Dr. Ezra, 3
stock market crash, of 1929, 63–64
Stone, Rev. Robert, 112
Stuyvesant, Governor Peter, 2
Supreme Court decisions, 163–164
    Boynton decision, 106
    desegregation of public school system, 105
Survival Drive campaign, 91–92
    additional mini-campaign, 92–93

synagogues. *See* Barnert Memorial Temple,
    Broadway at Straight Street; Barnert Memorial
    Temple, Derrom Avenue; Barnert Memorial
    Temple, Franklin Lakes; Touro Synagogue
Synagogue 2000 project, 142

Ten Commandments, 165
Todd, Joseph C., 16
Touro Synagogue, New Port, Rhode Island, 2, 2*f*, 3
Trachtenberg, Rabbi Joshua, 100
Truman, President Harry S., 4*f*, 70, 70*f*
    desegregation of armed forces, 114
    letter, 70
Ukraine, Jewish immigrants from, 5
Union for Reform Judaism, 62
Union of American Hebrew Congregations, 62
Union Prayer Book, 40, 165
United Jewish Appeal of Paterson, 69, 69*f*
Urban Mitzvah Corps, 160

Washington, President George, 2, 2*f*
Webster, Daniel, 12
Week Ahead, on Barnert Memorial Temple
    Franklin Lakes groundbreaking ceremony, 126
Weiner, Ernest, 139
West Side Presbyterian Church fire, Ridgewood,
    158–159
Wexler, Edward, 88
White, Gail Cohen, 78
Whitman, Governor Christine Todd, 145, 148*f*
Wiesel, Elie, 137, 137*f*
William Paterson College, 117
Wise, Dr. Isaac M., 49
Wise, Rabbi Stephen S., 54
World War I, 67*f*
World War II
    Bad Kissingen, Germany, 99
    Pearl Harbor bombing, 66
    Rabbi Max Raisin, awareness of, 53–54
Wyckoff News, Barnert Memorial Temple Franklin
    Lakes groundbreaking ceremony, 126

youth activism, 160–161